中国-东盟法律研究中心

重庆市人文社会科学重点研究基地

最高人民法院东盟国家法律研究基地

本书是中国-东盟法律研究中心规划课题成果

中国—东盟法律评论

CHINA-ASEAN LAW REVIEW

(2018 Cambodia Volume)

第八辑 二〇一八年(柬埔寨法专辑)

厦门大学出版社 XIAMEN UNIVERSITY PRESS 国家一级出版社 全国百佳图书出版单位

中國一东盟法律评論

韩杼滨

越南—中国—东盟法律信息咨询中心主任陈大兴用越南文字为《中国—东盟法律评论》题写刊名

Journal Undang Undang Asean-China

冯正仁

马来西亚联邦法院前大法官、第五届“中国—东盟法律合作与发展高层论坛”组委会主席冯正仁先生以马来语为《中国—东盟法律评论》题写刊名。

柬埔寨司法部大臣昂翁·瓦塔纳用高棉语为《中国—东盟法律评论》题写刊名

China-ASEAN Legal Research Centre plays vital role in legal communication and cooperation between China and Myanmar

17.12.16

H.E. Mr. Win Myint
Deputy Attorney General
Union Attorney General's Office
Republic of the Union of Myanmar

缅甸联邦最高检察院副检察长吴温敏为中心题词

Many thanks for China-ASEAN Legal Research Center to pruide the Stenthing legal Caperaton between Indenesia and China

Nanning. China
6th. Dec. 2017
Indonesia Attorney General
H.M PRASETYO

印尼最高检总检察长 穆罕默德·普拉赛特为中心题词

中国—东盟法律研究中心：

法学之花盛开！

佟晓玲
驻东盟大使
二〇一二年五月七日

Editor's Note

The study ofCambodian legal system issue is the main subjects of this volume of the China-ASEAN Legal Review (CALR).It is based on the cooperation and publication consensus reached by the delegation of the China-ASEAN Legal Research Center the Ministry of Justice of Cambodia during its visit to Cambodia. It was compiled by the Center in cooperation with the Ministry of Justice of Cambodia. It is mainly composed of eight latest research articles on the development of Cambodian legal system and departmental law by officials of the Cambodian Ministry of Justice officials or teachers of the Royal University of Law and Economics of Cambodia. Most of them are PhD-candidate of Southwest University of Political Science and Law.

In the article on Administrative Complaint Mechanisms in Cambodia: The Current Situation and Its Challenges, Khlok Dara, Director of International Relations and Development Partners of the Ministry of Justice and PhD—Candidate of the School of International Law of SWUPL, study the current situation of administrative complaints mechanisms in Cambodia, focusing only on the mechanisms inside the administration in order to find out the challenges and issues for improving and building effective mechanisms to ensure citizens' rights and trust. To do this, the article will highlight first the current legal and policy framework, the type of administrative complaint and its structure, and finally assess the current type of administrative complaint by focusing on two specific cases for deeper analysis. At the end, the article will provide some recommendations for improving the existing mechanisms.

In the article on *Introduction to Administrative Law in Cambodia* ,Kai Hauerstein,Permanent Secretariat of the Committee for Legal and Judicial Reform,explains and analyzes the problems existing in the construction of the administrative law system in Cambodia, and proposes that the Cambodian Administrative Law has evolved from emphasizing that social order is above personal autonomy to protecting individuals from the state, and there is a strong correlation between the constitution and the administrative law through detailed introduction to the Cambodian Administrative Law. On the basis of specifying the procedures and specific implementation of the Cambodian Administrative Law, the author thinks that it is necessary to formulate important laws requiring legal and judicial reforms, and to improve the mechanism where the information can be issued and picked up to ensure fair and transparent administrative procedures.The author also proposes an independent judicial review of administrative litigation and a law governing the enforcement of administrative decisions.

In the article on *A Brief Introduction to Cambodia's Legal System* , Khim Kiri,Lecturer of Royal University of Law and Economics Ph.D-Candidate of International Law School of SWUPL,and Li Dongmei,Program Director of China-ASEAN Legal Research Center of SWUPL, explains that since the enactment of the modern national constitution in Cambodia in 1993, Cambodia's legal system has gradually improved,forming a process of building a democratic law, which takes Constitution as the center and take law,royal decree,government regulations and departmental regulations as a system through the detailed interpretation and analysis of Cambodia's legal system.

In the article on *Introduction to Contract and Tort Law under Cambodia Civil Code* , Ung Radsorin, Assistant to H.E Minister of Justice of the Ministry of Cambodia, Ph. D-Candidate of International Law School, SWUPL,explains that the stated purposes of the the Implementation of the New Civil Code are to ensure continuity in legislation governing civil matters and to guarantee the proper enforcement of the provisions of the Civil Code and of any matter related to the implementation of the Civil Code. The Implementation Law reflects three salient principles for the enforcement of the

Civil Code: the principle of non-retroactivity, the continuity of the rule of law and legal consistency. According to these principles, although the Civil Code will not apply to any transaction (or contractual or similar arrangement) that completed prior to the effective date of the Civil Code, to the extent a transaction (or contractual or similar arrangement) was ongoing (and not completed) as at that date, it would be subject to the provisions of the Civil Code on and from that date (even though these obligations may have been entered into prior to that date). Further to the implementation of the Civil Code, a number of provisions in existing Cambodian laws will be abrogated or amended.

In the article on *Introduction to the Civil Tort in Cambodia*, LAY NISAY, Legal official of Minister's cabinet of the Ministry of Justice of Cambodia Master Student of International Law School of SWUPL, and Li Dongmei, Program Director of China-ASEAN Legal Research Center of SWUPL, holds that in the daily living, we all cannot avoid the civil tort in everyday life, even though it is a petty or heavy tort. According to the glossary of Cambodia Civil Code, it has given the definition of Tort as the act of an unlawful abuse of rights or interests of others people. In additional, in the Civil Code of Cambodia has clearly stipulated on the elements of general tort and burden of proof that is a person who intentionally or negligently infringes on the right and benefits of the another people in violation of law is reliable for the payment of damages for any harm occurring as a result. In the light of this law, even a mistake or infringement permit by a person is petty but as a result, if damages or harm occurring to another person is huge, the person who had committed will be reliable to all the huge damages to the victim. The victim or injured party caused by tortious act must proof that the damage prove by intent or negligence of the tortious actor by any means according to the laws.

In the article on *Domestic Adoption in Cambodia*, Sotheavy Chan, Secretary of Sate of Ministry of Justice of Cambodia, Ph.D-Candidate of International Law School of SWUPL, holds that adoption is the establishment of family relations and family relations, the same as the relationship of parents and children as well, therefore, in the state's obligations related to the protection and ensuring the higher interests of the child. States must set a good system to care for children so that children grow and develop in a family with warm and no abuse rights.

In the article on *Important Judicial Officers in Criminal Procedure of the Court of First Instance In Cambodia*, Nup Sothunvisoth, Director Department of Research Publishing and Training on Penal Law of the Ministry of Justice of Cambodia, Ph.D-Candidate of International Law School of SWUPL, holds that The purpose of Code of Criminal Procedure of the Kingdom of Cambodia aims at defining the rules to be strictly followed and applied in order to clearly determine the existence of a criminal offense. The power and the responsibility of the state officers are provided by this law in order to process a smooth procedure on any criminal case, as well as to find justice for both victims and the accused. Although those officers are provided the power to investigate or to prosecute or to put somebody in jail, their power is restricted very strictly according to the law. There are some important judicial officers who involving in criminal procedure, however this paper focus only the most important person such as Judicial Police, Prosecutors, Investigating Judge, and the Trial Judge of the Court of First Instance.

In the article on *Effective Measurement for International cooperation in Cambodia in the context of Corruption Case*, Mr. Ku Khemlin: Deputy Director General of Justice Development of the Ministry of Justice of Cambodia, Ph.D-Candidate of International Law School of SWUPL, holds that the corruption offence is a main problem that threat to economic development, prosperity, democratic by effect to electoral process in selecting right leading in the country, and justice and rules of law by creating bureaucratic quagmires whose only reason for existence is the soliciting of bribes. The effective measures to combating the corruption is set up clear policy and sufficient measure to craft down roof of corruption by using the exiting national legal framework and also close cooperation among regional and international scheme for quickly response to the offences. The strengthening network among execution agencies is also a crucial tool help facilitate mutual legal assistance without the need for a formal request.

编者按

本期《中国—东盟法律评论》为柬埔寨法律制度研究专刊，是根据中国—东盟法律研究中心代表团出访柬埔寨时与柬埔寨司法部达成的合作出版共识，由中心与柬埔寨司法部合作编撰而成，主要收录了八篇由柬埔寨司法部官员或柬埔寨皇家法律经济大学教师所作的有关柬埔寨法制发展与部门法特色的最新研究文章，他们大部分都是西南政法大学的在读博士生。

柬埔寨司法部国际关系与发展伙伴局局长、西南政法大学国际法学院博士生 Khlok Dara 的文章“柬埔寨行政申诉机制的现状及挑战”以柬埔寨行政申诉机制的现状为切入点，通过着重研究柬埔寨在当前形势下的行政申诉机制及政府内部运行机构和机制，指出了柬埔寨行政申诉机制仍存在的许多问题和挑战，包括缺乏明确、良好的申诉机构和机制、行政申诉部门和步骤都缺乏明确的安排等，以探索建立并完善保障公民权利和增强信任的有效申诉机制为目标，提出了一些改进现有机制的建议。

柬埔寨法律和司法改革委员会常设秘书处法律顾问 KaiHauerstein 的文章“柬埔寨行政法介绍”，通过对柬埔寨行政法的详细介绍，阐释并分析了柬埔寨在构建行政法体系中存在的问题，提出了柬埔寨行政法已经从强调社会秩序在个人自治之上演变为将个人从国家中保护起来，并且在宪法和行政法二者要求中间建立了很强的相关性。在具体阐述柬埔寨行政法的制定程序和具体执行基础上，针对柬埔寨行政法法律和司法改革要求的综合投诉制度尚未落实的问题，作者提出需要制定法律和司法改革要求的重要法律，并且改进信息发布和获取机制，保证行政程序法公平透明，对行政诉讼进行独立的司法审查并制定规制执行行政决定的法律。

柬埔寨皇家法律经济大学教师、西南政法大学国际法学院博士生 Khim Kiri 和西南政法大学教师、中国—东盟法律研究中心项目官员李冬梅的文章“柬埔寨法律制度简介”，以柬埔寨的法律制度为切入点，通过详细阐释和分析

柬埔寨的法律制度,阐述了自1993年柬埔寨颁行现代国家宪法以来,柬埔寨的法律制度逐步完善,形成以宪法为中心,法律、皇家法令、政府法规、部门规章为体系的民主化法律构建的过程。

柬埔寨司法部司法部长助理、西南政法大学国际法学院博士生Ung Radsorin的文章"柬埔寨民法典中的合同与侵权法",以柬埔寨新民法典的颁行与生效,有关旧民法典中关于合同的规定将被取代为切入点,通过详细阐释和分析柬埔寨新旧民法典中合同规定的变化窥见了柬埔寨司法改革的重心,论证了柬埔寨新民法典更加注重保护公民私权利、新民法典对合同的规定更加的细致的观点。

柬埔寨司法部部长办公厅法律官员,西南政法大学国际法学院硕士生Lay Nisay和西南政法大学教师、中国—东盟法律研究中心项目官员李冬梅的文章"柬埔寨民事侵权导论",以《柬埔寨民法典》为依据,通过分析《柬埔寨民法典》中有关民事侵权的一系列内容,包括民事侵权类型、一般侵权行为的责任构成要件以及行为人对其故意或过失下不法侵害他人权利或权益而导致的任何损害结果承担责任的证明责任分配等,来描绘出柬埔寨民事侵权行为的法律架构,为社会中每个人避免故意或过失行为造成他人损害提供预防建议。

柬埔寨司法部国务秘书、西南政法大学国际法学院博士生Chan Sotheavy的文章"柬埔寨的国内收养制度",以《柬埔寨民法典》为依据,通过阐述《柬埔寨民法典》中有关国内收养制度的规定,包括国内收养制度的两种类型中完全收养和简单收养构成关系的条件、手续和标准等,为社会中的弱势群体儿童给予保护并保证其获取更好的权益,同时为缺乏亲生父母照顾的儿童营造充满幸福、爱和理解的家庭气氛。

柬埔寨司法部刑法研究出版和培训局局长、西南政法大学国际法学院博士生Nup Sothunvisoth的文章"柬埔寨初审法院刑事程序中的重要司法官员简介",以《柬埔寨王国刑事诉讼法》为依据,阐释了柬埔寨刑事诉讼程序中涉及到的许多司法工作人员如司法警察、检察官、调查法官和审判法官在该各自领域内被明确赋予的权力和责任,同时这些权力也被严格限制在了法定范围之内。这样规定的目的一方面有助于刑事程序的顺利推进,确保刑事程序的公正性,另一方面,也能平衡权力机关的权力和公民接受公平审判的权利。

柬埔寨司法部司法发展总局副局长、西南政法大学国际法学院博士生Ku Khemlin的文章"柬埔寨在反腐败国际合作中的有效措施",通过详细介绍柬埔寨现有的法律体系中存在着的有关反腐败的明确的政策和有效的措施,包括引渡和移交被判刑者、司法互助、财产没收与追缴以及反腐败调查等执法合作方式，力图在地区性和国际性体制间建立反腐败国际合作机制，目的在于迅速应对腐败犯罪，推翻腐败根基，并恢复国家在经济、政治和法治公正性上的正常运转。因此，在柬埔寨第五项皇家政府命令中，有关反腐的立法司法改革列为国家战略计划首要内容。

目 录

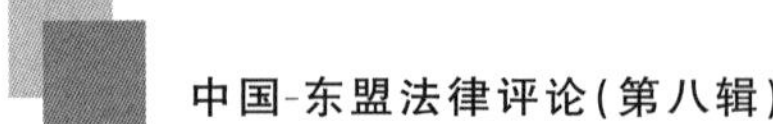

Administrative Complaint Mechanisms in Cambodia: The Current Situation and Its Challenges

Khlok Dara*

Abstract: A good relationship between citizens and the public administration is a core requirement for good governance of a country. A citizen should have the right to clarify or complain about any unclear decision/regulation or wrongful action from the administration, and consequently the administration has to be open and responsive to the citizen's claim or complaint in an effective manner. To have such an accountable, transparent and responsive administration, effective complaint mechanisms should be established.

This principle of this good governance has been stipulated in the Rectangular Strategy of the government, where the administration needs to fulfill all-important requirements for providing better services to citizens, including effective complaint resolution mechanisms. The rights to review and clarify the decisions and actions of the administration seem limited in the Cambodian context, even though the constitution envisages clearly these rights in Article 128[2-3] and other sector laws. The mechanisms are fragmented, which makes it very difficult for citizens to access justice in administration matters even in ordinary cases. Therefore, this chapter will study the current situation of administrative complaints mechanisms in Cambodia, focusing only on the mechanisms inside the administration in order to find out the challenges and issues for improving and building effective mechanisms to

* KHLOK Dara is the Director of International Relations and Development Partnership of the Ministry of Justice of Cambodia and a Ph.D candidate of the International Law School, SWUPL.

ensure citizens' rights and trust. To do this, the chapter will highlight first the current legal and policy framework, the type of administrative complaint and its structure, and finally assess the current type of administrative complaint by focusing on two specific cases for deeper analysis. At the end, the chapter will provide some recommendations for improving the existing mechanisms.

1. Introduction

In 1993, Cambodia adopted a liberal multi-party democratic system. Since then many reforms have been introduced and implemented. The Rectangular Strategy provided a comprehensive legal and judicial reform and public administrative reform program. One of the key areas is to improve institutions related to the organization and operation of the public administrative system, including those that "regulate the relationship between the State and its citizens."

The mechanism for the settlement of citizens' complaints is one of the essential institutions in the relationship between the state and society. There is a need for the government of Cambodia to seriously consider the development of effective mechanisms that can improve the relationship between the citizens and public administration, especially building trust.① The improvement of these mechanisms will contribute to enhancing the effectiveness and efficiency of public administrative practices, and simultaneously promote the implementation of citizens' civil and political rights.② The administration needs to be open, transparent and accountable to citizens.

The Constitution of Cambodia (1993) provides all citizens full rights to complain against wrongdoing by the administration.③ Currently many com-

① Khlok Dara, 2009, *Searching for Implementing an Ombudsman System in Cambodia* (Phnom Penh: Council for Legal and Judicial Reform supported by GIZ), p.13.

② Legal and Judicial Reform Strategy, pp.6-7.

③ Constitution, 1993, Article 39 [1].

plaints have been filed against the administration in both individual and collective manners. However, citizens are not satisfied with the settlement of their complaints. There are no clear, properly functioning mechanisms in place and citizens don't know where to file their complaints and how the process of the complaint should be followed since the mechanisms that do exist are without systematic arrangement[①]. Most of the complaints are lodged with the highest institutions of the state such as the prime minster, office of the Council of Ministers, king, National Assembly, Senate or main donors and international organizations.

Given this fact, the government has tried very hard to enhance and strengthen the existing systems. Despite some improvements, there are still many challenges and issues that the government needs to address at a time when it is working to develop the country. The improvement and strengthening of an effective complaint mechanism to deal with maladministration is behind schedule. It needs more effort from all relevant stakeholders to contribute to this reform process.

This paper will study the current mechanisms for settling administrative complaints in Cambodia and the challenges they face. In doing so, the paper will first highlight the current legal and policy framework supporting the mechanisms, the types of complaint and structure, and finally assess and analyze two specific cases of complaints against decisions and provision of services. The assessment will focus on four questions:

(1) Is the institutional set-up clear or is the mandate doubling-up/overlapping?

(2) Is the complaint process easy to understand and to comply with?

(3) Is the conflict resolved in an effective and efficient manner?

(4) Can a citizen appeal against a decision?

---

① Khlok Dara, 2009, *Searching for Implementing an Ombudsman System in Cambodia* (Phnom Penh: Council for Legal and Judicial Reform supported by GIZ), p.26.

2.Overview of the Current Administrative Complaints Structure

2.1 Legal and Policy Framework

2.1.1 Constitution

The Cambodian Constitution provides full rights to all citizens to exercise their rights to complain against the administration as stipulated in the two famous articles, Article 39 and Article 128, explained below. These rights can be exercised through the competent institutions that are responsible for handling the administrative complaint and, if complainants are dissatisfied, they can appeal to the court for a final decision.

- Article 39 [1] states:

> Khmer citizens have the right to denounce, make complaints, or claim compensation for damages caused by any breach of the law by institutions of the state, social organizations, or by members of such organizations.

- Article 39 [2] and Article 128 [3] state:

> Article 39 [2]: "The settlement of complaints and claims for compensation for damages is the responsibility of the courts."
>
> Article 128 [3]: "The judiciary shall consider all legal cases including administrative cases."

2.1.2 Laws

Sector law provides rights to citizens or any interested person to complain against actions of the administration. Some sector laws establish their own special institutions for handling complaints from citizens, such as the law on electricity in Article 7 [6], providing the power to the Electricity Authority of Cambodia(EAC) to handle complaints on behalf of the Ministry of Industry, Mines and Energy. Other sector laws provide the power to settle complaints

to the respective line ministry such as Law on Tourism, which provide this power to the Ministry of Tourism as mentioned in Article 46 of the Law on Tourism:

> Any person considered him/herself a victim of the decision of the Ministry of Tourism or the Sub-National Administration on the rejection, suspension, revocation and downgrading of the Tourism License or other relevant decisions as stipulated in Chapter 5 of this Law may file a written complaint to the Minister of Tourism or the Sub-National Administration within 30(thirty) days upon receipt of the written notification of any decisions as mentioned above.
>
> Upon receipt of the complaint, the Ministry of Tourism or the Sub-National Administration may suspend its decision and reconsider the matters within 60(sixty) days.

Again, the sector law not only stipulates the rights of citizens to complain and the place where citizens can lodge a complaint, but the law also mentions sanctions for harmful actions, namely the traffic law, which clearly defines the punishment for police who abuse their power during their performance.①

---

① Law on Traffic, 2006, Article 72 mentions that "Any officials or agents responsible for traffic order used their power to confiscate the driving icense, number plate, identification card or keeping the driver's vehicle, shall be jailed from six (6) days to one (1) month and or fined from Riel 25,000 to Riel 200,000. In case the vehicles are damaged or lost any parts due to the detaining, the entity shall be responsible for the payment. If the level of violation of the police officers or the traffic agents is too serious, the entity can demand the compensation from the police officers or traffic agents. The police officers or traffic agents shall be imprisoned from 1 (one) year to 3 (three) years and/or fine from two millions (2,000,000) Riels to six millions (6,000,000) Riels to any traffic officers or traffic agents that:

• Forced and demanded the fining money against the amounts set by the law.

• Obtaining money by using the incorrect fining tickets or do not issue fining tickets to the fined driver.

• Shall be punished by jailing from 1 (one) year to 3 (three) years and or fine from two millions, (2,000,000) Riels to six millions (6,000,000) Riels to any government staff or staff working directly or those who have duty or task in managing the driving schools or engaging in the issuance of the driving license and vehicle identification card and have committed wrong to the article 40 or 48 of this provision."

There are provisions on sanctions outlined in the chapter on punishment provision.

The organic law provides rights to the citizen for filing complaints against maladministration as well. The Law on Administration Management of Capital, Province, City, District, and Khan Article 85 clearly envisages the rights of citizens to complain against a territorial administration. However it is still unclear whether complaints can be filed by all citizens evenwhen they don't have residence in the place where they want to complain.

Article 85 of the organic law stipulates, "... Any person or persons who have been adversely affected by, or have paid taxes or service charges because of illegal actions or decisions, may submit their claim to the council to provide compensation and pay back in full amount. Any person or persons whose claim for compensation has been rejected or has not been paid by the council within a two month-period, that person may inform and make a complaint to the Minister of the Ministry of Interior to coordinate and solve the problem. In the event that the person does not agree with the solution made by the Minister of the Ministry of Interior, that person has the right to file their complaint."

2.1.3 Legal and Judicial Reform

Supporting the Constitution and sector laws, the improvement of the relationship between citizen and administration and the rights of citizens to claim for justice in the framework of administration is a strong commitment of the government. Improvement in this area is a priority action in the legal and judicial reform program adopted by the Council of Ministers in 2003.

A detailed Plan of Action Implementing the Legal and Judicial Reform Strategy was adopted in 2005 by the Council of Ministers. The plan includes 93 priority actions. Among them are seven priority actions that were clearly defined to establish a comprehensive and effective mechanism to settle administrative complaints. The priority actions (PA) are:

(1) PA 1.6.1 on establishment of an Ombudsman

(2) PA 1.2.4 on specific complaints for women and other disadvantaged groups

(3) PA 2.1.1 on an administrative (procedure) code, which standardizes administrative litigation as well as complaints procedures

(4)PA 2.1.4 on Law on the Organization of Courts introducing an Administrative Tribunal

(5)PA 2.1.11 on establishment of an Ombudsman's Office

(6)PA 5.4.5 on establishing an administrative tribunal

(7)PA 7.2.1 on the law for an Ombudsman.

2.2 Types of Complaints/Structure

2.2.1 Complaint Against What?

In principle, citizens can complain against all aspects of administration action such as abuse of power, corruption, decisions, provision of public services, illegal regulations issued by the administration, and misbehaviour. Administrative complaints can be divided into five main types, which include complaints against:

(1)administrative decisions

(2)service provision

(3)corruption and abuse of power

(4)administration behaviour

(5)administrative regulations.①

Complaints against administrative decisions refer to administrative complaints from citizens who are not satisfied with the decision from the administration in terms of getting a licence or any other decision that can harm rights of citizens, such as the decision to evocate the request for a marriage certificate or a request to organize a wedding ceremony.

The complaint against the provision of services from the public administration refers to administrative complaints about the services that government provides to citizens such as education, health care, electricity, and so on. Citizens can file a complaint to public administration agencies regarding their dissatisfaction with the services provided by the administration, for example health care service provision.

Complaints against criminal activities/corruption are complaints against

① Kai Hauerstein, 2013, *Aspects of Administrative Law and Its Reform in Cambodia*, p.41.

the collusion or bribery of public administration officers or agencies. It addresses criminal actions for which the administration is accountable. However, criminal responsibility is mostly envisaged as referring to the officer who committed the crime.

Complaints against administrative behaviour allow citizens to complain about any action of an administration agency which does not perform well in its duties. All interested citizens can complain to the court about the misbehaviour of police while carrying out their duties. So far this type of complaint seems not regulated clearly in Cambodian law and regulations. This paper will not cover this type of complaint.

Complaints against administrative regulations allow citizens to complain against illegal provisions established by the administration(executive power). In general, the administrative agency gets the delegation of power from the authorized law provided by the legislative branch. If the provision issued by the administration is against the authorizing law or any other regulations, citizens have the rights to clarify the legality of the regulation. In Cambodia this type of complaint seems to be not clearly provided for in the legal framework.

2.2.2 Complaints to Whom? Institutional Set-Up: Internal/External

Currently, citizens can file administrative complaints with sector ministries, sector law institutions, public enterprises and other authorities, committees, councils, cabinet of prime minister, office of the Council of Ministers, and the king as well as bodies outside the legislative branch such as the National Assembly, Senate and courts.

We can categorize these mechanisms into three kinds: (1) court, (2) intra-administrative or internal complaint mechanisms and (3) external monitoring mechanisms like the parliamentary system, and ombudsmen(see table below).[①]

---

① Joerg Menzel agreed in his presentation on international formal and informal frameworks to settle administrative complaints from citizens against administration action that in general there are three mechanisms for dealing with administrative complaints, which include (1)court, (2)intra or internal mechanisms, and (3)external mechanisms. (3-4 June 2013, Sokha Hotel, Siem Reap Province, Cambodia.)

Table 1 Summary of administrative complaint mechanism structures in Cambodia

Internal (intra-administration)	External	Court
• Ministry of National Assembly-Senate and Inspection • Sector ministry • Sector law institutions • Territorial administration	• Anti-Corruption Unit • Cambodian Human Rights Committee	Normal court (there is no specialized court or chamber for administrative cases yet in Cambodia)

Court

Lodging a complaint with the court on administrative matters is a classic method that citizens can use to review administrative maladministration. However the procedure on how to conduct the administrative complaint seems not clearly defined yet, even though the Constitution clearly envisages full rights of citizens to file complaints against the administration in Articles 39 [1] and 128 [2-3]. So far, no administrative complaints have been filed with courts.

Internal Administration

Complaints to internal administrations are normally allowed to citizens or any interested person, who can file a complaint inside the administration. Normally the process of handling the complaint is carried out by the administration of the respective institution that the complaint was addressed to. In this regard, there are four main mechanisms for handling the complaint:

(1) Ministry of National Assembly-Senate and Inspection (MONASRI)

(2) sector ministry①

(3) sector law institution

(4) territorial administration②.

MONASRI has a special mandate to deal directly with administrative

① There are 23 ministries in Cambodia.

② The territorial administration is divided into three layers: (1) capital and province, (2) city/district/khan, and (3) commune/sangkat.

complaints on corruption, abuse of power and administrative decisions.① The jurisdiction is provided to the General Department of Inspection of the Ministry. The jurisdiction for handling the administrative complaint seems to cover the whole administration.

Most sector laws provide the power to respective sector ministries to handle complaints within the scope of the sector. Generally, each sector ministry has at least one section called the Inspectorate Department within the ministry to receive and handle complaints from citizens. In addition, each ministry has one office or department in charge of internal audit, which mostly has similar power to the Inspectorate section of the ministry to deal with the complaint.

External Administration

External mechanism refers to mechanisms outside the institution of a sector ministry or sector law.② Currently there are two main external mechanisms in Cambodia:

(1) Anti-Corruption Unit

(2) Cambodian Human Rights Committee.

This does not include extra mechanisms inside the legislative branch, such as the commission in the National Assembly and one commission in the Senate.

Beside the internal and external and court mechanisms, citizens or any interested persons can file administrative complaints to the highest political institutions like prime minister, Office of the Council of Ministers, and the king. These complaints are mostly made by collective complainants and on sensitive issues such as human rights violations.

---

① Sub-Decree on Organizing and Functioning of the Ministry of National Assembly-Senate and Inspection, 1999, Article 2.

② Joerg Menzel, 2013, *International Formal and Informal Frameworks to Settle the Administrative Complaint from the Citizens Against Administration Action*, a presentation in the seminar on 3-4 June 2013 in Sokha Hotel, Siem Reap Province, Cambodia.

3. Assessing the Current Administrative Complaint Structure

This section will evaluate only the three main types of complaint against administration decisions, provision of services, and corruption and abuse of power of administration. The other two complaints, on misbehaviour of the administration and illegal regulation by the administration, are not really defined clearly in the Cambodian context. The section will raise for deeper analysis and evaluation a specific case of complaint against trademark registration decisions in the type of complaint against administration decisions, and another case of a complaint against electricity services in the type of complaint against provision of services, since these two types of complaint are the most frequently used in Cambodia.

3.1 Complaints Against Decisions of the Administration

This complaint is about the dissatisfaction of citizens on the decision of administration when they apply for a licence or permission. There are many mechanisms in place to deal with these complaints. The complaints are mostly against decisions where the administration wants to restrict the complainants' rights and freedom for doing something in the country.

Legally, each line ministry applies specific sector laws under its jurisdiction and therefore decisions are mostly related to implementing sector laws, which include (ⅰ) sanctions or (ⅱ) issuing/not issuing licences/permits. Citizen's rights are mostly provided to file the complaint when they don't agree with the objection of application for licence or permission or decision of the administration. In general, each sector law stipulates one chapter or articles, which provides citizen's rights to file a complaint against the administration when a decision does not satisfy them. For example, the Law on Taxation from 1997 sets out the rights of taxpayers to complain and the process *for handling the complaints in chapter* 5, section 8 from Articles 120 to 124.[①]

Currently, citizens can complain to the respective sector ministry or the special agency created by the sector. Sometime it can be both sector ministry institutions and special institutions created by sector law. For the sub-national level, citizens can bring their case to the respective sector department at the sub-national level and some of the special agencies that have operations at the sub-national level. However, citizens can bring a complaint to the Ombudsman's office at district level against the decision of the One Window Office or any other offices in the district level. Citizens can also file the case to the Provincial Accountability Working Group at provincial level on the decisions of the administration at both district and provincial level.

For the purpose of the paper, the author will take one example of a decision on trademark registration in the Ministry of Commerce for evaluation and analysis of the current situation.

3.1.1 Trademark Registration Case

All citizens or any interested persons who want to get protection for their trademark need to register in the Department of Intellectual Property Rights of the Ministry of Commerce.[②] The requirement is mentioned in Article 3 of the law on Marks, Trade Names, and Acts of Unfair Competition.

The application process begins with the filing of an application form, fif-

---

① Law on Taxation, 1997, Articles 120-124. The law provides the rights only to the taxpayer but not for third parties to file a complaint. The complaint must be in written form. The process is to first complain directly to the department Director of Taxation Administration who made the decision or action within 30 days, and the taxation administration has to respond within 60 days. If there is no agreement, appeal can be made to the Taxation Conciliation Committee of the Ministry of Economic and Finance within 30 days after decision of the taxation administration; finally the complainant can appeal to court within 30 days from the decision of the Committee if they do not agree with the decision of the Committee. These provisions were stipulated in the *Handbook on Rights and Duties of Tax Payers*, 2010 by the Ministry of Economy and Finance, pp. 28-32.

② Law on Marks, Trade Names, and Acts of Unfair Competition (2001), Article 3.

teen specimens of the mark, and if filed by an agent, an original notarized power of attorney. Unless the application is rejected and requires an appeal, it usually takes about four months from filing to issuance of the final certificate.

Legal Basis

When the application is denied by the registrar's office of the Department of Intellectual Property Rights of the Ministry, the applicant can file a complaint to the registrar's office of the Department for clarification.① The Department is responsible for dealing with the complaint from the interested party who is not satisfied with the decision of the department.②

The law on trademarks does not mention rights of the applicant for the trademark registration to file a complaint against the decision of objection of trademark registration. However, there is an implementing sub-decree. It seems to conflict with the principle of legality. Instead, the law provides the rights to claim to the court if the interested party does not agree the decision of the Ministry of Commerce. Article 62 states:

> Any decision taken by the Ministry of Commerce may be the subject of an appeal by any interested party before the Courts and such appeal shall be filed within three months of the date of the decision.③

Articles 17 and 18 of the Sub-Decree issued by the prime minister-stipulate briefly the procedure for receiving and handling the complaint against the trademark decision. The law provides rights to complain, however the complaint must be made it in written form to the registrar's office of the Department of Intellectual Property Rights.④

---

① Sub-Decree on the Implementation of the Law Concerning Marks, Trade Names and Acts of Unfair Competition, 2006, Articles 17-18.

② Sub-Decree on Organizing and Functioning of Ministry of Commerce, 2007, Article 21.

③ Law on Mark, Trade Name and Acts of Unfair Competition, 2002, Article 62.

④ Sub-Decree on the Implementation of the Law Concerning Marks, Trade Names and Acts of Unfair Competition, 2006, Article 17 [3].

Beside the two articles of the Sub-Decree, there are no others laws or regulations or procedures for a complaint handling process. The two Articles 17 and 18 of the Sub-Decree state:

Article 17: "Objection to or Conditional Acceptance of Application and Hearing

1. If, upon examination in accordance with Article 8(a) of the Law, the Registrar decides to make objection to the application for registration of a mark, he/she shall notify the applicant in writing of this objections with all detailed information relevant to this decision and invite the applicant to amend the application, then to submit the response in writing back to the Registrar or to apply for a hearing within forty five(45) days starting from the date of receiving the notification. If the applicant does not comply with the notification, he/she shall be deemed to have withdrawn his/her application.

2. If, upon examination in accordance with Article 8(b) of the Law, the Registrar decides to accept the application subject to amendments, modifications, conditions, disclaimers(on any element(s) of the mark) or limitations or other conditions, he/she shall communicate this decision to the applicant in writing. If the applicant objects to the amendments, modifications, disclaimersor limitations or other conditions, he/she shall, within sixty (60) days starting from the date of receiving the notification of the Registrar, apply for a hearing or submit his/her observations in writing. If the applicant does not object to such amendments, modifications, disclaimersor limitations or other conditions, he/she shall notify the Registrar in writing and amend his/her application accordingly. If the applicantdoes not response in one way or the others as mentioned above, he/she shall be deemed to have abandoned his/her application.

3. The request for a hearing shall be made in writing to the Registrar. Upon receivingthis request, the Registrar shall notify the applicant, in writing, at least one month before the date on which the applicant will be invited to be heard."

Article 18: "Refusal of Application or Conditional Acceptance of the Registrar to which Applicant Objects

1.If,after hearing or after consideration on the applicant's amendments or observations in writing, the Registrar still refuses the application or accepts it subject to any amendments, modifications, disclaimers or limitations or other conditions to which the applicant objects to this refusal or conditional acceptance,he/she shall communicate his/her refusal decision to the applicant in writing.The applicant may, within one month from the date of such communication,request the Registrar to confirm in writing the grounds of his/her decision and the referred materials used by the Registrar in making this decision.

2.The applicant is entitled to appeal against the Registrar's decision to refuse the application to the Appeal Board of the Ministry of Commerce or to the competent court within three(03) months counting from the Decision date.

3.Pursuant to Article 62 of the Law, interested party is entitled to appeal against the Appeal Board's decision to the competent court within three(03)months counting from the Decision date."

Responsible Department

Legally,the law on trademarks provides a mandate to the Ministry of Commerce to handle the registration of the trademark as well the mandate to handle the complaint from the applicant who is registering the trademark.[①] The responsible Department of Intellectual Property Rights of the Ministry is in charge of handling the complaint from the interested party as stipulated in the law.However,the study of the Council for Legal and Judicial Reform in 2009 found that there were at least three other departments in the Ministry who typically receive and handle complaints as well.The three departments are the Department of Legal Affairs,the General Inspectorate Department,and Cabinet of the Minister.[②]

---

① Sub-Decree on Organizing and Functioning of Ministry of Commerce,2007,Article 21.

② Sub-Decree on Organizing and Functioning of the Ministry of Commerce,Articles 7,21,and 23 and Khlok Dara,2009,*Pre-Assessment of Complaint Mechanisms and Ombudsman Systems in Cambodia*.

The Department of Legal Affairs mostly claims to have a single office to handle complaints. The Department established an officer to handle the complaint for the Ministry, however it seems to be not working well as it is too small an office in which there are only two officers in charge and the complaint-receiving was low.[①]

The General Inspectorate Department has a broad mandate to handle mostly the internal complaints within the Ministry, however, the Department mostly exercises its power to handling other complaints. Most of the complaints have been received and settled in the Cabinet of the Minster.

Complaint Handling Procedure

The interested party can complain against the administration of the Department of Intellectual Property Rights of the Ministry of Commerce in three different situations:

- First, in cases where the registration of trademark is in the process of proceeding for registration in the Department of Intellectual Property Rights of the Ministry
- Second, in cases where the registration of trademark is rejected
- Third, in cases where the registration of trademark is finished and it has already been published in the official gazette of the Ministry of Commerce.

Given the facts from the two Articles 17 and 18, the complaints handling process can be divided into four main steps:

- The first step starts with the complaint from the interested party who applied for the trademark registration. In the case where the application has been rejected by the Department, the interested party can file a complaint for hearing within forty-five(45) days from the date the notification was received from the registrar's office of the Department. If the applicant objects to amendments requested by the registrar, the applicant has sixty(60) days from the date of the notification received to file a complaint for hearing.
- The second step is receiving and hearing the complaint from the inter-

① Khlok Dara, 2009, *Pre-Assessment of Complaint Mechanisms and Ombudsman Systems in Cambodia*.

ested party by the registrar's office. Upon receiving the complaint the registrar's office has to notify the complainant within one month before an invitation for a hearing.

• The third step applies if the applicant is not satisfied with the decision of the registrar's office. In this case the applicant can appeal to the Appeal Board of the Ministry of Commerce or directly to court within three months from the date of the decision of the registrar. So far the Appeal Board of Ministry of Commerce is not established, therefore the appeal must go directly to the court, although the court does not yet have a clear procedure in place either.

• There is a fourth step if the applicant appeals to Appeal Board of the Ministry of Commerce without filing directly to the court, and the applicant does not agree the decision of the Appeal Board. In this case the applicant can appeal to the court within three months after the decision of the Appeal Board of the Ministry of Commerce.

The procedure for handling complaints seems to be not yet developed clearly by the ministry. Normally the ordinary administrative complaint process has been used to settle the complaint. When the complaint comes, the receiving office (all offices in the ministry can receive and handle complaints regardless the jurisdiction or mandate) will make a report with recommendations and submit this to superiors for a decision. However, the procedure will normally take a long time, and there is no system of reply or notice or any other clear reference on whether the complaint has been received by the administration of the ministry.

The final decision reached depends on the decision from the superior, whether the superior agrees for mediation or conducts more investigation into the case. There is no specific rule or any other guideline on the procedure of handling the complaints in place yet, even in the special department that is supported by some donors, for example, the Department of Intellectual Property Rights.

3.1.2 Analysis

The mechanism for handling trademark registration decisions within the ministry is clearly defined in the legal framework of the sector law on trade-

marks. However, in practice, the jurisdiction for handling complaints seems fragmented inside the Ministry of Commerce.① It is not clear enough for the interested party who is affected by the decisions of the administration since within the ministry, there are couple of departments that provide a possibile path for complaint handling. The Department of Legal Affairs has an office to receive and handlle complaints where the jurisdiction seems to cover all matters under the Ministry of Commerce, including trademark registration decisions. In addition the General Inspectorate Department of the ministry seems have the power to deal with all issues under the ministry too. The Cabinet of the Minister is mostly seen as the main entrance for all issues, including complaint handling.

There is no rule or any guideline mentioning clearly the process for dealing with complaints. Citizens or interested persons who are not satisfied with the decisions of the administration don't have any clue or idea on what process or procedure they should follow. They don't know where they should complain to as the ministry doesn't provide any clear signal or information for the complainant. The complainant most of the time goes to the administrative office or cabinet or respective department that issued the decision.

It takes a long time for the complaint to be dealt with and sometime there is no notice from the administration of the ministry-no clear reference on whether the complaint has been received and registered by the ministry or not, even though there is a rule that the registrar's office, after receiving the complaint, will notify the complainant one month before the hearing starts. The complainant just lodges the complaint without knowing whether their complaint will be processed or just kept without processing. Most of the time, the complainant needs to contact the administration of the Ministry again and again to take action on their complaint otherwise there is no progress.

There is no clear jurisdiction for handling the complaint and there is no rule on how the decision should be made by the registrar's office of the Department or the Appeal Board of the Ministry of Commerce during the hear-

① Khlok Dara, 2009, *Searching for Implementing an Ombudsman System in Cambodia* (Phnom Penh: Council for Legal and Judicial Reform supported by GIZ), p.48.

ing process. In general, when the administration get the complaint they will make a report and recommendation to a superior for a decision, and if the superior doesn't do anything then the case will be kept without action as long as the complaint reconfirms again and again to the administration that they do not want to drop the complaint.[①] Even if there is a decision from the superior to process the case, the procedure to settle seems to work very slowly since there are no rules or guidelines on the hearing process.

The law provides rights to an interested party to appeal to the Appeal Board of the Ministry of Commerce when the party does not agree with the decision of the registrar's office, but the Appeal Board has not been established yet.

There is no clear procedure on how to conduct an investigation or clarification before the decision for accepting or rejecting the complaint on the decision of the administration. The sub-decree on the Implementation of Concerning Marks, Trade Names, and Acts of Unfair Competition does not provide a clear process on the investigation step. Information on the procedure of settlement of the complaint seems invisible to the complainant. They cannot access or know what process they should follow next or how to do it. Furthermore, the statistics of complaints handling within the Ministry are even more difficult to access.

The legal framework supporting the process dealing with the complaint seems not established, and even the existing legal framework in the Ministry doesn't provide clear jurisdiction and mandate for each responsible department.

3.2 Complaint Against the Provision of Services

This category of complaint refers to complaints against the administration that provides public services to the citizens, where the service provision does not satisfy the citizens. In Cambodia public services delivery includes education, health care, welfare services, electricity, water, and so on. The complaint can be filed to the respective office or department or sector ministry

---

① Khlok Dara, 2009, *Searching for Implementing an Ombudsman System in Cambodia* (Phnom Penh: Council for Legal and Judicial Reform supported by GIZ), p.48.

that provides the service and other institutions provided in sector law. In general, the responsible mechanisms for complaint handling are located inside the administration and use or follow the ordinary administrative procedure for handling complaints. There is some overlapping of complaint handling functions among the department inside the sector Ministry. The complaint handling functions of the Department of Legal Affairs, Cabinet of Minister and General Inspectorate Department commonly overlap. The report of a baseline survey on legal units and law making capacity of ministries/institutions by the Council for Legal and Judicial reform in 2009 found that most of the legal affairs departments of the ministries/institutions had the function to settle complaints for which they had jurisdiction under the ministries/institutions.①

The power to handle complaints in mechanisms located in the sector ministry and the specific institution is mostly provided by the specific sector law, for example the Ministry of Education, Youth, and Sport as mentioned in the Education Law in Article 40:

> Right to request, right to protest, right to complain, right to solution:
>
> Parents or guardians, learners and educational personnel, whose rights specified in this law, are violated, have the right to request or protest to the competent educational authority at different levels as well as to the court. The Ministry in charge of education shall issue regulations on procedures for requests, protests and solutions.

The following section provides an example of a complaint against the provision of electricity services.

3.2.1 Electricity Services Case

Electricity provision is a main service that the government of Cambodia needs to ensure for its citizens. Any missing or ineffective service or any bad

① Council for Legal and Judicial Reform, 2009, *Baseline Survey on Legal Units and Law Making Capacity of Ministries/Institutions*, p.13.

service in the electricity provided by the government is subject to filing for clarification or complaint from citizens or consumers. The government under the jurisdiction of the Ministry of Industry, Mines and Energy gives the power to the Electricity Authority of Cambodia (EAC) as the responsible agency to ensure the effective provision of electricity to citizens.① However the EAC has to cooperate with the Ministry in terms of technical support.②

Legal Basis

Sometimes a citizen or consumer is not satisfied with the service provided by the supplier or disputes the correctness of the meter, meter reading or the bill in relation to the supply, or the cutting off of the electricity without reason. In such cases the citizen or consumer can file a complaint first with the supplier which is located nearest to the place where they live. To file complaints and resolve disputes efficiently and transparently, EAC has the power to handle these issues within their approved Procedures and Regulations to be followed by consumers and suppliers.③

The Law on Electricity envisages the power to settle an administrative complaint around service provision by any agency that provides electricity in either private or public sectors.④ Citizens can complain against any provision decision of EAC within thirty (30) days from the date they receive the decision.⑤

The power to deal with the complaint is found in the procedures of complaint handling of EAC:⑥

1. Under Electricity Law of the Kingdom of Cambodia, the duties of Electricity Authority of Cambodia (EAC) include evaluation and resolution of consumer complaints and contract disputes involving licensees to the extent the complaints and contract disputes relate to violation of the conditions of license.

2. The Electricity Law provides that any licensee or consumer, who is

① Law on Electricity, 2001, Article 1.

② Law on Electricity, 2001, Article 3.

③ Procedure for Filing Complaint to EAC and for Resolution of EAC, 2004.

④ Law on Electricity, 2001, Article 7-f.

⑤ Law on Electricity, 2001, Article 18.

⑥ Procedure for Filing Complaint to EAC and for Resolution of EAC, Clause A.

party to a dispute regarding the provision of electric power services, under an EAC approved tariff or under a contract, may refer the dispute to EAC for resolution; provided that the related License requires such dispute to be referred to EAC.

3. Any interested person may file to EAC a written complaint against a licensee alleging a violation of any provision of the Electricity Law. EAC shall investigate this complaint and determine whether there may have been a breach of the Electricity Law.

4. The Electricity Law also provides that EAC may investigate any facts, natures, actions or matters which it may find necessary or proper to determine whether any person has violated or is about to violate any provision of the Electricity Law or any Sub-Decree, regulation, order, or judgment of EAC.

Responsible Institution

There are two institutions that are responsible for handling complaints, which are the private supplier who is licensed by EAC to provide an electricity service (the supplier) and the EAC. The Department of Legal Affairs of the secretariat of EAC is responsible for receiving and handling complaints from citizens or customers about electricity provision.① However the guidelines for the complaint handling process of EAC do not mention that specific Department when citizens want to complain. It just mentions that any interested person who is affected by the electricity services provision can complain to the supplier or EAC.②

Complaint Handling Procedure

It is different from other mechanisms which are located in the sector Ministry or even in specific institutions of the sector, where the complaint handling procedure for the settlement of the provision of electricity service is mentioned clearly in two guidelines:

---

① Report of EAC, 2010, p.14.

② Procedure of settlement of complaint of EAC mentions only that all interested citizens can complain against the agencies that provide electricity services to EAC. The procedure does not mention a specific unit or office, which is responsible to receive and deal with the complaint.

(1)Guidelines for the Information of Consumers about their Rights to Complain to the Supplier or Electricity Authority of Cambodia(the Guidelines)

(2)Procedure for Filing Complaints to EAC and for Resolution by EAC (the Procedure).[①] Beside the two main important complaint handling procedures, EAC has established other Standards of Performance of Licensees relatingto the quality of supply and services, which mention the obligations of suppliers or EAC to handle consumers' complaints.[②]

Both the Procedure and the Guidelines provide clear complaint handling processes which include within their jurisdiction subjects that citizens can complain about, the modality of making a complaint, phases of receiving and resolution of complaints, documentation, and rights to appeal. According to the procedure for settlement of complaints against the electricity service provision of EAC, all citizens can complaint to EAC after 30 days of the decision of any electricity provider. The Procedure and Guidelines for settlement of the complaint by EAC provide two options for complaints where the complaint can first filed directly with the electricity supplier(the supplier who is licensed by EAC)or directly to the EAC. If it is filed with the electricity supplier and the complainant does not agree the decision from the supplier, they can then file the complaint to EAC.

Consumers who want to file a complaint directly with the supplier can complain on only six subjects as mentioned in the Guideline for the Information of Consumers about their Rights to Complaint to Supplier or EAC.[③]

---

① Procedure for Filing Complaint to EAC and for Resolution of EAC and Guidelines for the Information of Consumers about their rights to Complaint to the Suppliers or EAC.

② Overall Performance Standard for Electricity Suppliers in the Kingdom of Cambodia mentions 13 standards for suppliers when dealing with consumers.

③ The Guideline for the information of consumers about their rights to complain to the supplier or EAC mentions six categories of complaint against the electricity service provision, which are (1)complaint on voltage, (2)complaint on interruption/failure of supply, (3)complaint about meters and meter reading, (4)complaint about non-receipt of energy bill or receipt of incorrect bill, (5)complaint on disconnection or reconnection, and (6)complaint on delay in giving new connection.

When the complainant does not agree with the decision of the supplier, the complainant can appeal to EAC. All thirteen(13) subjects of electricity service provision, including the six subject matters for complaint as mentioned in the Procedure, can be the subject of a complaint filed directly with EAC①. It means that all subject matters stipulated in the Procedure can be the subject of complaint about electricity services.

---

① (1) The supplier has an obligation to give power supply to consumers in its authorized area of supply and can refuse to give power supply to a consumer only under certain conditions stated in the General Conditions of Supply. If the Supplier refuses to serve an applicant, he/she must inform the applicant the reason of its refusal. If the applicant is dissatisfied with the decision of the supplier, he/she may file a complaint with the EAC, giving copies of the decision of the supplier, other correspondence related to this complaint and the reason of considering the decision of the supplier incorrect. (2) For giving a new connection to a Medium Consumer, if extension/ upgrading of the network is required, the supplier indicates the participation amount in network extension/ upgrading cost to be paid by the consumer. If any difference or dispute arises as to the participation amount, the consumer can file a complaint to EAC for resolution of the dispute, giving copies of the letters in the matter and the reason of disputing the amount. (3) The General Conditions of Supply provide that if the supplier finds out that any person is taking supply without authorization or dishonestly, the supplier shall issue a bill for the electricity used with authorization. If the consumer disputes the bill, he/she may file a complaint with the EAC giving full reasons for disputing the bill. (4) Apart from raising the bill as stated above, the supplier may also file a complaint to EAC to impose a monetary penalty on the consumer under Article 68 of the Electricity Law of the Kingdom of Cambodia, giving full justification for this. (5) Any interested person may file to EAC a complaint against a licensee alleging a violation of any provision of(ⅰ) the Electricity Law of the Kingdom of Cambodia, Rules and Regulations issued under the Electricity Law(ⅱ) the licence issued by EAC or(ⅲ) regulations made by EAC. The person in their complaint should clearly state the provisions of the Law, Rules or Regulation that have been violated. (6) When a reference is made to EAC by the Ministry of Industry, Mines and Energy or the Local Authority about violations by a licensee, or when EAC decides to start proceedings against a licensee or consumer for violations that came to its notice from information derived from any other source, EAC shall designate an officer of EAC not below the rank of Office Manager to act as Complainant. (7) Complaints relating to contract disputes can be filed by a party to the dispute provided the related licence requires such dispute to be referred to EAC. The party in its complaint shall state the provisions of the licence that require the dispute to be referred to EAC and details of the dispute.

Given the facts from the Guideline and Procedure for complaint handling by EAC, the complaint settlement procedure is divided into five(5)phases.[①]

First, filing of complaint and notice to the defendant. When the complaint is submited to EAC, the responsible unit will register it and provide notice within 15 days from receiving it whether they accept the complaint or not. The complaint must be in written form with relevant attachments. The complaint should contain (1) information about the complainant, (2) information about the defendant, (3) details of the complaint such as the subject of the complaint, (4) specific reference to relevant law and regulations or any rules, (5) prayer of the complainant, (6) relevant attachments, and (7) signature of the complainant.

When the complaint is received by EAC, EAC will send the complaint to the defendant to give clarification in a reply within the period specified by EAC. If no reply is received within the specified period, it will be deemed that the defendant has no comments to offer and a decision on the complaint shall be taken by the EAC as deemed fit and proper unless the time for receiving the reply is extended in writing by the EAC.

Second, conciliation: if the reply does not satisfy the complainant, the reconciliation process will start after the agreement from the chairman of EAC. The reconciliation officer will be appointed for this. The agreement of both parties will be documented.

Third, investigation: If agreement is not reached in the conciliation stage, EAC starts to conduct an investigation. There is no specific duration for the investigation. In addition there is no rule mentioning how the investigation process will be done.

Fourth, session of EAC and Judgment: EAC will conduct a final meeting with participation from the three members of EAC to decide the case. Before the trial starts, EAC has to give notice 15 days in advance to the complianant and other relevant parties. Three members of

① Procedure for Filing Complaint to EAC and for Resolution of EAC, 2004.

EAC will decide on a majority basis.EAC decision will be documented in the EAC.All relevant documents will be made available in the EAC and all interested parties can access the information.However,there is no information on the EAC website regarding complaint handling data.

Fifth,appeal to court:If the complainant does not agree with the decision of EAC,they can appeal to the court within three months of the decision of EAC.

3.2.2 Analysis

From the case described above,the process for handling complaints against the provision of services is in general quite well organized,mostly in state owned enterprises,which operate independently from the government, particularly in termof budgeting. However, complaint mechanisms are not working well in sector ministries.① Some specific sector law institutions who have the power to settle administrative complaints are not working well either,since mostly they are not independent from the government budget. EAC is an independent institution, which gets a separate budget from the government. Therefore, EAC works quitewell. But so far there are no statistics on the handling of complaints.②

The power of handling complaints seems mostly to be given to the chairman of EAC to decide on behalf of the other two members of the EAC. The reconciliation process cannot start without the agreement from the

① There is no clear law or procedure on how a complaint against education service provision should be handled.The Law on Education provides the power to receive and settle complaints to the Ministry of Education,Youth and Sport and the Education Council.(See more in the Law on Education and Sub-Decree on Organizing and Functioning of Ministry of Education,Youth,and Sport.)

② There are many annual reports in which there is no statistic mentioned on the number of complaints handled.The author tried to make contact by phone and email to get statistics on complaint handling but the responsible officer in EAC said that there are no statistics to report.

chairman of EAC as mentioned in the procedure for complaint handling.[1] The power is still centralized even in the independent public enterprise institutions such as EAC. In addition, the chairman has the power to appoint an investigation officer, where this power should be kept in the Department of Legal Affairs, the body that gets a full mandate from EAC for complaint handling.

The power to make decisions to solve the complaint is not really clearly defined even in EAC law or any regulations, even though there is a clear and quite detailed procedure for handling cases. There is no clause that mentions on what extent the jurisdiction of decisions can be made.

Even the power to conduct an investigation seems clearly defined in EAC but it seems not to define clearly how the power of investigation should be exercised. The procedure just provides the rights to the investigator appointed by the chairman of EAC to conduct the investigation, and all relevant parties should cooperate with the officer. The process of investigation should clearly define the jurisdiction of EAC or any responsible officer. In the Procedure, the chairman has the power to appoint one of the officers of EAC not below the rank of office manager as the investigating officer, who may be assisted by other officers of EAC. If considered necessary, experts or consultants may be asked to assist in the investigation. The responsible Department of Legal Affairs who gets the mandate for the complaint handling seems not to be involved in this process.

The way consumers can make a complaint is rather limited since the complaint needs to made in writing and there is no rule allowing the citizens to complain to EAC by any others options. In addition, there is no clear timeframe for how long the investigation should be conducted.

There is a clear rule that all relevant documents of complaint handling, including the statistics of complaint handling, should be made public where all interested persons can access them, but the information is not available for access on the EAC website. At least the information on how to complain

---

① Procedure for Filing Complaint to EAC and for Resolution of EAC, 2004, Clause D [25].

or who to complain to should be available on the website of the EAC where interested persons can learn about the process.

3.3 Complaints Against Corruption and Other Forms of Abuse of Power

This category refers to a complaint against the collusion or any other bribery of public administration officers or agencies. It involves criminal action, for which the administration is required to be responsible. However, normally the criminal responsibility applies to the personal officer who commits the crime.

Citizen can complain to both internal administration institutions and external institutions. Currently, there are at least five institutions in which two mechanisms are external mechanisms and three institutions are internal mechanisms. The mechanisms include

(1) Anti-Corruption Unit (ACU), ①

(2) Ministry of National Assembly-Senate and Inspection (MONASRI) ②

(3) Cambodian Human Rights Committee (CHRC) ③ and the subnational administration institutions

(4) Provincial Accountability Working Group (PAWG)

(5) District Ombudsman (DO). ④

---

① Law on Anti-Corruption, Articles 2, 3, 13.

② Sub-Decree on Organizing and Functioning of Ministry of National Assembly-Senate and Inspection, Article 2.

③ The mandate of the Committee covers mostly the human rights violation protection, including any complaint regarding corruption and abuse of power by the administration. However while the mandate is for receiving the complaint, this institution is not the complaint handling institution. They receive the complaint and study and then make a report with recommendations on the jurisdiction of the complaint for a decision by a superior.

④ PAWG is established within the framework of working and monitoring the performance of subnational administration, including corruption in procurement issues at the district level. DO is a citizens office that is responsible for monitoring the performance of One Window Office at district level and its mandate has been expended to the whole district performance monitoring, including the corruption issue.

Legal Basis

This type of complaint relates to specific criminal activity where the punishment is mostly covered in the Criminal Code and the process of complaint handling is mostly stipulated in the Criminal Procedure Code. The Criminal Code mentions the punishment in clauses from Articles 278-283. Regarding the punishment of administration abuses of power during their performance, some sector law provides clear clauses on punishment. For example, the Law on Traffic provides:

> Any officials or agents responsible for traffic order used their power to confiscate the driving license, number plate, identification card or keeping the driver's vehicle, shall be jailed from 6(six) days to one(1) month and or fined from Riel 25,000 to Riel 200,000. In case the vehicles are damaged or lost any parts due to the detaining, the entity shall be responsible for the payment. If the level of violation of the police officers or the traffic agents is too serious, the entity can demand the compensation from the police officers or traffic agents.
>
> The police officers or traffic agents shall be imprisoned from one (1) year to three (3) years and/or fine from two millions (2,000,000) Riels to six millions (6,000,000) Riels to any traffic officers or traffic agents that:
>
> • Forced and demanded the fining money against the amounts set by the law
>
> • Obtaining money by using the incorrect fining tickets or do not issue fining tickets to the fined driver.
>
> • Shall be punished by jailing from one (1) year to three (3) years and/or fine from two millions (2,000,000) Riels to six millions (6,000,000) Riels to any government staff or staff working directly or those who have duty or task in managing the driving schools or engaging in the issuance of the driving license and vehicle identification card and have committed wrong to the article 40 or 48 of this provision.①

① Law on Traffic, Article 72.

Complain to Whom?

As mentioned above, complaints can be filed to internal and external mechanisms. However, if we look at MONASRI, the Ministry envisages three different departments handling complaints. The first department is called the Department of Receiving and Investigating the Complaint; the second is the Department of Litigation; and the last department is the Department of Legal Affairs.① Another four institutions at both national and subnational level have specific departments for handling complaints.

The complaint can also be filed with an external mechanism such as ACU or CHRC. The ACU has jurisdiction for the whole country. All citizens or any interested person can complain against corruption at the national level with an ACU office located in the capital or a province.② Besides complaining in person in the ACU, citizens can complain by phone, fax, post box, email or where a box is installed publicly. Similarly, MONASRI has jurisdiction covering the whole country as well through their delegated capital/provincial departments and district/Khan/city offices. CHRC is not a resolution mechanism, however its role is to receive complaints on human rights issues, including corruption and abuse of power by the administration, and then CHRC staff will study and identify the jurisdiction, making a report and recommendation of the jurisdiction to a superior for a decision.③

Complaint Handling Procedure

The complaint handling procedure can be divided into three categories according to the nature of the responsible institution. The first procedure for handling the complaint in the MONASRI follows the ordinary administrative process. After receiving the complaint, the complaint will be studied to identify the jurisdiction and there will be a report with recommendations that goes to a superior for a decision. If the superior agrees to more investigation,

---

① Sub-Decree on Organizing and Functioning of Ministry of National Assembly-Senate and Inspection, Articles 7, 14, and 15.

② Law on Anti-Corruption, Article 22.

③ Khlok Dara, 2009, *Searching for Implementing an Ombudsman System in Cambodia* (Phnom Penh: Council for Legal and Judicial Reform supported by GIZ), pp.51-52.

then the investigation will start and finally a report with recommendations for a decision will again go to the superior. It is similar to the process in the CHRC, where the complaint handling procedure is the same as the ordinary administrative process, but CHRC is not a resolution institution. CRHC can just receive the complaint and send it to the responsible institution[①].

Most of the complaint handling by ACU follows the Criminal Procedure Code, except for measures that are not stipulated in the Code.[②] The process is divided into three phases:

> First is receiving complaint. The complaint can be made in person, dropped into ACU boxes, through electronic form, post office, phone, fax or email.
>
> Second, the complaint will be studied by the Complaint Analysis Center of the ACU who then make suggestions to the president of ACU for a decision before any action (such as transfer to court). If the president of ACU agrees then, the investigation starts in cooperation with the court.
>
> Finally the after the investigation is completed in cooperation with the prosecutor, the case will be transferred to the court for final decision-making.[③]

This is just a temporary procedure that needs to be established more clearly by ACU in the near future, said an ACU officer.

PAWG and DO set up their own procedure for complaint handling. The procedures are clearly defined with a detailed process from receiving the complaint through to the decision-making.

Analysis

There are five institutions that are responsible for dealing with corruption and abuse of power complaints. The jurisdiction is not clearly separated

---

① *Ibid*.

② Law on Anti-corruption, Article 21.

③ *Ibid*., Article 25.

among the government institutions. Even inside MONASRI, there are many departments in charge of handling complaints.

Even though there are some good developments in combating corruption, there is no clear guideline or procedure the ACU should follow. Even the anti-corruption laws mention that the procedure for dealing with corruption can follow the process stated in the Criminal Procedure Code.

There is no clear timeframe for the process of dealing with complaints. Transparency of information is not provided for the public, as the public cannot get access to all the necessary information such as how to file a complaint properly. Complaints can be made through email, phone, post office or dropping in a white box, but there is no certainty whether the complaint will be taken up for action or not.

There are no statistics on complaints handling so far. Access to information is very limited in Cambodia in general. ACU is an institution that should be open and transparent for the public to access necessary information. However, the situation is the same as with other public institution where access to information is still questionable. Information regarding complaint-handling statistics was disseminated sometimes by the news media, but the website of ACU does not have this data. According to the news, there were 800 cases received in 8 months in 2012 and half of them were processed. The complaint numbers increased from 700 cases in 2011.①

3.4 Complaints Against Illegal Regulationsand Misbehaviour of Administration

Currently there is no clear law or any rules that provide citizens with an avenue to make a complaint against misbehaviour of the administration. Most sector law provides the rights to complain against wrongdoings of the administration where the jurisdiction is rather broad whether it covers

---

① DAP Website: http://www.dap-news.com/en/index.php?option=com_content&view=article&id=9623:-cambodias-anti-corruption-unit-receives-800-complaints-in-8-months&catid=1:local-news&Itemid=18, accessed on 24 June 2013.

misbehaviour of administration or not.[①] Again a process to complain against illegal regulations seems to be not mentioned in any laws yet. The regulations here means any law created by execution. It covers royal decrees, sub-decrees, prakas (proclamations), circulars, and decisions of the government, as well deika (bylaws issued by the territorial administration). There are some provisions that ensure the principle of legality of administration through the principle of hierarchy of law where the regulations cannot be made above or beyond the higher law and regulations.[②]

A draft Circular on Procedure on Law and Regulations Making Process was adopted by the Council of Ministers meeting on 10 June 2013. The Circular covers royal decrees, prakas (proclamations), circulars, government decisions and is legally binding. However there are still questions on the legal binding for some other administrative acts such as announcement letters from the Office of the Council of Ministers. Which institution has the power to check the legality of the regulations or administration acts? The Constitutional Council can check both constitutionality of law or legality of any regulations of ministries/institution when the case is in the court.[③] However, there seems to be little clarity of who has jurisdiction over administration organizations or even the court system.

Even though the Constitution authorizes ordinary courts to act, there is no procedure or law which stipulates the process for doing so.[④] Many other countries use courts to clarify the validity of a regulation or act from the administration. Dr. Bory agreed that the full jurisdiction for conducting this judicial review is generally given to the court as mentioned in Article 128 of

---

① Law on Taxation Articles 18 and 120 mentions that if the taxpayer doesn't agree with any decision or wrong doing of the taxation administration, they can file a complaint with the administration.

② Law on Organizing and Functioning of the Council of Ministers, Article 29 and Say Bory, *General Administrative Law*, Third Edition, Blossom Lotus Printing, 2002, pp. 109-127.

③ Law on Organizing and Functioning of the Constitutional Council, Article 19.

④ Constitution, Article 128 [2-3].

the Constitution.[①]

4.Conclusion and Remarks

The administrative complaint mechanisms in Cambodia are not yet well organized. They are still fragmented inside and outside the administration. Each institution or administration office can play a role in dealing with all types of administrative complaints. There is no standard rule in any law that stipulates how the mechanisms should be organized and managed within the administration. Each sector law and sector ministry produces different standards of procedure. The right of citizens to file a complaint is still limited. The power and functions of each mechanism are still blurred, with some of them overlapping, even inside one ministry or institution. Each ministry has at least three overlapping sections (the Department of Legal Affairs, General Inspectorate Department, and Cabinet of the Minister) that have a similar mandate dealing with administrative complaints. There is no coordination in the system, systematic coordination noted as a very important factor for good government and public management.

To improve these challenges, commitment from all relevant stakeholders, in particular the government, is essential. What is needed:

• First, set up a legal framework that provides clear rights to citizens to file a complaint against the administration.

• Second, there must be a clear mandate for each government ministry/institution to reform. A functional mapping and functional review should be undertaken to ensure sound public management. The starting point for functional mapping and functional review of delegating the power and function to sub-national administration is a good step already begun by the National Committee for Sub-National Democratic Development (NCDD). However, this process should start at the national level as well.

• Third, at least a simple procedure for administrative complaint-han-

① Say Bory, 2002, *General Administrative Law*, Third Edition, Blossom Lotus Printing, pp.139-140, 166, 200.

dling should be produced for short-term implementation by all mechanisms. A comprehensive Administrative Procedure Code should be considered in the long term.

• Last but not least, there is a need to not only improve the internal mechanisms but also to improve and establish effective external mechanisms. ACU should be improved in term of setting up a clear complaints handling procedure that is transparent and accountable to the public. In addition, setting up a National Ombudsman as mentioned in the priority actions of the Legal and Judicial Reform Strategy should be seriously considered to complement the court system where the administrative court/chamber does not yet really exist.

Bibliography

Policy, Law and Regulations

Circular on Procedure and Rules of Law and Regulations Making Process(Office of the Council of Minsters, 2013)

Constitution of Cambodia, 1993

Guidelines for the Information of Consumers About Their Rights to Complaint to the Suppliers or EAC

Law on Anti-Corruption

Law on Education

Law on Electricity

Law on Marks, Trade Names, and Acts of Unfair Competition

Law on Taxation, 1997

Legal and Judicial Reform Strategy, 2003

Ministry of Economy and Finance, *Handbook on Rights and Duties of Tax Payers* 2010

Plan of Action for Implementing Legal and Judicial Reform Strategy, 2005

Procedure for Filing Complaint to EAC and for Resolution of EAC

Sub-Decree on Organizing and Functioning of Ministry of Commerce

Sub-Decree on Organizing and Functioning of Ministry of Industry, Mines, and Energy

Sub-Decree on the Implementation of the Law Concerning Marks, Trade Names and Acts of Unfair Competition, 2006

Research/Studies and Others

Bory, Say, *General Administrative Law*, Third Edition, Blossom Lotus Printing, 2002.

Council for Legal and Judicial Reform, *Baseline Survey on Legal Units and Law Making Capacity of Ministries/Institutions* (Phnom Penh: Council for Legal and Judicial Reform supported by GIZ), 2009.

DAP website: http://www.dap-news.com/en/index.php? option=com_content&view=article&id=9623:-cambodias-anti-corruption-unit-receives-800-complaints-in-8-months&catid=1:local-news&Itemid=18, accessed on 24 June 2013.

Dara, Khlok, *Pre-Assessment of Ombudsman and Other Complaint System in Cambodia* (Phnom Penh: Council for Legal and Judicial Reform supported by GIZ), 2009.

Dara, Khlok, *Searching for Implementing an Ombudsman System in Cambodia* (Phnom Penh: Council for Legal and Judicial Reform supported by GIZ), 2009.

Electricity Authority of Cambodia, *Overall Performance Standard for Electricity Suppliers in the Kingdom of Cambodia*.

Hauerstein, Kai, *Aspects of Administrative Law and Its Reform in Cambodia*, 2013.

Menzel, Joerg, *International Formal and Informal Framework to Settle the Administrative Complaint from the Citizens Aagainst Administration Action*, Presentation for the seminar on 3-4 June, 2013 in Sokha Hotel, Siem Reap Province, Cambodia, 2013.

Report of Electricity Authority of Cambodia, 2010.

柬埔寨行政申诉机制的现状及挑战

Khlok Dara*
林俊**编译

内容摘要: 公民与公共行政之间的良好关系是一个国家善政的核心要求。公民应有权对行政机关任何性质不明确的决定/规定或不法行为要求澄清或者提出申诉,而行政机关则必须对公民的要求或申诉作出公开有效的回应。为建立可问责的、透明灵活的行政管理模式,应该建立有效的行政申诉机制。目前,柬埔寨行政申诉机制仍存在许多问题和挑战,包括缺乏明确、良好的申诉机构和机制、行政申诉部门和步骤都缺乏明确的安排等,因此,本文着重研究柬埔寨在当前形势下的行政申诉机制及政府内部运行机构和机制,以探索建立并完善保障公民权利和增强信任的有效申诉机制,最后提出一些改进现有机制的建议。

关键词: 柬埔寨行政申诉;机制架构;问题;建议

一、引言

1993年,柬埔寨引进并采用了自由的多党民主制度。此后开展实施了许多战略改革方案,其中,“矩形战略”提出了全面的立法司法改革和公共行政改革方案,并将改善公共行政制度的组织和运行机构放入关键领域,其中就包括了“处理国家与公民关系的机构”。

国家公共行政与公民之间的良好关系是一个国家善政的和核心要求,而

---

* Khlok Dara,柬埔寨司法部国际关系和发展伙伴局局长,西南政法大学国际法学院博士生。

** 林俊,西南政法大学国际法学院2017级硕士研究生。

处理公民申诉的机制乃是处理国家与社会关系的重要制度之一。因此,建立健全公开有效的行政申诉机制,有助于提高公共行政的效果和效率,同时促进公民行使自身公民权利和政治权利。

在当前形势下,柬埔寨的行政申诉机制还存在诸多问题和挑战,公民不服对其申诉的处理、政府内容缺乏明确且运作良好的机制、现有机制缺乏系统安排,公民不知道去哪里提交自己的申诉请求,以及应该如何遵循申诉的步骤等问题层出不穷,因此,本文将研究柬埔寨现行行政申诉机制及其存在的问题、关注现行的法律和政策保障机制、申诉的类型和结构,并对政府行政决定和公共服务提供提起的两种类型的申诉作重点分析与评价。

二、现行行政申诉构造概述

(一)法律和政策框架

1.宪法

《柬埔寨宪法》规定,任何公民都有充分的权利行使第 39 条和第 128 条所规定的行政申诉权。[①] 该权利可以通过负责处理行政申诉的主管机构行使,如果申诉人不服,可以向法院上诉,寻求终局裁判。

2.法律

部门法规赋予公民和任何利害相关人对行政行为提出申诉的权利。一些部门法规规定了其受理公民申诉的特别机构,如《电力法》第 7 条第 6 款授权柬埔寨电力局代表工业矿场能源部处理申诉;其他部门法授予其部门自己受理公民申诉的权力,如《旅游法》第 46 条即授予旅游局这一权利。

部门法规不仅规定公民申诉的权利和部门,还规定了对造成损害的行政行为的制裁,如《交通法》明确规定了对执行职务期间滥用权力的警察的处罚。

《组织法》规定了公民对不当行政行为提起申诉的权利。《省、市、区行政管理法》第 85 条明确规定了公民对关于领土的行政行为的申诉权。然而,其

---

① 《柬埔寨宪法》第 39 款第 1 款规定:高棉公民有权就国家机关工作人员、社会组织或其成员因任何违法行为而造成的损害进行谴责、申诉或索赔。

《柬埔寨宪法》第 39 条第 2 款规定:处理申诉和因受损害而提出的索赔是法院的责任。

《柬埔寨宪法》第 128 条第 3 款条规定:司法机关应审查所有案件,包括行政案件。

仍未能明确是否所有公民即便在自己并不居住的地方也享有申诉权。

3.立法司法改革

2005年，内阁通过了《执行〈立法司法改革战略〉行动计划》，该计划明确以7项优先行动建立全面有效的行政申诉处理机制，这些优先行动是：第一，申诉专员的设置；第二，妇女和其他弱势群体的特定申诉；第三，规范行政诉讼和申诉程序的行政法规；第四，行政法庭《法院组织法》的制定；第五，申诉专员办公室的设置；第六，设置行政法庭；第七，申诉专员法的设置。

(二)申诉类型/结构

1.申诉对象

原则上，行政申诉的对象可分为五大类，包括行政决定、公共服务的提供、腐败和滥用权力、行政行为和行政法规。

对行政决定的申诉是指公民因对行政部门作出的决定如获得许可证或任何可能损害公民权利的其他决定不服而提起的申诉。

对公共行政部门提供的服务提出申诉，是指关于政府为公民提供的教育、保健、电力等服务的行政申诉。

对犯罪活动或腐败的申诉是针对公共行政官员或机构之间的串通或贿赂而提出的申诉，其处理行政部门负有责任的犯罪行为。不过，刑事责任推定由犯罪官员承担。

对行政行为的申诉是公民对于行政机关不适当履行职务的申诉。所有相关的公民都可以就警察执行职务时的不当行为向法庭申诉。在柬埔寨，这种申诉机制无明确法律规定。

对行政法规的申诉是公民对行政部门制定的非法规定的申诉。一般来说，行政机关通过立法机关授权的法律获得授权。如果行政部门发布的规定违反了授权的法律或其他规定，公民有权要求澄清规定的合法性。在柬埔寨，这种申诉机制无明确法律规定。

2.申诉受理主体/机构设置：内部/外部

申诉受理机制可以分类三类：(1)法院；(2)内部行政管理机制或内部申诉机制；以及(3)外部监督机制，如议会制度(见下表)。

表 1 柬埔寨行政申诉机制机构汇总

内部(内部管理机制)	外部	法院
·国民议会一参议院和监察部:主要处理关于腐败、滥用权力和行政决定的行政申诉。 ·部委部门:柬埔寨有 23 个部委。 ·部门法制机构:大多数部门法规赋予了各部门处理其内部申诉的权利。 ·区域法制机构:行政区域可分为首都和省、市和区以及分区三个层次。	反腐败机构 柬埔寨人权委员会	常规法院

内部管理机制,是对内部管理部门提出的申诉,通常允许公民或任何利害关系人向内部行政部门提起,一般由申诉所针对的各机构的上级管理部门处理申诉,上表为处理这方面申诉的 4 个主要机构。

外部管理机制,指部门机构或部门法规之外的机制,不包括立法机关内部的附加机制,如国民议会委员会,上表为处理这方面申诉的 2 个主要机构。

就行政事宜向法院申诉是公民可用来审查行政管理不善的典型途径。然而,柬埔寨还没有专为行政案件设立的法院或议院,同时向法院提起行政申诉的程序也没有明确的法律规定。

三、分析目前的行政申诉架构

本节仅探讨行政决定、公共服务的提供、腐败和滥用权力等三种类型的申诉。另外两种关于行政行为不当和政府非法规定的申诉,柬埔寨没有明确规定,不作探讨。

(一)对政府决定的申诉

该申诉涉及公民对申请执照或许可证的行政决定不服的情况。公民的权利主要是对行政机关否决许可、不颁发许可证,或对某项决定不服的情况下申诉。目前,公民可以向各部门或该部门设立的特定机构申诉,这种机构有时可能既是部门设立的机构,也是依部门法规设置的专门机构。对于地方一级案件,公民可以向地方各级行政部门和某些负责处理地方事务的专门机构申诉。但是,市民可以针对单窗口办公室或其他区级办事处的决定向地方一级的申诉专员办公室申诉。公民还可以针对省区级行政机关的决定向省级问责工作

组提起申诉。

(二)对提供的公共服务的申诉

这类申诉是指公民在对行政部门提供的公共服务不满的情况下对其提出的申诉。柬埔寨公共服务包括教育、医疗、福利服务、电力、水资源等。该申诉可以提交给该服务的相应办公室、部门或区域部门以及部门法中规定的其他机构。一般来说,申诉处理的责任机制位于行政部门内,使用或遵循的是处理申诉的一般行政程序。商务部内部部门之间申诉处理职能有一些重叠,如法律事务部、部长内阁和总监察部的申诉处理职能常常重叠。立法司法改革委员会 2009 年曾对各法制部门/机构组成和立法能力做过一次基线调查,调查报告显示,各部门/机构的大部分法律事务部门都有能力解决归该部门/机构管辖的申诉。

处理区域部门和具体机构机制申诉的权力主要由具体部门法提供,例如《教育法》第 40 条所述的教育青年体育部的权力来源即是如此。[①]

(三)对腐败行为以及其他形式的权力滥用行为的申诉

这个类别是指对公共行政工作人员或机构之间的串通或其他贿赂行为提起的申诉。它涉及刑事诉讼,行政当局须对此负责。但是,刑事责任通常只适用于犯罪的工作人员个人。

公民可以向内部管理机构和外部管理机构投诉。目前,至少有 5 个机构负责处理此类申诉,其中 2 个机制是外部机制,3 个机构是内部机制。这些机制包括:

(1)反腐败组织(ACU)

(2)国民议会—参议院和监察部(MONASRI)

(3)柬埔寨人权委员会(CHRC)和地方行政机构

(4)省级问责工作组(PAWG)

(5)地区申诉专员(DO)

1.法律基础

这种申诉所涉及的特点犯罪活动,其处罚主要包含在《刑法典》中,申诉处

---

① 《教育法》第 40 条规定:请求权、抗辩权、申诉权和解决权,这些权利受到侵害的父母或监护人、学习者和教育人员有权要求或抗议各级主管教育机关和法院。负责教育的部门应当出台有关请求、抗辩和解决流程的规定。

理的过程则主要规定在《刑事诉讼法》中。《刑法典》第278～283条提到了相关处罚。关于滥用行政权力的行为,部分法律规定了处罚的明确条款。

2.申诉受理主体

如上所述,可以向内部和外部机制提出申诉。但是,如果我们看MONASRI,该部设有三个不同的部门处理申诉。第一个部门被称为接收和调查申诉部;第二个是诉讼部门;最后一个则是法律事务部。还有另外四个在国家或地方层面的机构也有具体的处理申诉的部门。

申诉也可以提交给外部机构,如ACU或CHRC。ACU对全国有管辖权。所有公民或任何利害关系人可以就国家一级的腐败案件向位于首都或某省的ACU办事处提起申诉。CHRC不是一个决议机制,但其作用是接受有关人权问题的申诉,包括针对行政部门的腐败和滥用权力的申诉。CHRC的工作人员将研究和确定管辖权,向上级作出报告,并提出有关管辖权的建议,以供其作出决定。

3.申诉处理程序

申诉处理程序可以根据负责机构的性质分为三类。MONASRI处理申诉的第一个程序遵循的是普通的行政程序。首先,在收到申诉后,根据申诉情况确定管辖权,并向上级提交建议报告供其作出决定;其次,如果上级同意进行更多的调查,调查程序即启动;最后,向上级提交调查报告。这类似于CHRC的申诉处理程序,与普通行政程序相同,但不同于MONASRI的是,CHRC不是决议机构,CRHC只能接收申诉并将其发送给负责机构。

ACU处理的大部分申诉遵循《刑事诉讼法》的规定,其申诉处理程序分为三个阶段:

首先,接收申诉。申诉可以当面进行,亦可通过电子表格、邮局、电话、传真或电子邮件送达ACU。

其次,申诉由ACU的申诉分析中心进行审查,并向ACU主席提出决定建议(如转交法院)。经ACU主席批准同意,ACU启动与法院的联合调查。

最后,与检察官的联合调查完成后,案件移交法院进行最后裁决。

PAWG和DO同样设立了自己的申诉处理程序。这些程序明确规定了从接收申诉到决策的详细过程。

4.分析

负责处理腐败和滥用权力的申诉有5个机构,机构之间的管辖权并不明确。即使在MONASRI内部,也有很多部门负责处理申诉。

尽管在打击腐败方面有一些良好的发展,ACU却仍没有明确的准则或程

序可以遵循，即使反腐败法律也提到了处理腐败的程序可以按照《刑事诉讼法》的规定。

处理申诉的程序没有明确的时间表。政府未能为公众提供透明化的信息；公众无法获得所有必要信息，例如如何妥善提出申诉。公民可以通过电子邮件、电话或邮局提出申诉，但不能确定申诉是否被接收并采取行动。

在柬埔寨，公民获取信息的渠道非常有限，目前尚无有关申诉处理的具体统计数据信息。虽然 ACU 是一个公开透明的机构，供公众查阅必要的资料，然而，与其他公共机构的情况相同的是，信息获取仍然存在着许多问题。

四、结论和评论

柬埔寨的行政申诉机制存在着诸多问题和挑战。各组织机构在政府内部和外部仍然分散。每个机构或行政机关都可以在处理各类行政申诉方面发挥作用，但关于行政机关应该如何对行政申诉机制进行体系化管理，并无任何的法律规定。各部门法律和行业部门制定不同的程序标准。公民提出申诉的权利仍然有限。每个机制的权力和职能仍然模糊，有些甚至在一个部门或机构内部重叠。每个部门至少有三个重叠部分（法律事务部、总监察部和部长内阁）具有类似的处理行政申诉的管辖权。

为了改善这些问题和挑战，所有利益攸关方，特别是政府的投入至关重要。为此，笔者提出以下建议：

第一，建立一个法律框架，为公民提供明确的申诉权。

第二，强制各政府部门/机构进行改革。应进行职能测绘和职能检查，以确保良好的公共管理。全国地方民主发展委员会（NCDD）已经开始的职能测绘和职能检查的起点是将权力和职能委托给地方行政部门。但是，这个过程也应该从国家层面开始。

第三，至少应采取一个简单但统一的行政申诉处理程序，以便所有机制的短期执行。长远来看，则应该考虑制定综合的《行政诉讼法》。

最后，但也是最重要的一点，不仅需要改进内部机制，而且还要建立和改进有效的外部机制。ACU 应进一步制定具体的、对公众透明的、可追责的申诉处理程序。另外，也应认真考虑《立法司法改革战略》优先行动中设立国家申诉专员的决定，以健全欠缺行政法庭的法院系统。

Introduction to Administrative Law in Cambodia

Kai Hauerstein*

Abstract: Cambodia is in the process of building a comprehensive administrative law system. This implies that some fundamentals are still lacking. The purpose of this article, therefore, is twofold:

- To propose a framework of how to structure administrative law. These structural principles are expressed in guiding questions, for instance, 'What is administrative law?'
- To use this framework and apply it to the Cambodian context in order to take stock of the current situation.

The 1993 Constitution of Cambodia (CC) and—as a reflex—the Legal and Judicial Reform Strategy (LJRS) call for the introduction of a comprehensive administrative law system that would provide and protect citizens' rights against unlawful government action. A system like this would be a novelty in Cambodia's turbulent history and a milestone towards good governance. How do we establish a comprehensive administrative law system against the background of the Cambodian context? To answer this question, we have to ask another question first: Where are we now? This question is important, as positive change requires moving from an existing situation to an ideal situation. The purpose of this synopsis is to provide only an answer to the second question-that is, to provide an overview of the existing situation concerning administrative law in Cambodia and to contribute to an

* Kai Hauerstein is a German lawyer and currently the legal advisor of the Permanent Secretariat of the Committee for Legal and Judicial Reform under the Ministry of Justice.

ongoing discussion of how to structure and define administrative law.

Thus, it provides definitions and a synopsis of aspects concerning administrative law and reform in Cambodia by answering the following questions:[①]

- **What is administrative law?** Definitions, administrative processes, general administrative law, specific administrative (sector) law, structure and elements, history of administrative law.
- **What are the sources of administrative law?** Hierarchy, Constitution, international obligations, specific administrative (sector) laws, unwritten administrative law (court decisions, customary law), and academic research.
- **What is the status of specific administrative (sector) laws?** Publication, systematization/compilation, public service compendium.
- **Who is applying administrative law?** Administrative bodies, government officials, functional and territorial organizations.
- **What instruments are available to the administration?** Policies, plans, regulations, administrative decisions (acts), enforcement/punishment.
- **How can citizens complain against administrative measures?** Administrative appeal mechanisms (complaint, ombudsman), access to justice.
- **How can citizens claim damage for unlawful actions?**

The last section briefly analyses the current situation and concludes by answering the following question:

- **What is the status of the reform process?** Policy framework, current situation (burning issues/gaps), reform leading to a comprehensive administrative law system, elements and outline of options how to codify an administrative (procedure) code, proposed first steps.

---

① The guiding questions for structuring administrative law were taken from *Administrative Law of the European Union, Its Member States and the United States: A Comparative Analysis* (Rene J. G. H Seerden, ed., 2007), pp. 2-3.

1. What Is Administrative Law?

This section clarifies the term administrative law. It proposes a definition of administrative law, outlines types of administrative actions and puts administrative law into context. At the end, it provides a brief evolution and history of administrative law in Cambodia and proposes a working definition.

Rationale of Administrative Law: The rationale of administrative law is two-fold. On the one side, administrative law should protect citizen's rights and on the other hand it must ensure that the administration can function effectively.① Thus, administrative law needs to balance these two interests. In Cambodia, the scale balancing these two sides leans more towards one side-the emphasis is more on empowering the administration to function effectively. In contrast with Western legal traditions organised around the understanding of autonomous right-bearing individuals, Cambodia's legal tradition emphasised social order over individual autonomy. Against this background, administrative law does not primarily protect individuals from the administration, but is an instrument to establish responsibilities and control. Under the Khmer Rouge, Cambodian citizens had to suffer tragically under the excesses of this understanding. Therefore, the new Constitution of 1993—in theory—changed the old paradigm, and strengthened the second element, protecting the individual from the state.

Thus, there is strong correlation between the requirements set out in the Constitution and administrative law. Guiding principles such as individual rights, rule of law, and democracy need to be operationalised by administrative law. The idea that administrative law is concretised constitutional law goes back to Fritz Werner,② stating that most aspects of adminis-

---

① Eberhard Schmidt-Assmann, *Das Allgemeine Verwaltungsrecht Als Ordnungsidee* (Berlin Heidelberg New York: Springer, 2004), p.1.

② Fritz Werner, "Verwaltungsrecht Als Konkretisiertes Verfassungsrecht," *Deutsches Verwaltungsblatt* (1959), p.527.

trative law operationalises provisions of the Constitution. This article points out that the key requirements set out in the Constitution, such as the protection of individual rights, complaint against unlawful actions, judicial review, and state liability, are still not yet available and therefore need to be operationalised by administrative law.

1.1 Defining Administrative Law

There is no official definition of administrative law in Cambodia. The government published two volumes of an official Lexicon on Legal and Administrative Terms.①

Neither of the volumes defines administrative law. A non-official English-Khmer Law Dictionary defines administrative law under the term administrative proceeding, "The body of rules created by administrative agencies to implement their powers and duties."②

This definition only covers the literal meaning of administrative law and thus has very narrow scope. Theng Chan-Sangvar defines administrative law as "The area of public law that regulates the relationship between the citizen and the state."③ This definition-as the previous one-appears to be too narrow, as it does not include the body of law that deals with the organisation of the administration. Therefore, the two definitions are of limited use.

The purpose of this chapter is to provide a wider understanding of administrative law as key element of law itself, such as criminal law or civil law.

Approaching a Definition: administrative law is the branch of public law

---

① "Lexicon of Legal and Administrative Terms; English, Francais, Khmer (D E F G H)," in *Lexicon of Legal and Administrative Terms* (Phnom Penh: Council of Ministers, Royal Committee for the Adoption of Legal Work, 2008).

② Theng Chan-Sangvar, *Administrative Law and Decentralization*, eds. Kong Phallak Hor Peng, Joerg Menzel, Introduction to Cambodian Law (Phnom Penh: Konrad Adenauer Foundation, 2012), p.245.

③ "Lexicon of Legal and Administrative Terms; English, Francais, Khmer (D E F G H)."

dealing with the actual operation of government.[①] Responsible for the actual operation of government is the administration, as the permanent body of government, which implements laws in relation to citizens as well as in relation to other administrative entities. As such, administrative law can be defined as the legal framework for the:

• organization of the administration itself, as well as

• interaction between administration and citizens and vice versa. The interaction between the two is defined by rights and obligations (see Table below) which are interchangeable, as well as the type of administration (intervening vs. servicing).

Figure 1 below illustrates the two elements of administrative law (its organisation and the interaction between the administration and citizens) as well two sub-elements of administrative law (intervening and service administration):

• One part of administrative law governs the organisation of the administration itself, and deals with, among others things, (ⅰ) the territorial organisation of the administration (decentralisation/deconcentration of authority on national and sub-national level), (ⅱ) the functional organisation such as the role and responsibility of ministries and agencies, and (ⅲ) the civil service.[②]

• The other part of administrative law governs the interaction between the administration and citizens and deals with the implementation and enforcement of public law. From the perspective of a citizen, this interaction can be either positive (service administration/public service provision) or negative (intervening administration). The two sub-elements are:

• Intervening Administration: The classic 19th century type of adminis-

---

① Stanely de Smith and Rodney Brazier, *Constitutional Law and Administrative Law* (London: Penguin Books, 1998), p.504.

② The Council for Administrative Reform (CAR) published a *Handbook for Civil Servants*, which provides an overview of the legal framework governing the legal status of permanent civil servants in the administration (excluding servants in the judiciary, legislature, and the armed forces). CAR in addition maintains a legal database on laws governing decentralization (see also Chapter 3, Section 3.2).

tration has always been of intervening character. It sought to ensure public order and safety. Thus it mostly dealt with police matters and restricted citizens' rights in the public interest.[①]

• Service Administration: In modern social welfare states administration has an additional role. It provides services to the citizen, for instance welfare, schools, hospitals, and transport.[②]

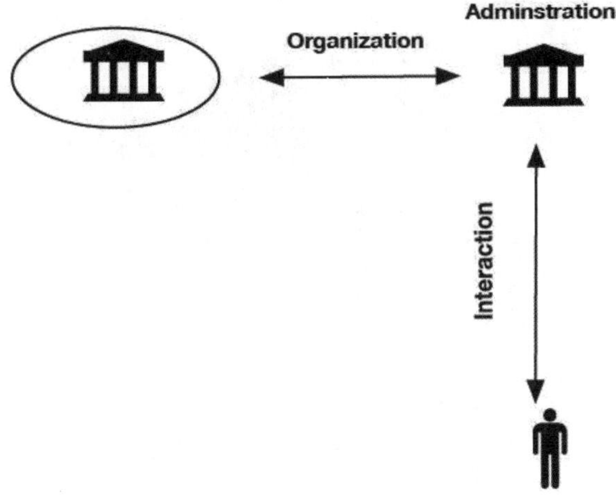

Figure 1 Two elements of administrative law: (1) organization and (2) interaction

Examples for administrative law and procedure:

• A government denies the licence application for a small business (interaction between administration and citizens in the form of an negative intervention).

• A government official is being promoted (organization of the administration).

• A commune council schedules a meeting (organization of the administration).

• A transportation agency charges a bus company for operating unsafe

---

① Nigel Foster and Satish Sule, *German Legal System and Laws*, 4th ed (Oxford: Oxford University Press, 2010), p.283.

② Ibid., p.284.

vehicles (intervening administration). This is an example where the administration restricts the property right of a citizen in the public interest. The public interest is to protect citizens from unsafe vehicles in the name of public safety.

• The provision of public roads on the other hand is a public service provided by the government and is a typical example of the service administration

Excluded from the scope of administrative law: What is not included in the scope of administrative law are the following elements of public law:①

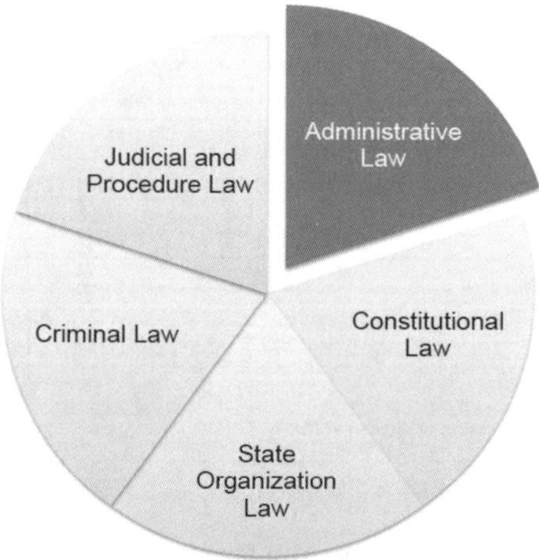

Figure 2 Overview of public law

• **Criminal law** is part of public law. It provides the legal framework for criminal prosecution by defining what behaviour is criminal, setting out punishment for criminal behaviour, and setting out procedures by which crimes are investigated, prosecuted, adjudicated, and punished.

• **Constitutional law** is part of public law. It refers to the provisions of the Constitution insofar as they provide the basic legal framework for the set-up of the legislative branch and the government of a state and for the interplay of the latter. It also comprises fundamental rights enshrined in the Constitution.

① Public law is the body of law that governs the conduct of the state and the relationship between the state and citizens.

• **State organization law** is also part of public law and concretizes the constitution by detailing the roles and responsibilities of the legislature, the judiciary, and the executive.

• **Judicature/procedure law**: within the division of public law, this area deals with the organization of judicial bodies and the process of litigation.

1.2 Administrative Processes and Proceedings

Administrative processes and proceedings breathe life into administrative law as they shape the interaction between the administration and citizens. The flow of a generic process defining the interaction between administration and citizen can be outlined as follows: After the legislature enacts a new law, the administration adopts rules implementing and explaining the new law, publishes the new law and develops implementing regulations, applies the new law/implementing regulations in a specific case, reviews the decision in the case of a citizen's complaint. If the administration rejects the complaint an independent court or tribunal reverses or upholds the administration's decision. After the citizen has exhausted all legal measures, the administration enforces its decision.

1.2.1 Enactment, Operationalization and Publication

The starting point is the enactment of a new law, which authorizes the administration to regulate a public issue, for example a social, economic, and environmental issues. In most cases, the public sector law is not yet operational as it provides only the framework for the interaction between the administration and citizens. To add technical details, the framework law authorizes a specific sector (line) ministry to issue implementing regulations for its operationalization. The authorizing law as well as the implementing regulations need to be published in an official gazette and made accessible for the citizen. In addition, the responsible line ministry is required to disseminate the information to the lower levels of the administration and-if necessary-train public service officers in applying the law.

1.2.2 Application and Complaint

The administrative decision-making process starts with the application of the public sector law in a specific case. There are three scenarios: an individual either applies for (ⅰ) a benefit, for example social welfare, or (ⅱ) a licence/permit, or (ⅲ) the administration imposes a sanction, for example it imposes the demolition of an illegal building. The procedure of this decision-making process is either regulated in the specific sector law or complemented in a general administrative procedure. This process often includes the following procedures:

• application

• hearing

• decision and respective administrative measures (e.g. administrative act)

• complaint

• costs

• notification

• enforcement.

The end of the administrative decision making process is either positive as the agency approves the benefit/licence, or revokes the sanction. Or, the decision is negative as the agency either denies the licence/benefit or imposes a sanction.

In the case of a positive decision, the agency notifies the individual, who will pay the required costs and receive the permit/benefit.

In the case of a negative decision, the individual has the right to complain and (usually) appeal to the next higher administrative body. The complaint mechanism, which is either regulated in the sector law or a general administrative procedure act, outlines the process for the complaint and allows the individual to ask for the decision to be reconsidered.

If the individual complains against a decision, the enforcement of the decision is suspended (even though there are exceptions to this rule).

In case the next higher administrative agency decides against the citizen, the citizen usually has the opportunity to bring his/her case to an administrative court or an administrative tribunal (depending on the legal system of a country).

1.2.3 Independent Review (Administrative Adjudication)

Laws on the organization of courts usually assign judicial review (inclu-

ding appeal and revision) of an administrative measure to an Administrative Court or a similar independent institution. The Cambodian Constitution as well as Law on the Organization of the Courts assign-in theory-administrative adjudication to the general jurisdiction of the court. Id at Art. 128(3)CC and Art. 4 Law on the Organization of the Courts. As Cambodia has no Law on Administrative Law Procedure, the Civil Procedure Code is analogously applied. Id at Art. 89(III) Law on the Organization of the courts. These are theoretical references as in practice courts do not review government decisions.

However in countries with an operational administrative court system, the independent court or tribunal can reverse or uphold the administration's decision.

1.2.4 Enforcement

If the individual has complained or the litigation process is ongoing, the enforcement process is blocked until a final decision is reached (there are however, exceptions to the rule). After the individual has exhausted appeal/revision the decision can be enforced. The agency can enforce its own decision in case the demanded action has not been performed, or by penalty in the form of fines.

1.3 Function and Structure of Administrative Law

1.3.1 Function of Administrative Law

Throughout history the relationship between administration and citizens has changed substantially:

• **Intervening administration**: Historically, the administration had a policing function regulating private activities and enforcing control. Its main purpose was to establish law and order, if necessary with force. A typical example would be the Prussian bureaucracy in the 19th century, which had a quite detailed regulatory agenda interfering with private activities. This type of administration is therefore called 'intervening (policing) administration', because it restrains citizens' rights in the public interest. The liberal '*Rechtsstaat* (Rule of Law)' movement during this time tried to restrain administrative interventions and fought for the introduction of formal legal criteria to justify an intervention.

• **Service (welfare) administration**: The other type of administration is called service administration. Its purpose is to contribute to the overall welfare of citizens. Service administration arose with the modern social welfare state in the 20th century. Service administration provides social security, operates hospitals and schools, and builds roads.

• **Fiscal administration**: Finally, there is fiscal administration, which generates revenues through taxes and user charges to pay for, among others things, public services such as health services or infrastructure.

Depending on the function (welfare, law and order, fiscal), administrative law either restricts citizens' rights or provides rights. See also the definition above.

1.3.2 Structure of Administrative Law

Administrative law can be divided into: (1) general administrative law and (2) specific administrative law. General administrative law is concerned with basic rules, general principles, and concepts applicable to all aspects of administrative law, such as administrative principles, proceedings, and so on.

Specific administrative law is the body of law that deals with specific policy areas, such as maintaining public health, immigration, protection of the environment, and so on. Specific administrative law is mostly set out in public sector laws such as land law or environmental law.

In addition, the majority of civil law countries have introduced general administrative (procedure) codes that set out general standards such as administrative principles, standardized proceedings for the decision making process or the complaint process. The development of general standards is important, as administrative law should be as comprehensive and coherent as possible. General administrative (procedure) codes only provide a standard for the whole body of administrative law and apply uniformly across sectors. This standard, however, can be complemented with more specific mechanisms in sector laws.

1.3.2.1 General Administrative Law

Some countries have introduced a general administrative law, which defines:

• administrative principles[①]

• standardized proceedings in the decision making process

• standardized instruments such as the administrative act or the administrative contract

• complaint mechanisms

• enforcement of administrative decisions

• state liability.

General administrative law provides a general standard for all existing and future public sector laws and every government agency must comply with this general framework as a minimum standard. However, this minimum standard can be complemented by specific mechanism in sector laws as long as they do not conflict with the general standard. For example, a law on land management can only specify a complaint mechanism, but cannot abolish the complaint mechanism itself.

1.3.2.2 Specific Administrative Law and Regulations

Starting from the definition of administrative law and its distinction between general administrative law and specific administrative law (see before), this sub-chapter defines in more detail specific administrative law.

Specific administrative law deals with those sectoral details that are not covered by general administrative law.

Specific Administrative Law: The main body of administrative law is specific administrative law. Specific administrative law deals with various specific policy areas such as maintaining law and order (for example, through the police), protecting public goods (such as the environment), managing development and the economy (for example, investment), providing public services (such as education). In Cambodia, administrative law is administered by sector ministries and includes:

Law on Agriculture, Law on Forestry, Law on Fishery, Law on Commerce, Law on Cults, Law on Religious Affairs, Law on Economy,

---

① Administrative principles will be covered in more detail in another chapter of this publication.

Law on Finance, Law on Education, Law on Youth, Law on Sport, Law on Environment, Law on Health, Law on Industry, Law on Mines, Law on Energy, Law on Information, Law on Justice, Law on Labour, Law on Vocational Training, Law on Land Management, Law on Urbanization, and Construction, Law on Planning, Law on Posts and Telecommunication, Law on Public Works, Law on Transportation, Law on Rural Development, Law on Social Affairs, Law on War Veterans, Law on Youth Rehabilitation, Law on Tourism, Law on Water Resources, Law on Meteorology, Law on Women's Affairs, Law on Functional and Territorial Organization of the State.

To structure specific administrative law, these sectors could be clustered according to the main functions of the state:

- **Infrastructure and Development** (Public works/transportation, land management, transport, post/telecommunication);
- **ManagementofNaturalResources** (Mines/energy, waterresources, agriculture/forestry/fishery, environment, land management);
- **Economic Development** (Economy/finance, commerce, labour, rural development, tourism, banking, investment);
- **Social Development** (Religion, culture, education, health, social affairs, women, labour);
- **Security and Public Order** (Nationality and immigration, media and assembly, health and medicine, police, weapons, prisons and youth rehabilitation, among others);
- **Organization of the Executive Branch** (Civil servants, organization of the executive branch [functional], organization of the executive branch [territorial]); and
- **Fiscal** (Taxes, customs, international trade among others).

Regulations: Regulations are the body of law issued by the administration. The law-making function of the administration can collide with the 'separation of power' principle. According to the Cambodian Constitution, the legislative and executive powers should be separated (Article 51). Thus, the National Assembly and the Senate enact laws (Chbab) and the executive imple-

ments them. The 'separation of power principle', however, is not absolute. Because the legislature cannot regulate every technical aspect in detail, it can authorize the administration to issue regulations in those areas where technical skills of respective line ministries are needed.

Therefore, laws in Cambodia only provide the legal framework and delegate the authority to regulate technical details to a responsible government agency (delegated legislation). In this case the administration exercises its own legislative (rule making) power.

Regulation is often defined as administrative law in a narrow sense because it represents the law created by the administration. Specific administrative laws (sector laws) authorize a responsible ministry① to develop and enforce control in one specific sector. For example, the Law on Tourism authorizes the Ministry of Tourism to develop policies and plans, draft regulations and issue licences. Each sector law therefore provides for a multitude of implementing regulations, which are also part of administrative law. As a delegated legal source, a ministry mainly regulates the technical details of an authorizing law. The legal requirements for issuing regulations are vaguely defined in the Constitution and the Law on the Organization and Functioning of the Council of Ministers. Article 150 II CC states that laws and decisions made by the state must be in strict conformity with the Constitution. Articles 13 and 39 of the Law on the Organization and Functioning of the Council of Ministers list types of regulations and put them in a hierarchical order.②

Issue 'Rule by Law' Rather Than 'Rule of Law': Boundaries for the leg-

---

① Ministry for: (1) Agriculture, Forestry & Fishery, (2) Commerce, (3) Cults and Religious Affairs, (4) Economy and Finance, (5) Education, Youth and Sport, (6) Environment, (7) Health, (8) Industry, Mines, and Energy, (9) Information, (10) Justice, (11) Labour and Vocational Training, (12) Land Management, Urbanization, and Construction, (13) Planning, (14) Posts and Telecommunication, (15) Public Works and Transportation, (16) Rural Development, (17) Social Affairs, War Veterans, and Youth Rehabilitation, (18) Tourism, (19) Water Resources and Meteorology, (20) Women's Affairs, (21) Interior.

② Tep Darong, "Cambodia and the Rule of Law," in *Occasional Papers Democratic Development Rule of Law*, ed. Konrad Adenauer Foundation (St. Augustin: Konrad Adenauer Foundation, 2009), pp.24-25.

islative authority vested in the executive are sometimes difficult to draw. According to the Constitution, the National Assembly and the Senate have the legislative authority. But the legislature can also authorize the administration to issue implementing regulations (delegated legislation). Thus, a law that delegates most of the legislative responsibility to the administration could violate the 'separation of power' principle stated in Article 51(5) of the Constitution, which provides that legislative, executive, and judicial powers should be separated. It is difficult to define what belongs to legislative powers and what belongs to executive powers. Some countries, for example Germany, have developed a rule that parliament should regulate all 'essential matters'. As a consequence, the more essential a matter is for a citizen and the public, the more detailed the parliament-made law has to be. This rule effectively limits the administration from issuing regulations in essential areas, for example areas in which fundamental human rights are concerned. In Cambodia, no such limits appear to exist, which in turn leads to extensive regulatory powers vested in the executive.

Summary: Against the background in this section, the following working definition for administrative law is proposed:

Administrative law: Legal framework for (ⅰ) the organization of administration itself and (ⅱ) the interaction between government and citizens.	
(ⅰ) Legal framework for organization/management of administration:	(ⅱ) Legal framework for the interaction between the administration and citizens when implementing/enforcing public law:
Public service management (for example, Law on Public Service)	**General administrative lawis** the background system that cuts across administrative law areas and includes, among other areas, basic processes and general principles/procedural rights
Territorial organization (for example, Law on Decentralization)	**Specific** administrative law (for example, Law on Land, Law on Tourism)
Functional organization (for example, Law on Ministry of Justice)	Administrative **'law making'** (for example, a government agency issues a sub-decree)

续表

Box: Historic Background on Administrative Law

Cambodia has experienced frequent and drastic changes of its legal and institutional systems. Different colonial powers and governments introduced, established, destroyed, and replaced existing legal systems. Administrative law as an integral part of those legal systems shared the same fate.

• Pre-1953 (colonial rule): Under colonial rule, Cambodia introduced the French-based civil law system, but did not introduce all aspects of administrative law. Complaints, for example against administrative (colonial) actions, were not allowed. Therefore, French institutions such as the *Tribunal Administratif* and the *Conseil d'Etat* were never introduced in Cambodia. Only in 1948, judicial review on administrative matters was assigned to the *Krom Viveat* (a separate administrative review body with wide powers of administrative review).

• 1953-1970: After Cambodia's independence the *Krom Viveat* continued its work to review administrative law, but was finally abolished in the 1970 coup.

• 1975-1979: Under the Khmer Rouge all legal institutions and frameworks were destroyed, including administrative law.

• 1979-1993: During the time of the People's Republic of Kampuchea a socialist government model was introduced. In principle, government and people were considered the same and a legal framework that would govern their interaction was deemed unnecessary. Nevertheless, the 1982 Law on Complaints granted non-judicial review to citizens and allowed them to complain against government actions if they were considered harmful to the state, the collective interests, or the individual.

• 1993-today: In 1993, the (old) civil law system was re-established. The new Constitution, which requires separation of powers, judicial review, procedural rights, and decentralization of powers, provided a blueprint for establishing a comprehensive administrative law system. Since 1993 a multitude of organic laws, which shape the institutional and territorial set-up of the administration, as well as numerous public sector laws, have been enacted.

2.What Are the Sources of Administrative Law?[①]

Administrative law, as a part of public law, feeds from numerous sources of law.There is debate over how to organize these sources in an appropriate order.This section structures sources of administrative law according to the hierarchy:

(ⅰ)Constitution

(ⅱ)International law (general rules and international agreements)

(ⅲ) Sector laws and their implementing regulations (for example, decrees and sub-decrees)

(ⅳ)Unwritten administrative law such as court rulings, customary law, and academic research.

Hierarchical Order of Administrative Law: The Constitution and the Law on the Organization and the Functioning of Cabinet of Ministers' define the hierarchy for laws and regulations. It appears that the(ⅰ)Constitution (Article 150)and the Universal Declaration of Human Rights, UN Covenants and other International Human Rights instruments(Article 31)are at the Apex; followed by (ⅱ) international treaties approved by the National Assembly and the Senate, (Article 26); followed by(ⅲ)statuary law(organic law and ordinary law); followed by(ⅳ)royal decrees, sub-decrees, ministerial proclamations, circulars, and(ⅶ)local regulations.

The legislative instruments have to be viewed in a hierarchical order.[②] General legal principles demand that lower-ranking laws always have to comply with higher-ranking laws. There is a strict hierarchy of legislative instru-

---

① Organic laws are part of administrative law. Organic laws establish state institutions and establish rules for their operation. As mentioned in the introduction, organic laws are not part of this review, as well as other laws on state organization and management such as public service laws and decentralization.

② According to the theory of Hans Kelsen and Adolf Merkl about the pyramidal character of the legal order, a strict hierarchy of norms exists with the constitution on the top followed by parliamentary statutes, prevailing over different types of regulations issued by the executive.

ments. The following figure provides the hierarchy of legislative instruments for Cambodia.

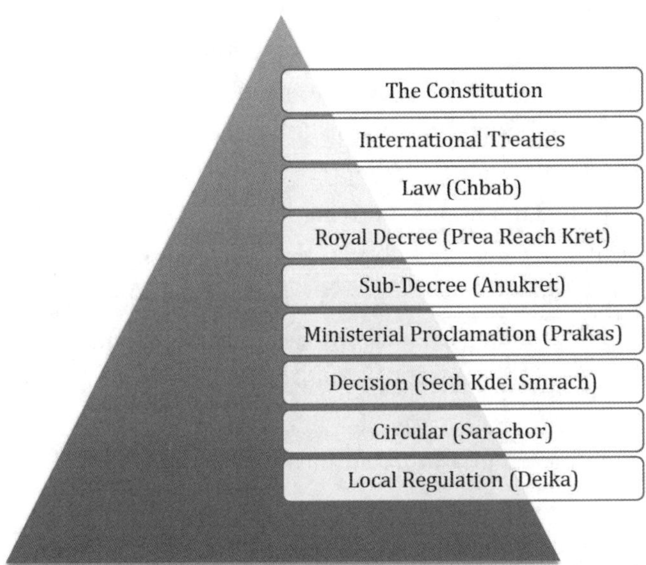

Figure 3　Hierarchy of Laws

The Constitution: The hierarchy of laws is the foundation of the supremacy of the Constitution. The Constitution is the supreme law. All laws and regulations made by state institutions must conform with the Constitution. Id. at Art. 150.

The Constitution itself is subject to revision and change. The initiative to review or amend the Constitution is the prerogative of the King, the Prime Minister, and the Chairman of the National Assembly at the suggestion of 1/4 of all assembly members. Revisions or amendments can be enacted by a constitutional law passed by the assembly with a 2/3 majority vote. Revisions or amendments affecting the system of a free, liberal and pluralistic democracy and the model of constitutional monarchy are prohibited. Id. at Art. 153. These principles are set out for "eternity".

International treaties (also called Conventions, Pacts or Accords) are agreements reached between a state and another state (bilateral), between several states (multilateral) or between a state and another subject of interna-

tional law(for example an international organization such as the United Nations).International treaty ranks immediately after the Constitution in the hierarchy of laws and regulations, provided that it has been ratified by both houses of the Parliament and promulgated by the King.For example, the Cooperation Agreement between the European Union and the Kingdom of Cambodia, which was signed on April 29th, 1997 has been transformed into national law by the Law on the Adoption of the Cooperation Agreement between the European Union and the Kingdom of Cambodia in 1999.

Article 26 of the Constitution of Cambodia states:

> "The King shall sign and ratify international treaties and conventions after a vote of approval by the National Assembly and the Senate."

Human rights aspects stipulated in international law become automatically part of Cambodian law and do not require ratification. This is stated in Art.31(I)of the constitution:

> "The Kingdom of Cambodia recognizes and respects human rights as stipulated in the United Nations Charter, the Universal Declaration of Human Rights and the covenants and conventions related to human rights, women's rights and children rights."

A 2007 decision of the Constitutional Council reaffirms that international law related to human rights issues is directly applicable in Cambodia by reminding judges that they must consider international laws in their decision-making process.①

---

① Constitutional Council Dec.No.092/003/2007.Background of the decision was a petition from civil society organizations with the aim of reducing custodial sentences for persons under the age of 18.The Law on Aggravating Circumstances for Felonies allegedly was in violation not only of the Cambodian Constitution but also the Convention on the Rights of the Child. The Constitutional Council upheld the respective law, but the Constitutional Council also ruled that it could not have been the legislature's intention to violate the Convention on the Rights of the Child.

Laws and regulations: It follows from the hierarchy of laws that statutory laws may not conflict with the Constitution. In addition, a Sub-Decree has to comply with the Constitution as well as with the authorizing law. A Ministerial Order has to comply with (ⅰ) the Constitution, (ⅱ) the authorizing law and (ⅲ) the authorizing sub-decree.

2.1 Constitution

The Cambodian Constitution[①] directly and indirectly defines administrative law. The main provisions shaping administrative law are: (1) 'Respect for law' mentioned in the preamble of the 1993 Constitution; (2) Human Rights (Articles 31-50); (3) Right to complain against government action (Article 39); (4) right to claim compensation for illegal government action, Article 39; (5) right to seek judicial protection from administrative malpractice, Articles 39 and 109; (6) separation of powers, Article 51:

• **Respect for Law**: The preamble of the Constitution declares "respect for law". Respect for law means that the Constitution prohibits all administrative actions that do not comply with the authorizing law or the Constitution itself. In combination with the separation of powers (Article 51) it further means that administrative action should be based on a law enacted by the National Assembly/Senate.

These two principles combined form what is known in other countries as the 'legality principle'. The legality principle for the administration declares two things: (1) all administrative actions should be based on law enacted by the legislature and (2) all administrative actions should comply with the authorizing legislation-no administrative action against the law.

• **Protection/Respect of Human Rights**: Articles 31-50 guarantee citizens a number of human rights, which the administration must respect. Consequently, the protection of human rights is another key element of administrative law. Respecting human rights in the relationship between government and citizens means the restraint of government power.

---

① English translation of the 1993 Constitution published by Konrad Adenauer Foundation.

• **Right to complain**: Article 39 provides for every citizen the right to complain against administrative measures. The right to complain corresponds with government's obligation to provide an effective complaint mechanism, as included in some(but not all)sector laws.

• **Right to claim compensation for unlawful administrative actions**: Article 39 provides for every citizen the right to claim compensation against administrative malpractice. This is called state liability. State liability means that administrative authorities are responsible for unlawful administrative actions and that they have to compensate citizens for unlawful measures and/or non-performance.

• **Judicial review of administrative measures**: Article 39(2) also provides the right to settle citizens' complaints against administration and claims for compensation accessing independent courts.

Respect for law(the legality principle), administrative complaint, judicial protection of human rights in administrative processes, and state liability are cornerstones in the Constitution that directly shape administrative law. These principles are considered 'supreme law'(Article 150) binding administrative measures.

2.2 International Law/Obligations

International agreements can set out rules as well as principles, which either become directly or indirectly part of Cambodia's administrative law. International law in relation to human rights is an integral part of the Constitution and can take precedent directly over statute law(Article 31(1) of the 1993 Constitution). International agreements can become indirectly part of Cambodian law, if the legislature adopts them(Article 26).

The following international agreements have had a significant impact on the creation of administrative law.

• **Legal Requirement to Good Governance**: As Joerg Menzel concludes, good governance is part of the developing modern international law,[①] which addresses issues of good governance and good administration. Governments

① Joerg Menzel, "Principles of Administrative Law(Unpublished Report)," (Phnom Penh: GIZ, 2011), p.10.

can adopt these principles a part of their policies. In the case of Cambodia, the Government, for example, adopted Good Governance, as part of its Rectangular Strategy(Phase III).

• **Legal Requirement to fight corruption**: The Kingdom of Cambodia signed the UN Convention on Corruption,[①] which requires the government to establish legal frameworks and institutions to combat corruption. The adoption of an anti-corruption law and the establishment of Anti-Corruption Unit are important national reflexes to comply with international obligations set out in this convention.

• **Legal Requirements to Provide Access to Information**: The UN Convention on Corruption also requires effective access to information. Article 13 stipulates: "states (ensure) that the public has effective access to information". Article 19 of the Universal Declaration of Human Rights, which Cambodia has signed and acceded to, sets out a similar requirement: "Everyone has the right to freedom of opinion and expression; this right includes the right to hold opinions without interference, and to seek, receive, and impart information through any media". Consequently, the RGC has prepared a draft law on access to information to comply with international obligations set out in international law.

• **Legal Requirements of Human Rights Treaties**[②]: To date, Cambodia is

① 2005 U. N. Convention on Corruption (acceded to by Cambodia in September, 2007); ibid.; Article 13 of the Convention requires that states should "(ensure) that the public has effective access to information".

② Cambodia has also signed the Convention on the Rights of Persons with Disabilities (CRDP) and the International Convention on the Protection of the Rights of Migrant Workers and Members of Their Families (CMW). Signing a treaty signifies a commitment by the government to ratify the treaty in the near future. Cambodia has also ratified a number of optional protocols to these treaties which impose additional obligations on the government: the Optional Protocol to the Convention against Torture (OPCAT); the Optional Protocol to CEDAW; and the two Optional Protocols to the Convention on the Rights of the Child dealing with child soldiers and with child exploitation (CRC-OPAC and CRC-OPSC). Each of these treaties is guaranteed under Article 31 of the Cambodian Constitution. In 2007, after a petition from child rights NGOs supported by OHCHR.

party to six human rights treaties.

- International Covenant on Economic Social and Cultural Rights(ICESCR)
- International Covenant on Civil and Political Rights(ICCPR)
- International Convention on the Elimination of All Forms of Racial Discrimination(ICERD)
- Convention on the Elimination of Discrimination against Women(CEDAW)
- Convention against Torture and Other Cruel, Inhuman or Degrading Treatment or Punishment(CAT)
- Convention on the Rights of the Child(CRC).

Article 31 of the Constitution directly respects human rights treaties adopted in Cambodia. The relevance of human rights treaties for the decision making of all state institutions has also been emphasized by the Constitutional Council in its decision of 10 July 2007 (Decision 092/003/2007), which issued a ruling clarifying that the human rights treaties are part of domestic Cambodian law and should be applied by judges in the courts.①

• **Legal requirements of ASEAN**: Cambodia signed the ASEAN Charter. While entry itself is a political event, integration into ASEAN is largely an ongoing legal endeavour. Most of the recent changes relate to commercial matters. However, some required changes could relate to administrative matters as well. For example, transparency of laws and procedures is an explicit requirement for all ASEAN members.② Such transparency includes the requirement that laws and procedures are disseminated and that legal procedures for decision making must be consistent and respected.

• **Legal requirement to WTO/Transparency**: In 2004 Cambodia joined the

---

① Joerg Menzel, *Counstitutionalism in South East Asia*, eds. Clauspeter Hill and Joerg Menzel, Reports on National Constitutions(Singapore: Konrad Adenauer Foundation, 2008), Volume 2, p.60.

② Jeffrey A. Kaplan, "Cambodia's Asean and Wto Integration: A Legal Perspective" in *Cambodian Legal and Judicial Reform in the Context of Sustainable Development*, ed. Soc Sopana(Phnom Penh 1998), p.58.

World Trade Organization(WTO), which requires legal and institutional reforms ensuring uniform and impartial implementation of trade commitments. As part of the WTO accession package, the Cambodian authorities committed to enact 46 laws.[①] Even during the WTO accession process, member states stressed the important issue of transparency. As a result, Cambodia committed itself to 3 transparency related actions: (ⅰ) to provide at least 30 days for comments on all proposed new measures affecting trade in goods, services or the protection of intellectual properties; (ⅱ) that no such measure will become effective until it is published in the official journal; and (ⅲ) to make available on an official website the body of all current laws, regulations and decrees, as well as administrative and judicial rulings, relating to trade.[②]

International Administrative Law: Traditionally, International Law is defined as law between states.[③] Against the background there is a strict separation between the external sphere (law between states) and the internal sphere (law governing the relationship between persons and the relationship between persons and the government). The traditional view would consider international administrative law as a contradiction in itself, with a strict boundary between the two: international law is external and administrative law is internal. This strict separation does not reflect contemporary development neither of international nor of administrative law. Contemporary International Law, also still considered principally the law governing the relationship between states, is no longer deemed limited exclusively to these relations.[④] It has a wider reach and is now defined as law that deals with the conduct of states and of international organizations and with their relation inter se, as well as with some of their relation with persons, whether natural or

---

① Soc Sopana, "The Role of Law and Legal Institutions in Cambodia's Economic Development: Opprtunities to Skip the Learning Curve" (Bond University, 2008), p.99.

② Ibid., p.143.

③ Thomas Buergenthal, Sean D. Murphy, Public International Law in a Nutshell, 4th Edition, West Publishing (2006), Chapter 1, p.1.

④ Ibid., p.2.

juridical.[①] In addition, scholars also observe an internationalization of administrative law, for example in international environmental law, increased cooperation in specific areas such standardization, as well as international administration of territories(for example UNCAT) and the application of law created by international organization or development cooperation.[②]

2.3 Specific Administrative Law/Sector Laws

The most visible part of administrative law is the body of laws governing the public sector. This includes laws and regulations.

2.3.1 Laws

The National Assembly has the legislative power, i.e., the National Assembly adopts new laws or amends existing laws. Id at Art.90(I) of the Constitution. After adoption, the Senate reviews the law. Id at Art. 113 of the Constitution. If the Senate approves the adopted law, then the Senate directly submits the draft law to the King for promulgation.[③] Promulgation is a royal act that law-making process complied with all formal requirements. The formal act formalizing a draft law is called Preah Reach Kram. The format for the Royal Kram promulgating a law can be found on page 31, Circular (2013).

2.3.2 Regulations

Regulations are not(formal) laws adopted by the National Assembly, but laws enacted by the executive. There are different types of regulations. They include: (ⅰ) Royal Decrees, (ⅱ) Sub-Decrees, (ⅲ) Proclamations, (ⅳ) Decisions, (ⅴ) Circulars, and (ⅵ) Local Regulations. Regulations have different purposes reaching from appointing a government official(specific purpose) to providing technical details for the implementation of a law(general purpose).

---

① American Law Institute, Restatement of the Foreign Relations Law of the United States(Third), Para.101, 1987.

② Christoph Moellers, Andreas Vusskuhle, Christian Walter (eds.), Internationales Verwaltungsrecht, Jus Internationale et Europaeum, 16, Mohr Siebeck (2007), pp.1-2.

③ If the Senate requests a revision of the draft law, the process is more complicated. For details see Section, 2.2.5.

General and Specific Regulations: The Circular (2013) differentiates between general and specific regulations in relation to Royal Decrees, Sub-Decrees, and Proclamations.

• Specific regulations govern the status of a person, such as appointment to a high ranking position.

• General regulations govern the implementation of a (formal) law including organizational aspects.

The following paragraphs explain each regulation in more detail and refer to their respective legal sources, common understanding, and definitions outlined in Circular (2013).

Royal Decree (Preah Reach Kret): The King issues Royal Decrees following the request of other constitutional bodies, but does not reign through decrees in his own right.[①] This follows from Article 7(1) of the Constitution, which states that the King reigns, but does not govern.

• **Specific Royal Decrees**: The Circular (2013) outlines examples for specific Royal Decrees governing the status of dignitaries as outlined in Articles 19, 21, 27, and 29 of the Constitution, and Article 14 of the Law on the Establishment and Functioning of the Council of Ministers. Specific Royal Decrees include Royal Decrees on the (ⅰ) status of high ranking government officials, judges, and monks, (ⅱ) awarding Khmer nationality,

(ⅲ) and awarding title Oknha or Nak Oknha. An example for establishing an institution is the Royal Decree on Establishment of National Committee for Sub-National Democratic Development. An example for dissolving an institution is the Royal Decree Dissolving Supreme Council for State Reform and Council of General Reforms dated 01/10/2013. Finally, the King issues a Royal Decree to designate the winner of an election and form a government. Id at, Article 119 of the Constitution. Formats for specific Royal Decrees can be found in the Circular (2013).

• **General Royal Decrees**: Section 3.2.5 of the Circular (2013) defines different types of general Royal Decrees. A Royal Decree can be issued to

---

① only exception to this rule is the Royal Pardon. Id at Article 27, of the Constitution. It is understood that even in this case, the King should consult the Government.

address a problem under the jurisdiction of the Royal Government. In this case the Royal Decree has almost "law-like" character. The rather wide scope is derived from Article 28(1) of the Constitution, which states that the King shall sign any Royal Decrees proposed by the Council of Ministers. If the Government submits a draft Royal Decree to the King for approval the Royal Government should attach Summary Causes, which briefly outline the rationale and the potential impact of the Royal Decree. Id at Section 2.2, Circular (2013). In addition, a Royal Decree can be issued to further implement an existing law including organizational aspects. Finally, the King can issue a Royal Decree to declare a state of emergency following a joint approval of the Prime Minister, the President of the National Assembly, and the President of the Senate. Id at Art. 22, of the Constitution. Formats for general Royal Decrees can be found in the Circular (2013).

Sub-Decree (Anukret): The Prime Minister is authorized to issue sub-decrees exercising his own regulatory powers.① There are two types of sub-decrees: specific and general.

- Specific Sub-Decrees govern the status of person. They either appoint, transfer, and/or remove civil servants ranking from Head of Department up to one rank below the Director General or Governor. Id at Art. 15, Law on the Organization and Functioning of the Council of Ministers (1994).
- General Sub-decrees provide technical details how to implement a formally adopted law including organizational aspects, such as the Sub-Decree on Organization and Functioning of the General Department of the APSARA Authority, etc. The authorization to issue a sub-decree should be stated in the law itself. For example, Article 32, Section 3 Law on the Organization of the Courts (2014) states that the organization and function of the administrative secretariat (...) shall be determined by sub-decree, upon the request of

---

① The Prime Minister as the head of government can instruct ministers. This follows from the fact he is the one who is elected. Therefore, the Prime Minister has a strong position in the system. His instructions can range from general policies to individual decisions. This authority, is for example expressed in Article 16, Law on the Organization and Functioning of the Council of Ministers.

Minister of Justice.

Proclamation(Prakas): A Proclamation is a legal instrument issued by the minister or the head of a government institution governing the work of the ministry/institution. There are two types of Proclamation: specific and general.

• Specific Proclamations govern the status of a person, for example to appoint, transfer, and/or remove civil servants below Head of Department. Id at Art.28, Law on the Organization and Functioning of the Council of Ministers(1994).

• General Proclamations provide instructions how to implement a law or to clarify the legal content of a law.

As with all regulations the authorization to issue a Sub-Decree/ Proclamation should be stated in the law itself. Formats for preparing Proclamations can be found in the Circular(2013).

Decision[①]**(Sech Kdei Smrach)**: Decisions are referred to in Art.150 of the Constitution. The legislative, executive, or the judiciary are authorized to issue decisions for a temporary purpose. The general opinion agrees that a decision ceases to exist as soon as the purpose is reached. This is also confirmed by the Circular(2013), which states that decisions issued by the Government are temporary. A working group, for example, would be established by a decision, as the establishment of a working group is only temporary. Formats for preparing Decision can be found in the Circular(2013).

Circular(Sarachor): A (ministerial/government) Circular clarifies legal contents, interprets higher-ranking provisions, or introduces instructions for the implementation of a law. A Circular issued by the Head of Government is an instruction to ministries, municipal/provincial institutions how to implement a law. Id at Art.29 the Law on the Organization and Functioning of the Council of Ministers(1994). A circular issued by a ministry is to clarify laws

---

① The Constitutional Council issues decisions. A decision of the Constitutional Council is considered final and binding. It has supremacy within the legal system, meaning that all laws and regulations must strictly conform with the decision of the Constitutional Council.

and regulations under the jurisdiction of a sector ministry. Formats for preparing Circulars can be found in the Circular(2013).

Local Regulations(Deika): Sub-national authorities issue local regulation within their scope of authority. Id at Art.48, the Law on the Administration and Management of Commune and Sangkat(2001) and Art.32 and Art 53-Art.61, the Law on the Administration and Management of the Capital, Provinces, Municipalities, Districts, and Khans. Local Regulations only have territorial jurisdiction.

2.4 Unwritten Rules Governing Administrative Law

All sources of administrative law mentioned so far have been of written nature. But administrative law can also recognize unwritten rules such as(i) court rulings and(ii)customary law.

• **Court Rulings**: "In applying Administrative Law judges develop new standards and specific principles. In fact, administrative courts developed most of the general Administrative Law Principles in continental Europe. French Administrative Law has been developed largely by the jurisprudence of the administrated courts with the State Council(*Conseil d'État*)at the top. The *Conseil d'État* was established more than two hundred years ago and it was not a fully independent court in the beginning, but it has evolved to be one and the independence of administrative courts has been clearly stated by the French Constitutional Council.① In 2008 alone the Conseil d'Etat decided around 12.000 cases, the *Cours Administratives D'Appel* around 27.500 (Mestre, in: Bogdandy/Cassese/Huber, Vol III 2010, p.113). Cambodia does not have a judiciary body reviewing administrative cases. Even though-in theory-the ordinary courts review all legal cases, including administrative ones, there were no court rulings on administrative issues since 1993.② Prior to 1970, there were administrative cases first handled by the *Krom Viveat* and

① Decision of 22 July 1980, Indépendence de la jurisdiction administrative, Rec.p.46.

② According to anecdotal evidence, the sex-offender Garry Glitter appealed the administrative decision to revoke his visa. The motion was said to be denied due to lacking jurisdiction.

then by the *Counsel D'Etat* (see also historic overview), but it is doubtful whether their rulings still have a relevant influence on Administrative Law today".[①]

• **Customary Law**: Customary law can play a role in administrative law. Article 47 of the Constitution, for example, can be viewed as customary social security law as it reflects the custom that children are required to take care of their parents. Instead of challenging an administrative decision in front of the court, it may also be a custom to go to the village chief or to informally appeal to the superior of a decision maker. Another example for customary law could be the extra-judicial control by the King. Reynolds (1998) mentions a case where in 1996 the King was successfully petitioned to intervene in a dispute between a local administrative body and market stallholders regarding a rental increase.[②]

2.5 Academic Research

"Within *civil law systems* academic research usually plays an important role in the development and interpretation of law" states Menzel.[③] He continues that

> law professors are involved in the preparation of laws, the interpretation of laws and in the elaboration of general principles. German Administrative Law was strongly influenced by academic elaborations, most notably Otto Mayer's two volume book on German Administrative Law, which was first published in the end of the 19th century and which has been influential in a range of jurisdictions, which have looked to Germany in the development of their own law (in Asia: Japan, South Ko-

---

① Menzel, Joerg. "Principles of Administrative Law (Unpublished Report)." pp. 22-23.

② Rocque Reynolds, "Dicey in Cambodia or Droit Administratif Meets the Common Law," *The Australian Law Journal*, vol. 72, 1998, p. 210.

③ Menzel, Joerg. "Principles of Administrative Law (Unpublished Report)." pp. 23-24.

rea, Taiwan).[①]

In Cambodia, there is currently only limited academic research in administrative law. Whereas there are numerous textbooks on public administration and the civil service, there are only very few on administrative law itself. During the preparation of this report two relevant textbooks (both only available in Khmer language) could be identified:

- Doeuk Pidor, *General Administrative Law*, 2009.
- Say Bory, *General Administrative Law*, 2nd ed. 2001.

Say Bory's book is the most comprehensive publication on administrative law in Cambodia, but unfortunately it is outdated. It provides a systematic approach to structure and defines administrative law. Section 1 defines administrative law, identifies entities, sources, and analyses the legality of administrative actions. Section 2 reviews administrative instruments such as administrative decisions and the administrative contract.

In the second part of Section 2, Say Bory looks into state liability. Section 3 deals with the organization of the administration, in particular with territorial organization.

Besides these two books, there has been little attempt to structure and systemize administrative law. Law universities teach administrative law only as an introductory course. Some legal scholars even go so far as to say that administrative law only exists in theory but not in practice as neither institutions nor legal frameworks exist.[②] This is not the place to discuss the question of whether a body of law needs to be applied and practised to be considered law. However, the lack of academic research in this particular field of law indicates a lower level of interest.

---

① Ibid.

② This view was shared by a number of participants in stakeholder consultation sessions held between 2012-2012 and organized by the General Secretariat of the Council for Legal and Judicial Reform.

3. What Is the Current Status on Specific Administrative (Sector) Laws in Cambodia?

The major legal source for administrative law in Cambodia could be considered specific administrative (sector) law including implementing regulations (mostly sub-decrees). These laws and implementing regulations are fragmented and often not accessible.

In general, there are two forms of legal publishing, primary and secondary:

- The primary form is the systematization, collection, and updating of laws and regulations, including publication and dissemination. Primary publication is one of the core functions of the state. These are official documents and the primary legal source.
- Secondary publishing is where an organisation collects the primary material and reproduces or repackages this for sale or other form of distribution. This happens worldwide, usually as a commercial venture or as part of development projects. Secondary publishing is impermanent and is tied to the life cycle of a project or the commercial success of the publisher. It tends to involve a selection of laws relevant for a specific sector and does not attempt to have official authority.

In contrast to most other countries, in Cambodia, there is

- (No) effective primary publication/dissemination of administrative law in the Royal Gazette; and
- (No) secondary compilation/systematization of administrative law.

3.1 Royal Gazette as the Primary Publication for Laws and Regulation Including Administrative Law

In theory, the Government should publish every law and regulation in the Royal Gazette (unless it is declared urgent) as stated in the following Articles:

Article 93(2) of the Constitution states that

Laws that are signed by the King for promulgation shall be published in the Royal Gazette and announced to the public throughout the country in accordance with the time set out above.

Article 13 of the Law on the Organization of the Council of Ministers states that

All norms and standards of the Royal Government that will have general effect must be published in the Royal Gazette.

The report on 'Access to Legal and Judicial Information' prepared for the UNDP Legal and Judicial Reform Project states that administrative laws are either not published or not disseminated:

Individual Ministries make a considerable number of legislative instruments, such as Prakas. Although there are constitutional requirements to publish laws in the Official Gazette, it is clear that not all laws are published that way. The Ministries tend to retain what they consider their documents and access to these is not always easy.①

Raymond Leos quotes, in addition, three provisions in the current Cambodian Constitution that provide the constitutional underpinnings of a protected right of "timely and effective access to high quality and accurate information held by the Royal Government of Cambodia and other public institutions":

• Article 31 of the 1993 Constitution of the Kingdom of Cambodia pledges to "recognize and respect human rights as stipulated in the United Nations Charter, the Universal Declaration of Human Rights, the covenants and conventions related to human rights, women's, and children's rights".

• Article 35 of the 1993 Constitution also gives Khmer citizens the

① Rubacki, Michael and Murali Sagi. "Access to Legal and Judicial Information." In *Prepatory Assistance on Legal and Judicial Reform*. Phnom Penh: UNDP, 2004.

"right to participate actively in the political, economic, social, and cultural life of the nation. Any suggestions from the people shall be given full consideration by the organs of the State".

• Further, under Article 41, Khmer citizens "shall have freedom of expression, press, publication, and assembly".[①]

International Obligation: In addition, ASEAN and WTO treaties require Cambodia to publish trade relevant information. Trade law is a part of administrative law as it provides the public rules for import licences, customs, duty, and tariffs. For example, ASEAN member states have committed to put a number of relevant ASEAN Trade in Goods Agreement (ATIGA) on the internet through an ASEAN Trade Repository (ATIGA Article 13). Moreover, all official communications and documentation exchanged among member states related to ATIGA shall be in English (ATIGA Article 15).

Low Level of Compliance: However, compliance with national and international regulations is low. The Royal Gazette is neither complete, nor is it published on a regular basis.[②] In addition, Cambodia's current practice of publishing laws and sub-decrees related to trade law is insufficient for ATIGA and WTO compliance.[③]

3.2 Secondary Publications of Administrative Law

In Cambodia, there are no secondary publications that can provide a comprehensive update on administrative sector laws. In France, for example, administrative statutes and regulations are systemized and compiled in an *Administrative Code*, published by a private publisher, *Dalloz*[④].

In Cambodia, sector ministries, private organizations, development part-

---

① Leos, Raymond. "The Role of Access to Information in Promoting Democracy, Good Governance, and Development in Cambodia." In *Access to Information*. Phnom Penh: UNDP, 2010, p.11.

② Adler, Daniel. "Access to Legal Information in Cambodia: Initial Steps, Future Possibilities." *Journal of Law and Technology*, 2006, p.3.

③ Concluded by an (internal) World Bank project document to support the Ministry of Trade establishing a trade repository.

④ Dalloz is a French publisher specializing in legal matters.

ners, as well as the Council for Administrative Reform, the Council for Legal and Judicial Reform, and the Council of Jurists have made attempts to systemize, compile, and update laws and regulations in specific fields. None of these efforts provides a comprehensive, updated, systemized legal database on laws and regulation, let alone on administrative law.

Sector Ministries: Ministries tend to retain what they consider 'their' documents, trying to secure power through concealing information. Some ministries maintain an incomplete list of legal documents on their webpages, for example the Ministry of Justice,① the Ministry of Tourism,② or the Council of Ministers.③

Donor supported projects in publishing laws: Access to legal information is paramount for achieving good governance, rule of law, access to justice, and compliance with international trade obligations. Therefore, at least five projects have supported the publication of legislation in Cambodia. None of those publications is comprehensive or updated. The most significant donor contributions include:

• The Cambodian Legal Resources Centre, funded by South East Asia Fund for Institutional and Legal Development and Canadian International Development Agency published three volumes compiling all legislation from 1993 until 2000.④

• The Office for the High Commissioner for Human Rights (OHCHR) publishes the most complete compilation of laws in Khmer. The fourth edition of selected laws contains laws and regulations in force from 2001—

① http://www.moj.gov.kh/index.php? option=com_content&view=article&id=126&Itemid=59&lang=en.

② http://www.tourismcambodia.org/industry/text/text_pdf/? type=legislation#comp.

③ Office of the Council of Ministers: http://www.bigpond.com.kh/council_of_jurists/somg.htm.

④ Cambodian Legal Resources Centre, The Compendium of Cambodian Laws, Volume 1: Laws and regulations adopted between 1993 and 1995; Volume 2: Laws and regulations adopted between 1995 and 1997; Volume 3: Laws and regulations adopted between 1997 and 2000; edited by Sok Siphana.

2005.A supplement to the fourth edition was issued in 2009.It contains a selection of laws and regulations adopted since the fourth edition up to the end of the Third Legislature in March 2008.In addition, a CD-ROM is available in English, which provides an electronic overview of selected laws and regulation from 1993 until 2002.

• United Nations Development Program(UNDP) Access to Justice Program funded a trilingual legal database and CD-ROM(1996—1998).

• World Bank funded a trilingual publication (1999—2001) and supported the Council of Jurist in publishing laws.

• In 2011 the German International Cooperation(GIZ), Administrative Reform and Decentralization Project started to fund a legal database on laws and regulations pertaining to decentralization, public service, and organization.Laws and regulations are collected on CD Rom, but have not yet been published on the CAR website.

Legal Data Base: The legal data base under the Royal University of Law and Economics, was funded by the EU for the establishment of a database of legal and regulation texts and dissemination of thematic reports for the strengthening of the rule of law and human rights in Cambodia.

http://cambodialaw. nokor-solutions. com: 8080/fo/presentation. do? param=1

National Trade Repository: The World Bank supported the Ministry of Commerce to establish a legal data base concerning trade related laws and regulations.

http://cambodiantr.gov.kh/index.php? r=site/display&id=11

Private Organizations: Some laws and regulations can also be found on private websites, such as

Leaden: http://www.lexadin.nl/wlg/legis/nofr/oeur/lxwecam.htm;

BNG Legal: http://www.bnglegal.com/legal-database.html;

Compendium of Information on Public Services[①]: Based on the Policy on Public Service Delivery[②], the Council for Administrative Reform (CAR) and the Council for Legal and Judicial Reform published a Compendium of Information on Public Services, which attempts to systemize and standardize administrative procedures in the public (service) sector.

The Service Compendium includes four books (volumes), covering seven service clusters:

Volume 1:[③]

Cluster 1: Public services regarding state sovereignty. These are services dealing with civil status such as birth certificates, marriage licences, and so on.

Volume 2:[④]

Cluster 2: Services regarding security and public order. These include interventions and sanctions to uphold law and order. The categorization as service is misleading as these interventions typically involve prohibitions, restrictions and sanctions. These types of interventions are unlikely to be considered as 'service'.

Cluster 5: Services regarding social affairs, culture, and womens' affairs.

---

① The Service Compendium creates a misleading understanding of the term 'service'. It considers all administrative actions as 'services' including sanctions, mandatory licences, and taxes. Tax collection or the issuance of a mandatory licence are examples where the meaning of service is stretched beyond its actual meaning. An administrative action that intervenes with personal freedoms or takes away a part of a person's salary/profit, can hardly be considered a service. In order to avoid misunderstandings regarding the term service, it would help to differentiate between different functions of the administration such as service administration, intervening administration, and fiscal administration (see also section 1) and only consider as services those administrative actions that provide a benefit.

② Royal Government of Cambodia, Council for Administrative Reform, Policy on Public Service Delivery, 2006.

③ Royal Government of Cambodia, Council for Administrative Reform, Volume 1, *Compendium of Information on Public Services*, Cluster 1, Government publication, 2010.

④ Royal Government of Cambodia, Council for Administrative Reform, Volume 2, *Compendium of Information on Public Services*, Cluster 2, 5, 6, 7, Government publication, 2011.

These are classical services of the so-called welfare state. These services include the provision of teaching, health services, or the distribution of social aid.

Cluster 6: Services regarding the development of physical infrastructure.

Cluster 7: Services regarding revenue collection. The categorization as a service is misleading. See also Footnote 52.

Volume 3: ①

Cluster 3: Services regarding judicial services and arbitration.

Volume 4: ②

Cluster 4: Services regarding trade matters, SME development, investment environment, and public-private partnerships. These services are traditionally associated with economic administration regulating business activities, for example through the issuance of economic sector licences.

4. Who Is Applying Administrative Law? Organizational Set-Up of the Administration

The role of the administration, as part of the executive branch of government, is to implement/enforce public laws that apply to citizens. Another term for administration is bureaucracy, referring to the permanent body administering public law (as opposed to the government, which, in a democracy, is elected and therefore by nature is impermanent).

The Constitution names both the Royal Government as well as the administration. Article 145 of the Constitution, which addresses the administration directly, is not very specific on the role and responsibility of the administration, and seems to focus on its territorial organization. Decentralization laws stipulate the territorial organization, but they are not part of this re-

① Royal Government of Cambodia, Council for Legal and Judicial Reform, Volume 3, *Compendium of Information on Public Services*, Cluster 3, Government publication, 2011.

② Royal Government of Cambodia, Council for Administrative Reform, Volume 4, *Compendium of Information on Public Services*, Cluster 4 (Part 1), Government publication, 2010.

view.

Organization: What follows is a brief overview of the organizational set-up of the administration. The administration comes under the Royal Government (through the Council of Ministers). There are currently 26 line ministries under the Council of Ministers, as well as other administrative bodies. The Law on the Organization and Functioning of the Council of Ministers was passed with the aim of defining the mission and mandate, roles and responsibilities of the government followed by a series of laws(a total of 21)organizing ministries and state secretariats.①

Direct/Indirect Administration(territorial/functional): The administration acts either directly or indirectly through legal bodies on different organizational or territorial levels(at national and sub-national level):

• Direct Administrationmeans government implements the law through its own organization-through either a ministry or its deconcentrated branches. For example the tourism law directly authorizes the Ministry of Tourism to manage matters related to the tourism sector(Article 9, Law on Tourism).

• Indirect Administrationmeans government transfers its implementation authority to an independent legal body. Independent legal bodies can be divided in(1)territorial or(2)functional administrative bodies. They carry out the implementation of a law(on behalf of the government). For example, the Law on Tourism delegates authority to sub-national administration to organize the sub-national tourism development plan(Article 9)or to issue the tourism licence(Article 38). The delegation of implementation authorities to sub-national level is called deconcentration. The delegation of authorities to sub-national level-not only the authority to implement national laws on sub-national level-is called decentralization. Decentralization can include own policy/legislative functions, budget functions, or just simply to manage own affairs with limited interference from national level. In one of his contributions Mr. Theng Sangvar will take a closer look at administrative law and decen-

---

① Sopana, Soc."The Role of Law and Legal Institutions in Cambodia's Economic Development: Opportunities to Skip the Learning Curve." p.100.

tralization.

5. What Instruments Are Available for the Administration?

The administration has a number of instruments to(ⅰ)preparegenerally applicable rules such as policies,plans,and regulations and(ⅱ)to make individual decisions such as imposing sanctions,providing a service,or issuing or refusing a licence.

5.1 General Applicable Rules

The preparation of generally applicable rules is the rule-making or legislative function of the administration.Generally applicable rules are:

• Policies: A policy sets out a goal to be achieved within a specific sector.The Law on Tourism,for example,authorizes the Ministry to prepare policies and tourism development plans for the Kingdom of Cambodia after consulting relevant ministries, institutions, sub-national administration, Tourism Industry Association,and the relevant private sector bodies(Article 5).

• Plans:These are documents that operationalize a government policy.A plan often includes periods,goals,activities,and responsibilities.The Law on Tourism,for example,authorizes the national as well as sub-national administration to prepare national and sub-national development plans for tourism (Articles 5-8).The procedure of planning is relevant when realizing projects of territorial impact (spatial planning) or political impact (national development plan).

• Regulations:Regulations reflect the rule-making/legislative authority of administration.Most statutes authorize the administration to draft implementing regulations, which often regulate technical detail. The Law on Tourism,for example,authorizes the Ministry to issue regulations in specific fields (Article 10)by stating that:

> the Ministry of Tourism shall be mainly responsible for introducing main regulations in tourism industry in order to effectively implement the tourism development plans. These shall include: promotion of the

tourism sector both within and outside the Kingdom of Cambodia; quality assurance in the tourism sector; various standards in the tourism sector; Tourism License; tourism business activities; guidance to concerned parties in the tourism sector; administration and supervision of tourism information; international cooperation in the tourism sector with neighbouring countries.

5.2 Individual Decisions

In Cambodia, specific sector laws provide detailed procedures leading to a decision. For example, the Law on Tourism states in Article 39 that:

> Ministry of Tourism or the sub-national administration shall inform the applicant of its decision whether or not to grant requested licence.

An administrative decision in this sense means a legally binding decision in an individual case (unilateral). This decision can either be a sanction, for example the order to close a restaurant, or a service, for example issuing a tourism licence or providing a grant/subsidy.

Administrative Act: None of the literature on administrative law in Cambodia defines an administrative decision as what continental European countries would call an administrative act. The administrative act is the backbone of administrative law in civil law countries as this relates to substantive and procedural requirements leading to an administrative decision. In the end, it is the starting point for determining whether an administrative decision in a specific case is lawful or not. It needs to be determined whether administrative law in Cambodia directly/indirectly recognizes an administrative act as a separate instrument or not.

Conditions for lawful administrative decisions: An administrative decision is only legal if it fulfils the formal and substantial (material) requirements set out in the specific sector law. This universal rule could be deducted from the legality principle set out in the Constitution (see above under 'respect for

law').But beyond that it becomes difficult to determine whether a decision complies with formal and substantial requirements, because many legality criteria or even administrative principles have not been defined yet. Other countries have developed administrative principles, legal frameworks such as an Administrative Procedures Act, or instruments such as the administrative act, to determine the legality of an administrative decision. Cambodia has not yet developed these frameworks and instruments. This legal gap has significant consequences, because legal protection against administrative decisions, enforcement of administrative measures, and state liability all depend on the determination whether an administrative decision is lawful or not.

Penalties: Penalties can be imposed for the violation of obligations set out in specific sector law. Penalties are often delegated and stipulated in implementing regulation.

Administrative Contract: In contrast to the administrative act, which is a unilateral decision, the administrative contract is a bilateral agreement regarding a public law issue. It is used instead of a purely civil law contract where the subject matter of the contract deals with the exercise of a public duty. For example, the administration concludes a contract with an applicant stipulating that a building permit will be issued under the condition that he provides parking space. Both Theng (2011) as well as Say Bory (2001) recognize the administrative contract as an administrative measure.

6. Legal Protection: How Can Citizens Complain Against Administrative Measures?

6.1 Introduction and Background

Government agencies derive their power from properly enacted laws. They have limited, clearly defined powers to implement these laws. Making sure that agencies do not exceed or misuse this power is the essential role of the rule of law principle in the context of administrative law. Against this background, the purpose of administrative law is to restrain the activities of administrative bodies and prevent them from violating individual rights and

interests.① To achieve this purpose citizens must have legal protection against the administration and its measures. The Cambodian Constitution provides the framework for legal protection against administrative measures, such as the right to complain(Article 39[1])and the right of judicial review (Articles 39[2] 128[3])The system envisaged by the Constitution provides citizens with legal protection against administrative measures and controls the executive power/administration through an independent judiciary.This is a new principle in Cambodian history as it establishes the supremacy of fundamental rights,which binds all public authorities.The Constitution(and administrative law as the concretization of the Constitution)declares the individual a legal subject,with subjective public rights.It also outlines a system that protects these subjective public rights.The legal basis of this system is outlined in Article 39,which states clearly that a citizen can complain against any type of administrative measure("Khmer citizens have the rights(...)to complain").Consequently,most administrative sector laws provide complaint mechanisms against administrative decisions.Even if a citizen does not want to complain against an administrative decision,but against a simple(inappropriate)action,or if a citizen intends to report a criminal behaviour such as corruption,other mechanisms provide additional opportunities for complaint, such as the Ombudsman(citizen officer)on sub-national level,or the Anti-Corruption Unit of national level.In the last two cases,a citizen can play an important role as a 'watchdog' or as a 'whistle-blower' to ensure accountability of government institutions.

In theory,the complaint system envisaged by the Constitution and various reform strategies is comprehensive.In practice,however,the existing instruments need to be further strengthened and integrated.

A study commissioned by the Council for Legal and Judicial Reform② assesses a number of complaint mechanisms such as the performance of the

---

① The other role is to empower the administration to efficiently and effectively fulfill its mandate to enforce public law.

② Dara, Khlok. "Searching for Implementing an Ombudsman System in Cambodia." Phnom Penh:Council for Legal and Judicial Reform supported by GIZ,2009,p.13.

Ombudsman's office of Battambang District, the National Authority of Land Conflict Resolution, complaint units in sector ministries such as the Ministry of Commerce, Ministry of Interior, Ministry of Industry, Mines and Energy (industrial property, patents), the Ministry of National Assembly and Senate Relation and Inspection, as well as the Anti-Corruption Unit. The study concludes:

- "There is a need for a functioning complaint system. The rising numbers of complaints confirms this.
- The more independent the complaint offices and teams are, the better the reception will be from the citizens.
- Complaint offices should be easily accessible and located in a neutral location.
- The work done by the complaint offices on citizens' complaints about the administration should be more transparent.
- The complaint offices should get more competences to investigate and solve cases."

The purpose of the following sections is to provide the context for the current system, outlining the policy framework, providing a definition for complaint, and systemizing the existing formal and informal instruments.

6.2 Structuring and Defining Complaints

Complaints are an integral part of the administrative law system, which governs the interaction between the individual and the administration. This interaction is complex as the administration has different means to interact with individuals. Measures can range from a simple action, such as buying a pen with public funds, to complex decisions such as issuing a licence for a nuclear reactor. Actions can include criminal behaviour such as taking a bribe, stealing public funds, or torturing a prisoner, or managing public investment projects or enacting long-term decision-making processes such as developing policies, drafting implementing regulations, or developing plans. One key question for structuring complaints is therefore: What administrative measures can be the subject of complaint?

6.2.1 Structuring Complaints: Complaint Against What?

Complaints provide the right for citizens to object to the following administrative (negative) measures: (ⅰ) inappropriate (informal) action, (ⅱ) negative decisions, (ⅲ) criminal activities, (ⅳ) illegal regulations, or (ⅴ) insufficient public management.

• Inappropriate (Informal) Administrative Action: Traditionally, administrative law categorizes all actions that are not directed to a legal, but to a factual outcome, as real acts or plain administrative actions.① Citizens may report this or claim for removal, compensation, or restitution. Typical inappropriate administrative behaviour is an insulting treatment, a warning, or a simple action. For example, when the administration builds a road, the level of the noise as well the time might be inappropriate. So a citizen suffering from noise pollution can either claim compensation or may insist that the level of noise is kept down.

• Negative Administrative Decisions/Sanctions are the result of the decision-making process outlined in specific administrative sector laws. Here the citizen applies for a licence, a service, or acts against a sanction. An example of a negative decision is when the administration denies the issuance of a licence or a permit.

• Criminal Activities: Government officials can be involved in criminal activities such as corruption, collusion, nepotism, theft, or embezzlement. The state prosecutes these violations in the public interest through prosecutors or special agencies such as the Anti-Corruption Unit. To prosecute these crimes, public institutions need the support of citizens. Therefore, citizens have the right to report criminal behaviour either if they are directly affected or if they gain knowledge of such behaviour.

• Illegal Regulations: most sector laws authorize the administration to draft implementing regulations. A regulation is a formal law enacted by the administration on the basis of legal authorization set out in respective sector laws. The administration can overstretch these legal authorizations, either by conflicting with the authorizing law itself, higher-ranking laws, or violating

① Schulte, Martin. *Schlichtes Verwaltungshandeln*. Tuebingen: Mohr Siebeck, 1995.

human rights.

• Insufficient Public Service/Public Mismanagement: The administration plays a key role in the development cycle at national and sub-national levels. Activities range from planning, to budgeting, to procurement, to implementation, and monitoring and evaluation. Throughout this cycle, government can infringe a number of rights such as rights to participate, rights to access information, and rights to hold government accountable in implementing public projects or providing public services.

6.2.2 Defining Complaint

In Cambodia, 'complaint' seems to be the general/overall term. Against this background the following definition for complaint is proposed:

> Complaint is defined as a remedy of an individual against negative administrative measures such as (i) negative administrative behaviour, (ii) negative administrative decision, (iii) administrative criminal actions such as corruption, (iv) illegal regulations or (iv) insufficient administrative public management/service provision.

Not included in the definition are complaints in the field of private law, in other words between citizens and citizens, such as labour disputes and commercial disputes. These disputes are often handled outside the court system in specific arbitration or mediation councils.

In Cambodia, the term 'complaint' has a negative connotation as it is understood mainly as complaint against the abuse of power. Thus, government officials find the implication of a complaint offensive. However, as outlined above, complaints are not only about the abuse of power, but having a different opinion regarding the interpretation of the law and/or correcting the negative effect of an administrative decision. Other words such as 'objection', 'response', 're-consideration' or simply 'legal protection' have a more positive sound and seem to describe the nature of the request in a better way. Rather than offending a government official with critique, a complaint is more a feedback to correct a decision and/or to make a better decision.

In addition, the following definitions are either commonly used or are proposed:

• Formal/informal complaints: In the Cambodian context, formal complaints are understood as complaints handled by a court. Informal complaints are handled by the administration.

In addition, a more narrow definition of formal/informal complaints could be considered reflecting the fact that some complaints have formal requirements and legal effects and others not.

• Formal complaint (in a narrow sense) means that the complaint requires a specific certain form (written, time-bound) and has a legal effect resulting in a formal decision. Informal complaints have no formal requirements and have no legal effects resulting in a recommendation/notification.

Finally, there are complaints handled by the administration in direct relation to the citizen, and complaints that involve a third party, often to mediate a conflict. In the current cultural setting of Cambodia external mechanisms like the District Ombudsman are more likely to be accepted and used by citizens if they are known, as they allow a citizen to speak/complain about the administration through a third /intermediary person and decrease the level of fear/respect of the complainant. Against this background the following definition is proposed.

• Internal/external complaint: Internal means that the complaint is processed directly within the responsible sector ministry. External means that a third/complementary institution/person processes the complaint.

6.3 Complaint System

A complaint system is a comprehensive set of different complaint mechanisms, which handle complaints. The complaint system envisaged by the Constitution is outlined in Article 39, and includes (ⅰ) administrative review and (ⅱ) judicial review:

• Article 39 [1] states:

"Khmer citizens have the right to denounce, make complaints, or claim compensation for damages caused by any breach of the law by institutions of the state, social organizations, or by members of such or-

ganizations."

• Article 39 [2] and Article 128 [3] state:

Article 39[2]:"The settlement of complaints and claims for compensation for damages is the responsibility of the courts."

Article 128 [3]: "The judiciary shall consider all legal cases including administrative cases."

This system implies that Khmer citizens can complain against all unlawful administrative actions and that these complaints should be first resolved within the administration(administrative review). If unsuccessful, an independent court should settle the complaint(judicial review/administrative litigation). Here it should be mentioned that Khmer citizens, at this point, have no access to judicial review of complaints.

6.4 Complaints Mechanisms: Legal Framework and Constraints

A complaint mechanism is procedure against a specific negative administrative measure handled by an institution or a person. Currently there is a plethora of complaint mechanisms handled by different institutions/persons inside and outside of the state. Within the state there is the king, the National Assembly, the Senate, the prime minister, ministries, government agencies and the courts. Outside the state, NGOs, international organizations as well as traditional mediators such as the village chief or the head of the pagoda, handle complaints.

6.4.1 Legal Framework for Complaint Mechanisms

Besides specific complaint procedures in sector laws, there is a multitude of complaint mechanisms, which are the result of good governance reforms, international law, and customary law.

Public Sector Laws: The majority of complaint mechanisms are regulated in public sector laws. Whenever a citizen applies for a licence, objects to a sanction or a tax notice, or uses a public service, respective sector laws provide complaint mechanisms. The following example is a typical mechanism processing a complaint in a sector law. The Law on Tourism states in Article 46:

> Any person considered him/herself a victim of the decision of the Ministry of Tourism or the Sub-National Administration on the rejection, suspension, revocation and downgrading of the Tourism License or other relevant decisions as stipulated in Chapter 5 of this Law may file a written complaint to the Minister of Tourism or the Sub-National Administration within 30(thirty) days upon receipt of the written notification of any decisions as mentioned above.
>
> Upon receipt of the complaint, the Ministry of Tourism or the Sub-National Administration may suspend its decision and reconsider the matters within 60(sixty) days.

Most sector laws provide a similar mechanism, which allows the administration to review its original decision. These complaints are formalized, because they have to be submitted in writing within a time limit of 30 days. The decision has a legal effect, because it can replace the decision of the sub-national agency and it is a pre-requisite for the settlement in court.

Organic Laws: There are a number of organic laws that provide the legal framework for the set-up of a government institution and that assume the legal basis for a complaint mechanism. For example, the Senate, the National Assembly, or the Prime Minister can establish units that handle complaints.

Good Governance Reforms and Related Laws: To operationalize the mandate of the Constitution, the Royal Government of Cambodia developed a number of good governance policies such as (i) Legal and Judicial Reform, (ii) Public Administration Reform (in particular Local Government Reform and the Reform of Public Services), and (iii) Anti-Corruption Reform. To implement these reforms, several laws that serve as a legal basis for complaint mechanisms have been enacted or are in the process of being enacted,.

• Legal and Judicial Reform: The Legal and Judicial Reform outlines a comprehensive complaint system reflected in the following priority actions (PAs) in the 2005 Action Plan:

- Establishment Ombudsman Office
- Specific complaints for women and other disadvantaged groups
- Administrative(Procedure)Code, which standardizes complaints
- Law on the Organization of Courts introducing an Administrative Tribunal
- Administrative Tribunal
- Law on Ombudsman.

Currently a number of ombudsman offices on sub-national level have been established. And, the Law on the Organization of Courts has been enacted. However, the establishment of a comprehensive administrative law system as required by the Constitution and the legal and judicial reform documents is still not completed.

• Public Administration Reform: Under the Public Administration Reform/Local Governance Reform, the organic Law on Administrative Management of Capital, Provinces, and Municipalities was enacted. The Ministry of Interior refers to the organic law as a legal basis for the establishment of a number of sub-national complaint mechanisms to supervise the performance of sub-national agencies and to ensure their accountability. One example is the District Ombudsman, who supervises the provision of services in one-stop shops on the sub-national level. The other is the Provincial Accountability Working Group(PAWG).

• Anti-Corruption Reform: Under the Anti-Corruption Reform, the Anti-Corruption Law was enacted. The Anti-Corruption Law provides the legal basis to establish anti-corruption units on a national and sub-national level to prosecute criminals in public office and allow citizen to complain about criminal behaviour. These instruments pursue a public interest to prosecute criminals holding public office as well as to discourage the misuse of public power and the misuse of public funds.

International Law: In addition to the previously mentioned policies are other initiatives covering complaints outlined on the basis of international Law. For example, the Cambodian Working Group for an ASEAN Human Rights Mechanism and the government-run Cambodian Committee on Human Rights are in the process of establishing an ASEAN Human Rights mechanism that would allow citizens to complain.

Customary Law: Finally, complaints handled by the King, the village chief, or the head of the pagoda, are traditional ways to resolve conflicts based on customary law.

7. State Liability: How Can Citizens Claim Damages for Unlawful (Administrative) Actions?

Governments must be accountable for the wrongdoings of their officials, especially if their wrongdoings cause physical or commercial damages for citizens. A deeper understanding that government officials are not above the law, but bound by law, and that governments must be accountable for their unlawful actions, provides for the development of state liability and citizen's rights for compensation.

The underlying principle for state liability is that if government acts[①] are unlawful and cause physical and/or commercial damage, a citizen should have the right to claim compensation for these damages. Thus, state liability always requires an unlawful administrative action.[②]

The Constitution reflects this basic understanding and consequently states in Article 39 that:

> "...every citizen(...)can claim compensation for damages caused by any breach of the law by institutions of the state."

As with most of principles, rights, and obligations outlined in the Constitution, they are not directly applicable, but need to be operationalized through laws and procedural rules. The mandate outlined in the Constitution requires government to establish the legal and institutional frameworks to

---

① See also section 6 on Administrative Measures and Instruments.

② State liability should not be confused with compensation as a consequence of a lawful action, for example the legal appropriation of land or other lawful restrictions of the right of property. This type of compensation follows different principles.

process the rights outlined in the Constitution. The development of these legal and institutional frameworks is still in process.

Currently, Article 749 of the new Cambodian Civil Code(2012), in combination with Article 39 of the Consitution, appears to be the legal basis for claims against the government as it deals with the official liability for unlawful action of civil servants.

Article 749 states in Paragraph [1]:

> "Should a public official who exercises the public authority possessed by the national government or a governmental entity intentionally or negligently harm another in violation of the law in the course of his/her public duties, the national government or governmental entity is liable for the payment of damages."

Article 749(1) of the Civil Code(2012) relieves the official of personal liability and imposes liability instead on national government(which may reclaim damages from the official under specific circumstances-Article 749 [2]).

The requirements for compensation are: (ⅰ) a public official, (ⅱ) breach of official duty, (ⅲ) fault(intention or negligence), (ⅳ) damage, and (ⅴ) causality between breach of official duty and damage.

From the legal basis of Article 749 it follows that civil courts have the jurisdiction for handling cases related to compensation for damages resulting from unlawful administrative actions. However, the details of state liability are highly complex due to overlaps between public and private law. And, in the absence of respective jurisprudence, codification is required.

8. Summary and Conclusion

The comprehensive complaint system that is outlined the Legal and Judicial Reform is not yet implemented. Key legislation envisioned by the Legal and Judicial Reform need to be enacted, such as laws on administrative procedure, ombudsman offices, alternative dispute resolution as well as laws providing for the legal and institutional set-up of an administrative court/tri-

bunal and litigation procedures. Because the legal and institutional frameworks are still missing, the existing complaint mechanisms are ineffective in protecting citizens against negative administrative measures.

The figure below illustrates the blueprint for a comprehensive administrative law system as envisaged by the Constitution and the current Legal and Judicial Reform Strategy as well as the Plan of Action for Legal and Judicial Reform. The process is ongoing and essential building blocks are still under construction.

• Improved Publication and Access to Information: The first essential building block is access to information. Citizens have to know the legal basis for a public service as well as related costs. The Service Compendium prepared by CAR is a good starting point, but as a secondary (unofficial) source of information is insufficient (see above). The Law on Access to Information is in the pipeline and the underlying policy is currently being discussed with stakeholders. These are important measures. But the most important thing is to compile, update, and disseminate specific administrative law as a primary official source.

• Fair and Transparent Process (Administrative Procedure Code): The second building block is to establish administrative principles and standardized proceedings governing the administrative decision-making process. Currently this process is fragmented and nontransparent. The process of including administrative principles and standardized proceedings are important measures to address these constraints. The draft policy on reforming administrative law and procedures is addressing these constraints and provides options for introducing an administrative code.

• (Independent) Administrative Adjudication: The third building block is to reform existing complaint mechanisms and to introduce an independent judicial review of administrative actions. This requires a standardized complaint mechanism as well as the institutional establishment of a court system that-not only theoretical-includes an administrative court. In addition, administrative litigation procedures need to be developed, including different types of action.

• Enforcement: The final step for reform is to introduce a law that gov-

erns the enforcement of administrative decisions.

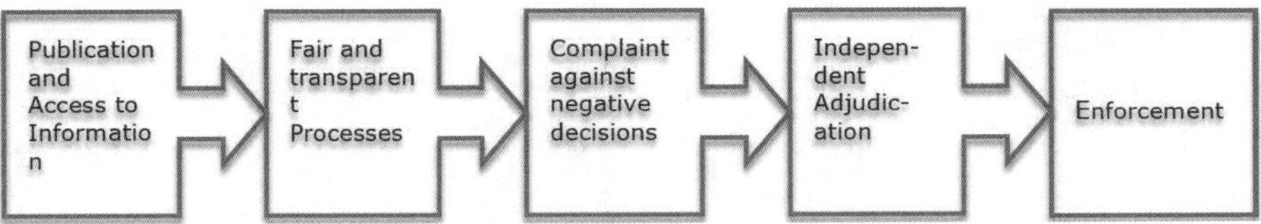

Figure 4　Comprehensive Administrative Law System

Positive change requires moving from an existing situation to an ideal situation. The Constitution, the Legal and Judicial Reform Strategy, and the Plan of Action provide the road map to establish a comprehensive administrative law system. Now, the building blocks need to be developed and assembled. Common wisdom, however, suggests that a strong base should be built prior to adding the roof. Therefore, the systematization and compilation of administrative law should be the first step. The next step is to discuss in more detail principles of administrative law and their application to the Cambodian context.

Selected Bibliography

Adler, Daniel. "Access to Legal Information in Cambodia: Initial Steps, Future Possibilities." *Journal of Law and Technology*, 2006.

De Smith, Stanley and Rodney Brazier. *Constitutional and Administrative Law*. London: Penguin Books, 1998.

Chan-Sangvar, Theng. *Administrative Law and Decentralization*. Introduction to Cambodian Law. edited by Kong Phallak Hor Peng, Joerg Menzel. Phnom Penh: Konrad Adenauer Foundation, 2012.

Chuan, Gan Ching. *Malysian Administrative Law: Commitment to the Rule of Law* Administrative Law and Practice from South to East Asia. edited by Clauspeter Hill and Jochen Hoerth. Singapore: Konrad Adenauer Foundation, 2008.

Von Danwitz, Thomas. *Europaeisches Verwaltungsrecht*. Berlin and Heidelberg: Springer, 2008.

Dara, Khock. "Searching for Implementing an Ombudsman System in Cambodia." Phnom Penh: Council for Legal and Judicial Reform supported by GIZ, 2009.

Darong, Tep. "Cambodia and the Rule of Law." In *Occasional Papers Democratic Development Rule of Law*, edited by Konrad Adenauer Foundation. St. Augustin: Konrad Adenauer Foundation,2009.

Schmidt-Assmann, Eberhard. *Das Allgemeine Verwaltungsrecht Als Ordnungsidee*. Berlin, Heidelberg and New York:Springer,2004.

English-Khmer Law Dictionary.Phnom Penh:Asia Foundation,1997.

Ginsburg, Tom. *Judicial Review in New Democracies*. Cambridge: Cambridge University Press,2003.

Kaplan,Jeffrey A."Cambodia's Asean and Wto Integration: A Legal Perspective" In *Cambodian Legal and Judicial Reform in the Context of Sustainable Development*,edited by Soc Sopana.Phnom Penh,1998.

"Legal and Judical Reform Strategy." Phnom Penh: Royal Government of Cambodia,2003.

Leos,Raymond."The Role of Access to Information in Promoting Democracy,Good Governance, and Development in Cambodia." In *Access to Information*. Phnom Penh: UNDP,2010.

Lexicon of Legal and Administrative Terms. Phnom Penh: Council of Ministers, Royal Committee for the Adoption of Legal Work,2010.

Lexicon of Legal and Administrative Terms. Phnom Penh: Council of Ministers, Royal Committee for the Adoption of Legal Work,2008.

Hill,Clauspeter and Joerg Menzel(eds.).*Constitutionalism in South East Asia* Volume 2:*Reports on National Constitutions*.Singapore:Konrad Adenauer Foundation,2008.

——."Principles of Administrative Law (Unpublished Report)." Phnom Penh: GIZ,2011.

Council for Legal and Judicial(ed.)."Plan of Action Implementing the Legal and Judicial Reform."Phnom Penh:Royal Government of Cambodia,2005.

Reynolds,Rocque."Dicey in Cambodia or Droit Administratif Meets the Common Law." *The Australian Law Journal*,Vol.72,1998.

Sagi,Michael Rubacki and Murali."Access to Legal and Judicial Information." In *Prepatory Assistance on Legal and Judicial Reform*.Phnom Penh:UNDP,2004.

Schmidt-Assmann, Eberhard. *Das Allgemeine Verwaltungsrecht Als Ordnungsidee*. 2nd edition.Berlin,Heidelberg and New York:Springer,2004.

Sopana,Soc."The Role of Law and Legal Institutions in Cambodia's Economic Development:Opportunities to Skip the Learning Curve." Bond University,2008.

Foster,Nigel and Satish.Sule *German Legal System and Laws*.4th edition.Oxford:Oxford University Press,2010.

Werner, Fritz."Verwaltungsrecht Als Konkretisiertes Verfassungsrecht." *Deutsches Verwaltungsblatt*,1959.

柬埔寨行政法介绍

Kai Hauerstein*
李文燕**编译

内容摘要:通过对柬埔寨行政法的详细介绍,本文阐释并分析了柬埔寨在构建行政法体系中存在的问题,提出了柬埔寨行政法已经从强调社会秩序在个人自治之上演变为将个人从国家中保护起来,并且在宪法和行政法二者要求中间建立了很强的相关性。在具体阐述柬埔寨行政法的制定程序和具体执行基础上,针对柬埔寨行政法法律和司法改革要求的综合投诉制度尚未落实的问题,本文提出需要制定法律和司法改革要求的重要法律,并且改进信息发布和获取机制,保证行政程序法公平透明,对行政诉讼进行独立的司法审查并制定规制执行行政决定的法律。

关键词:柬埔寨行政法;行政程序;国家责任;司法改革

一、柬埔寨行政法概述

行政法是调整行政主体行使行政职权的法律规范的总称。行政法作为负责政府实际运作的法律,是政府管理的重要组成部分。行政法的实施与公民和其他行政主体有密切联系,其有两个要素,即政府本身以及政府与公民之间的相互作用。

行政程序和诉讼程序赋予行政法生命,其为行政主体与公民之间的互动提供了条件。行政主体与公民之间相互作用的过程可概括如下:在立法机关颁布一部新法之后,行政主体通过实施和解释新法的规则,公布新法并制定实

---

* Kai Hauerstein,柬埔寨法律和司法改革委员会常设秘书处法律顾问,德国律师。

** 李文燕,西南政法大学国际法学院 2017 级硕士研究生。

施条例,在特定案件中适用,在公民申诉的情况下审查决定。如果主管部门拒绝申诉,则法院经审查后驳回或维持主管部门的决定。在公民用尽所有救济渠道后,行政部门执行根据最终的裁决或决定执行。简单来说就是新法的颁布、实施与公布,公民根据新法的规定进行申诉、适用,法庭独立审查行政措施是否合法,最后由相关行政机关执行最终决定。

下表总结概括了行政法的定义、架构及功能:

行政法:法律框架(1)政府本身并且(2)政府与公民的相互关系	
(1)政府/行政管理的法律框架	(2)当适用/执行法律时政府和公民之间相互关系的法律框架
公共服务管理(如公共服务法律)	一般行政法是跨越行政法领域的背景系统,除其他领域外,还包括基本程序和一般原则/程序权利
与领土和领域有关的法律(例如,分权法律)	具体行政法:规定不同领域的具体政策(如,土地法,旅游业法)
职能型法律组织(例如,司法部门法)	行政"立法"(如,一个政府机构发布一个次法令)

柬埔寨行政法的发展背景如下:

柬埔寨已经经历了它的合法的机构的系统,频繁而又剧烈的变化,不同殖民权力和政府介绍了,建立了,毁坏了,代替了存在的法律体系。作为一个完整的这些合法系统的完整部分的行政法有着同样的命运。

• 以前—1953 年(殖民规则):在殖民统治之下,柬埔寨引入了法国基础的民法体系。但并没有引入全方面的行政法。申诉,如对抗行政(殖民)措施,是不被允许的。因此,法国机构如行政法庭和最高行政法院从未被引入柬埔寨。只有在 1948 年,行政事务丹司法审查被分配给 Krom Viveat(一个分离的拥有广泛行政审查权力的行政审查主体)。

• 1953—1970:在柬埔寨独立后,Krom Viveat 继续它审查行政法的工作,但最终在 1970 年的政变中被废除。

• 1975—1979:在柬埔寨共产党下,所有合法机构和框架被毁坏,包括行政法。

• 1979—1993:在柬埔寨人民共和国期间,一个社会主义政府模型被引入。在原则上,政府和公民被看作相同的并且一个将会管理他们相互作用的

合法框架被认为是没有必要的。然而 1982 年申诉法授予公民无司法审查并且允许他们申诉政府行为,如果这些行为被认为对国家,集体利益或个人有害。

• 1993—今天:在 1993 年,旧的民法体系被重新建立。新的宪法,要求分权,司法审查,诉讼权利和地方分权,提供了一个建立全面行政司法体系的蓝图。自从 1993 年,许多塑造了机构型领土型行政建立的组织法和许多公共部门法已经被颁布。

二、柬埔寨行政法的渊源

作为公法的一部分,行政法有许多法律渊源。关于如何以适当的顺序组织这些来源存在争议。根据层次结构构建行政法的渊源如下:(1)宪法;(2)国际法(一般规则和国际条约);(3)部门法律及其实施条例(例如,法令和附属法规);(4)不成文行政法如判例,习惯法和学术研究。

法律的层次结构严格,低位阶的法律必须服从于高位阶法律。下图提供了柬埔寨法律的等级制度。

下面仅简要介绍宪法、国际条约、法律法规。

(一)宪法

法律的等级制度是宪法至上的基础。国家机构制定的所有法律法规必须符合宪法的规定。宪法自身可以修改和变更,根据所有议员中的四分之一的建议,国王、总理和国民议会主席有权提出审查或修改宪法的建议。修正案由议会以 2/3 多数票通过的宪法颁布。禁止影响自由、多元民主制度以及君主立宪制模式的修正案。

柬埔寨宪法直接和间接地定义了行政法,规定了与行政法相关内容的主要条款如下:(1)1993 年宪法的序文提到了“对法律的尊重”;(2)人权(第 31—50 条);(3)申诉行政行为的权利;(4)非法行政行为要求赔偿的权利,(39 条);(5)从行政人员玩忽职守中寻求司法保护的权利,第 39 和 109 条;(6)权力分立,第 51 条。

(二)国际条约

国际条约也称为公约、协定或协议,是一个国家和另一个国家(双边的)、若干国家之间(多边的)或在一个国家与另一个国际法主体(如一个国际组织,例如联合国)达成的协议。国际条约由议会两院批准并由国王颁布之后即在柬埔寨国内有法律效力,等级排列在宪法之后。例如,柬埔寨王国和欧盟的合作条约,在 1997 年 4 月 29 日签署,已经由欧盟和柬埔寨王国之间合作条约的实行法律转化为国家法律。

柬埔寨宪法的第 26 条规定:“国王应当在国家议会和参议院投票赞成之后,签署和批准国际条约和契约。”此外,宪法第 31 条(1)中规定:“柬埔寨王国认可并尊重联合国宪章、国际人权宣言和与人权、妇女儿童权利有关的条款和规定。”2007 年宪法委员会决定,有关人权问题的国际条约可以直接在柬埔寨国内适用。

(三)法律和规章

从法律等级出发,成文法律不能与宪法相冲突。另外,子法令必须遵守宪法和授权法。政府规章必须遵守(1)宪法,(2)授权法,(3)授权子法令。

三、柬埔寨具体行政法现状

柬埔寨行政法的主要法律渊源是包括实施条例(主要是次级法令)在内的

具体行政法。这些法律和法规十分零散而且通常是难以获得的。

法律发布有两种形式:原始发布和二次发布。原始发布是对法律法规的首次系统编撰、收集和修订,包括出版和传播。原始发布是国家的核心职能之一。这些是都是官方文件和重要法律渊源。二次发布是组织机构收集原始发布的资料,再复制或重新包装以进行销售或其他形式分发。

与大多数其他国家相比,在柬埔寨中行政法的发布包括:(1)皇家公报中原始发布有效的行政法;(2)行政法的二次系统化编撰。

首先,从理论上讲,政府应当根据下列条款的规定,在皇家公报上公开发布所有的法律法规(在紧急情况下颁布的除外),如下:根据柬埔寨宪法第93条第(2)项规定,经国王签署而被颁布的法律应当在皇家公报上发布,并在上述时间向全国公众宣布。内阁组织法第13条规定,具有普遍影响力的皇家政府的规范和标准,必须在皇家公报上发布。另外东盟和WTO条约要求柬埔寨公开与贸易有关的信息。

虽然宪法规定法律必须在皇家公报上发布,但很明显,并不是所有的法律都是经由这种方式公布的。各部门会倾向于保留其认为属于本部门的文件,而且想要获取这些文件或信息并非易事。另外,从当前柬埔寨发布与贸易法有关的法律和地方法令的惯例来看,其也并不满足东盟和WTO的要求。

其次,在柬埔寨,虽然政府部门、个人机构、发展伙伴、行政改革委员会、法律和司法委员会、法学家委员会等都曾尝试在特定领域对法律法规进行整理、编纂、修订。但是,这些尝试都没有为法律法规提供一种重大的、系统的法律数据库,行政法亦然。

但是,法律信息的获得对社会治理、法律规范、获得正义、履行国际贸易义务至关重要。因此,在柬埔寨,已经至少有五个项目支持了法律的公布,另外还有相关的法律数据库、国家贸易资料库、公共服务信息纲要等查询法律信息的渠道,促进法律法规文本的数据化并宣传法律知识以加强柬埔寨法律施行和保障人权的效力。

四、柬埔寨行政法的执行机构

作为政府权力执行部门的一部分,行政部门的作用是实施或执行适用于公民的公法。另一种关于行政部门的术语是官僚部门,指的是执行公法的常设性机构。

行政部门的组织结构:政府(通过部长会议)隶属于王国政府。部长理事

会和其他行政机构下设26个职能部委。《部长会议组织和运作法》的通过，目的是界定政府的任务和任务、作用和责任，随后又通过了一系列组织各部和国务秘书处的法律(共21项)。

直接/间接行政(地域/职能)：行政主体直接或间接地通过不同国家行政机构或下级行政机构(国家和地方)行事。

五、柬埔寨的行政措施

行使行政权的措施有很多，包括(1)制定普遍适用的规则，如政策、计划和条例；(2)作出个别行政决定，如实施制裁、提供服务或颁发许可证。

制定普遍适用的规则是行政主体的规则制定或立法职能。行政主体通过制定政策、计划或规定行使职权。

行政决定实际上是指行政部门对个别案件(单方面)作出具有法律拘束力的决定。柬埔寨关于行政法的文献没有一篇将行政决定定义为欧洲大陆国家所称的行政行为。行政行为是确定具体案件中的行政决定是否合法的起点。需要确定柬埔寨的行政法是否直接/间接承认行政行为是一项单独的文书。只有当一项行政决定在同时符合特定部门的法律所规定的实质要件和形式要件的情况下才是合法的。但是，由于尚未确定合法性标准，很难确定行政决定是否符合形式和实质的要求。

与行政行为相比，行政行为是单方的，而行政合同是一个关于公法问题的双边协议，它用来代替纯粹的民事合同，其主要问题是处理公权力的行使。例如，行政部门与申请人达成一项协议，协议规定在其提供车位时会签发许可证。

处罚是对违反具体部门法规定的义务的行为实施的，通常在执行条例中授权和规定。

六、法律保护：公民就一项行政措施提起申诉

政府机构的权力来自于法律，其执行法律的权力是有限的且明确的。确保行政机关不超越或滥用行政权力，是法治原则在行政法中的基本作用。在这种背景下，行政法的目的是限制行政机关的活动，防止行政机关侵犯个人的权利和利益。要实现这一目的，公民必须得到法律保护，不受行政主体及其措施的侵害。

(一)构建和界定申诉

申诉制度是行政法体系的组成部分,负责处理公民与行政部门之间的相互关系。行政部门行使的不同措施将对公民产生不同的影响,甚至可能损害公民的合法权利。因此,构建申诉机制的关键问是哪些行政措施可以成为申诉的对象。

在柬埔寨的行政法当中,没有明确的界定申诉的概念,仅概括性地对其进行定义。在此背景下,申诉可以定义为:为消除消极行政措施的影响而为个人提供的一种补救措施,这些行政措施包括(i)消极行政行为(ii)消极行政决定;(iii)行政犯罪行为,如贪污受贿等腐败行为;(iv)非法规定;(iv)不充分的公共服务。该定义不涉及私法领域,即公民与公民之间的申诉。

(二)申诉制度

申诉制度是一套全面处理投诉申诉的机制。宪法规定的申诉制度简要包括在第 39 条中,包括(i)行政审查和(ii)司法审查。宪法第 39 条规定,柬埔寨公民有权对国家机构,社会组织或该等组织的成员因任何违法行为而造成的损害进行谴责,申诉或索赔。法院有责任解决请求损害赔偿的诉和诉求。司法机关应考虑所有法律案件,包括行政案件。

这个制度意味着柬埔寨公民可以对一切非法行政行为进行申诉,并且首先应该在行政审查中得到解决。如果不成功,法院应当进行解决(司法审查/行政诉讼)。

(三)申诉机制的法律框架和限制

申诉机制是针对某一机构或个人处理的具体消极行政措施的程序。目前,国内外不同机构/人员负责处理的投诉机制过多。国家内部有国王、国民议会、参议院、总理、各部、政府机构和法院。在国外,非政府组织、国际组织以及村长或寺院院长等传统调解人处理申诉。也就是说,除行政法中的具体申诉程序外,还有许多其他的申诉机制,而这些机制是政改革,国际法和习惯法作用的结果。

七、国家责任:公民就不法行为请求损害赔偿

政府必须对其行政人员的不法行为负责,特别是当行政人员的不法行为

造成公民的人身或财产损害。行政人员的行为应受法律约束,不得超越法律,政府必须对其非法行为负责,这种理解有助于发展国家责任制度并赋予公民损害赔偿的权利。

宪法第39条规定,任何公民遭受的来自国家机关行政人员不法行为的损害均可要求赔偿。宪法的规定要求政府制定法律来保障在宪法中就已确定的权利。这些法律体系仍在发展建设之中。

目前,新《柬埔寨民法典》(2012年)第749条与"联合国条例"第39条,都是政府应对行政人员非法行为负责的法律依据。第749条第一段指出,国家政府或政府机关行使公共权力的公职人员,在执行公务过程中违反法律,故意或过失伤害他人,国家政府或政府机构应当赔偿损失。应当赔偿损失的构成要件如下:(1)公职人员;(2)违反公务职责;(3)故意或过失;(4)造成了损害;(5)违反公务职责与损害之间具有因果关系。

应该注意的是,民事法院对因非法行政行为提出损害赔偿的诉讼有管辖权。然而,由于公法与私法之间的重叠,国家责任的内容非常复杂,在没有相应判例的情况下,需要进行系统地编纂。

八、总结

目前,宪法、现行法律、司法改革战略以及"法律和司法改革行动计划"设想的全面行政法制度蓝图正在进行,由几个方面组成:第一,带个信息发布和获取机制;第二,制定公平透明的行政程序法;第三,改革现有的申诉机制,对行政诉讼进行独立的司法审查;最后,制定规制执行行政决定的法律。

"宪法"、"法律和司法改革战略"和"行动计划"提供了建立全面行政法制度的路线图。现在需要做的就是一步步地对该路线图进行开发和整合。然而,许多人认为,在添加"屋顶"之前应该建立一个强大的基础。因此,行政法的制度化应该是第一步,下一步才是更详细地讨论行政法原则及其在柬埔寨的应用。

A Brief Introduction to Cambodia's Legal System

Khim Kiri[*] and Li Dongmei[**]

Ⅰ. Introduction

This article purports to provide a brief introduction to the current legal system of Cambodia and the procedures for making laws in the country. Similarly to other countries in world, Cambodia's legal system has various forms, including statutory laws and customary laws, while having been largely influenced by foreign laws in recent times due to the extensive support and assistance from the international community in the process of law making in the country.

Historically, Cambodia's legal system has evolved constantly. Before the French Protectorate(1863), Cambodia was ruled under customary laws. From 1863 to 1953 during which French Protectorate when the governance of the country was exercised by the French administration, Cambodia's legal system was based entirely on and emulated the French Legal System.① The influence, however, of the French Legal System did not only cover Cambodia's legal system, but it also had significant impacts on the judicial

* Khim Kiri is the Director of International Relations Department of Royal University of Law and Economic of Cambodia, and a Ph.D candidate of the International Law School, SWUPL.

** Li Dongmei is Program Director of the China-ASEAN Law Research Center, SWUPL.

① Hor Peng, Kong Phallack, Jorg Menzel, Introduction to Cambodian Law, Konrad Adenauer Stiftung, 2012, p.7.

system of the country.

From 1970 to 1993, Cambodia underwent several political regimes that were triggered by internal political conflicts, including civil wars, such as the Khmer Republic regime from 1970 to 1975, the Democratic of Kampuchea regime from 1975 to 1979, the People's Republic of Cambodia regime from 1979 to 1989, and the State of Cambodia regime from 1989 to 1993 (the people's Republic of Cambodia was named as the State of Cambodia under the amendment of the 1981 Constitution in 1989, this amendment only the country's name was changed).

From 1993 up to present, Cambodia is following a democratic political process, where national elections are held every five years. The legal and judicial systems that had been destroyed in prior years of civil war and conflicts started to be revitalized, with the introduction of the country's modern Constitution in 1993① which sets out the democratic and liberal cornerstone for the development of the country's legal and judicial systems. Further, in 1998 when the Khmer Rouge Administration ended and the entire country became united, the political stability and unity contributed to the acceleration of the improvement of legal and judicial systems in the country.

Ⅱ. Overview of the Legislative System②

All laws of Cambodia are adopted by the legislative body and promulgated by the head of state through Royal Code (called Preah Reachkram). Since 1993, Cambodia has been a constitutional monarchy, where the King is the head of state as set out in the Constitution of 1993. Under the Constitution, the king shall reign over the country but not govern and the king shall reign for life.③

---

① Hap Phalty, Legal System of Asian, A Short Guide, Introduction to Cambodia Law, Korea Legislation Research Institute, 2016, p.21.

② Hap Phalty, Legal System of Asian, A Short Guide, Introduction to Cambodia Law, Korea Legislation Research Institute, 2016, p.21, part II.

③ The Constitution of the Kingdom of Cambodia, 1993, Art.7.

Like the legislative hierarchy of other countries around the world, in Cambodia all laws must accord to the Constitution. Where a question or challenge to the constitutionality of a law or any particular provision thereof emerges, the Constitutional Council-a constitutional authority comprising of nine members and serve for a term of nine years each-is empowered by the Constitution to review the constitutionality of the law. Typically, all organic laws must be submitted to the Constitutional Council for review of its constitutionality. International treaties and conventions to which Cambodian government has acceded are required to be submitted by the government to the Parliament for adoption and ratification.

According to the Constitution, the Parliament is comprised of two houses: the National Assembly and the Senate. Currently with 123 members, the National Assembly has the constitutionality authority to adopt and amend laws for Cambodia and approve the national budget and administration accounts,[①] approve or repeal international treaties and conventions,[②] and to initiate legislations, among other constitutional powers.[③] All laws that have been debated and adopted by the National Assembly shall be further forwarded to the Senate for further review and adoption.

The Senate with legislative powers was established since 1999 as a political compromise.[④] The Senate was established as the result from the political deadlock arising from the 1998 national election which was run by Cambodia. Currently with 61 members, the Senate is vested with the legislative power which exercises its functions according to the provisions of the Constitution and the laws in force.[⑤] to review and comments on the legislative drafts or proposed laws sent by the National Assembly.

The following charts specifies the process flow in respect of a law

---

① The Constitution of the Kingdom of Cambodia, 1993, Art.90.

② The Constitution of the Kingdom of Cambodia, 1993, Art.90.

③ The Constitution of the Kingdom of Cambodia, 1993, Art.91.

④ Hap Phalty, Legal System of Asia, A Short Guide, Introduction to Cambodia Law, Korea Legislation Research Institute, 2016, p.22.

⑤ The Constitution of the Kingdom of Cambodia, 1993 and amendment thereto, Art. 99 new.

review submitted to the Senate by the National Assembly:

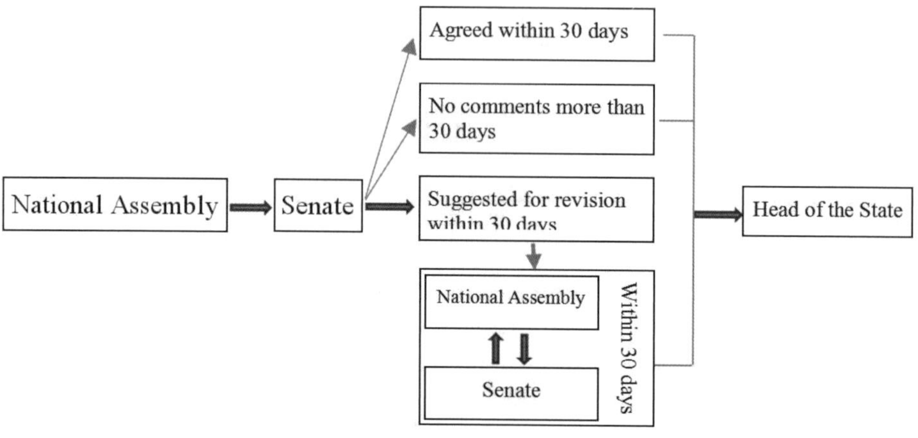

Ⅲ. Hierarchy of Law

a. Constitution

The Constitution of 1993 is the supreme law of Cambodia. Laws, regulations, and decisions made by state institutions are required to be in strict conformity with the constitution.①

The 1993 constitution, Cambodia is under a constitution monarchy, which stipulated the principle elements of how an independent state works. The 1993 constitution of the Kingdom of Cambodia included the provisions concerning the King, basic (fundamental) rights of the Cambodian citizens, political system, economic system, legislative body (including how the role and functioning of the National Assembly and the Senate, judicial organ and executive organ of the state.

Historically, Cambodia has faced vastly different constitutions as a result of numerous changes in political regimes. The 1947 constitution is the first constitution of Cambodia during the period when the country was under French protectorate. Although the country became independent in 1953, the

① The Constitution of the Kingdom of Cambodia, 1993, Art.150.

1947 constitution continued to remain in effect until 1970(when coup d'état was staged by General Lon Nol on March 18,1970)[①].

The second constitution was adopted in 1972 under so called "Khmer Republic" regime and remained in force until 1975.This constitution was replaced by another constitution in 1976 under the Democratic of Kampuchea (known as "Khmer Rouge" regime)from 1975 to 1979.From April 1975 to December 1978,the dictatorial proletariat regime essentially eradicated the entire legal system,and existing laws completely destroyed.[②]

Following the collapse of Khmer Rouge regime in 1979,Cambodia was governed under the People's Republic of Cambodia when the constitution was adopted in 1981.This constitution was further amended in 1989 when the formal name of Cambodia was changed to State of Cambodia which was operational until 1993.[③]

After national election in 1993, under the auspices of the United Nations,the country adopted a democratic political system with multiple political parties,and the modern constitution of 1993 was introduced to cement the new political regime and to guide the future political and economic trajectory of the country.

In sum, from 1947 until present day,Cambodia has five constitutions. The table below shows these five constitutions in different regimes.

No	Year	Name of the Regimes	Date of Constitution
1	1947-1970	The Kingdom of Cambodia	May 6, 1947
2	1970-1975	The Khmer Repuplic	June 10, 1972
3	1975-1979	The Democratic of Kampuchea	January 5, 1976
4	1979-1989	The People's Republic of Cambodia	June 27, 1981
	1989-1993	The State of Cambodia	April 30, 1989
5	1993-Present	The Kingdom of Cambodia	September 24, 1993

The modern constitution of 1993 has encountered numerous challenges.

① Cambodia Coup d'état 1970,Wikipedia,visited on May 24,2017.

② Hor Peng,Kong Phallack,Jorg Menzel,Introduction to Cambodian Law,Konrad Adenauer Stiftung,2012,p.12.

③ Hap Phalty,Legal System of Asian,A Short Guide,Introduction to Cambodia Law,Korea Legislation Research Institute,2016,p.23.

The key challenges were posed by the differing interpretations among Cambodian politicians and political parties. Accordingly, they led to a number of constitutional amendments. Within 20 years, the constitution of 1993 has been amended eight times from its inception to the present. The dates of the amendments are illustrated in the table as follows:

No	Date of constitutional amendment adopted by National Assembly	Date of constitutional amendment promulgated by the Head of the State
1	July 14,1994	July 14,1994
2	March 4,1999	August 8,1999
3	July 2,2001	July 28,2001
4	July 8,2004	July 8,2004
5	May 18,2005	June 19,2005
6	March 6,2006	March 9,2006
7	January 15,2008	February 15,2008
8	October 1,2014	October

As the supreme law of the country, the constitution of 1993 supersedes the rest of the laws and regulations, which shall accord with the constitution. Below is the table which reflects the hierarchy of laws in Cambodia:

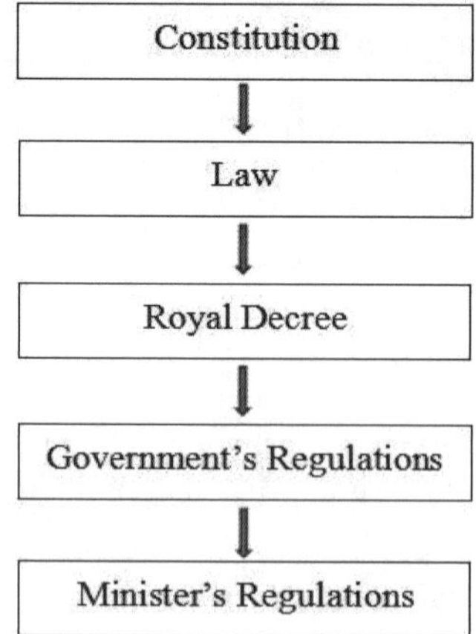

b. Law

Law, are the legal norms which require to be adopted by the legislative body and then promulgated by head of state.[①] The law is ranking below the constitution. The Cambodia constitution 1993 provides clear stipulation of the timeframe in which each law comes into force. Generally, the laws come into force ten days after the date of promulgation in Phnom Penh, the country's capital, and twenty days throughout the country. In the case of immediate promulgation, those laws will come into force immediately after the day of promulgation.[②]

For example, the Law on Association and Non-Governmental Organizations was promulgated on August 12, 2015, came into force in Phnom Penh on August 23, 2015 and throughout the country on September 2, 2015. The law on the Trade Union was promulgated on June 17, 2016. Article 100 of the law stipulated that "this law shall be promulgated immediately" therefore this law came into force in June 18, 2016.[③]

c. Royal Decree

The Royal Decree was known as a Legal Regulation, which ranks below the law in terms of the legislative hierarchy. For it to be effective, the head of state signs the Royal Decree after the submission by the Council of Ministers.[④] The Royal Decree is divided into two types. First, Royal Decree is for the appointing, transferring and dismissing high-ranking officers in the civil service, military service, Ambassadors,[⑤] judiciary organ,[⑥] and the Council

---

① The Constitution of the Kingdom of Cambodia 1993, Art.28.

② The Constitution of the Kingdom of Cambodia 1993, Art.93(1).

③ Hap Phalty, Legal System of Asian, A Short Guide, Introduction to Cambodia Law, Korea Legislation Research Institute, 2016, p.26.

④ The Constitution of the Kingdom of Cambodia 1993, Art.28.

⑤ The Constitution of the Kingdom of Cambodia 1993, Art.21(1).

⑥ The Constitution of the Kingdom of Cambodia 1993, Art.21(2).

of Ministers[①]. Second is an executive ordinance. The Royal Decree ranks above the Government's Regulations called sub-decree.

The constitution of Cambodia does not provide for the regulations that are issued by the Prime Minster or Ministers. However, the law on the Functioning and Organization of the Royal Government of the Kingdom of Cambodia July 20, 1994 makes references to sub-decrees, which can be issued by the Prime Minister. This law state that "the Prime Minister shall appoint, transfer and dismiss by sub-decree, high ranking officers, civil servants, military officials, members of diplomatic corps, deputy governors of the province and municipalities, and district governors who are not specified in Article 14, except for the officers who are stated in Article 18 of this law."[②] Furthermore, the Prime Minister has the power to issue the declarations, decisions, circulars, and other instruments with binding legal force. However, the ministers also have the authority to issue documents with binding legal effect such as proclamations, decisions, and notifications, but all ministerial regulations must be comply with the Prime Minister's regulations.

d. Government's Regulations (Sub-Decree)

The government's regulations (called 'sub-decree') is known as a legal instrument below the hierarchy of law and royal decree. The Government's regulation is an executive regulation usually prepared by the relevant ministries, adopted by the Council of Ministers and signed by the Prime Minister.[③] The government's regulation is divided into two categories, the appointing government regulation and executive government's regulation. The appointing government's regulation allows the Prime Minister to appoint elites or civil servants to serve at any position within the

---

① Law on Functioning and Organization of the Council of Ministers, No.02NS94, July 20, 1994, Art.14.

② Law on Functioning and Organization of the Council of Ministers, No.02NS94, July 20, 1994, Art.16.

③ Law on Functioning and Organization of the Council of Ministers, No.02NS94, July 20, 1994, Art.13.

government's administrative structure and while the executive government's regulations are concerned with other matter relating to the implementation and enforcement of laws.

In addition to the government's regulation, the Prime Minister issues decisions which are used to decide any matter under Prime Minister's regulatory authority. The constitution does not have provisions pertaining to the decision issued by the Prime Minister. However, the government's regulation as defined in 2013 is "a legal instrument in the form and content of a government action which is used for nonpermanent scope and status.①

Furthermore, the Prime Minister has the authority to issue a circular, which is required to offer further explanation or clarification concerning any matter under Prime Ministerial authority. The circular is a binding legal instrument which clarifies the legal content, explains and interprets legal regulations, raise more instructive measures and work activities in order that lower rank civil servants may implement.② The Prime Minister can also issue an order. There is no law stipulated with regards to orders. However, in the practice, an order is issued to deal with particular cases.

e. Ministerial Regulations (Proclamation)

The ministerial regulation is an executive regulation made at the ministerial level. This regulation is prepared by the relevant ministries and it has to be signed by the relevant ministers.③

The ministers have the authority to issue ministerial regulation (so called 'proclamation'), which is the legal instrument with lower legal hierarchy than the Government's Regulation (sub-decree).④ The ministerial reg-

---

① Office of the Council of Ministers, Guideline on the Procedures and Rules of Preparing Draft Laws and Other Legal Regulations, May 10, 2013, 93.

② Office of the Council of Ministers, Guideline on the Procedures and Rules of Preparing Draft Laws and Other Legal Regulations, May 10, 201, 99.

③ Law on Functioning and Organization of the Council of Ministers, July 20, 1994, Art.28, 29.

④ Law on Functioning and Organization of the Council of Ministers, July 20, 1994, Art.29.

ulations cannot go beyond the entrusted authority of the ministry where the minister's regulation is made. The structural organization and function of the ministries and the state secretariat from the department below are required to be issued by ministerial regulation.①

In addition, the ministers have the authority to issue circulars in order to provide explanation or clarification to any particular affairs and providing directives.② As they have lower legal hierarchy, the Ministerial regulation cannot conflict with government's regulations. Notifications can also be issued by ministers under their own administrative authority. These legal regulations cover any particular case but cannot go beyond the government's regulations.③

Ⅳ. Main Laws

The primary sources of the law in Cambodia are the constitution, the civil code and the code of civil procedures, the criminal code, and the code of criminal procedures. These laws are currently in force.

a. Civil Code

The current Civil Code of the Kingdom of Cambodia was promulgated on December 8, 2007 with the technical support and assistance from the Government of Japan.

The 2007 Civil Code consists of 9 books with 1,305 Articles. Book one deals with general provisions, mainly focused on general principles of the private law. Book two describes the concept of persons (physical and juristic persons). Book three centers on the real rights. Book four stipulates various obligations. Book five is concerned with various types of contracts and torts. Book

---

① Law on Functioning and Organization of the Council of Ministers, July 20, 1994, Art.30.

② Law on Functioning and Organization of the Council of Ministers, July 20, 1994, Art.29.

③ Hap Phalty, Legal System of Asian, A Short Guide, Introduction to Cambodia Law, Korea Legislation Research Institute, 2016, p.28.

six is related to security.Book seven describes relatives.Book eight deals with succession.Finally,Book nine concerning the final provision.[①]

For the implementation of this Civil Code,a special law is required.Notably,the special law on the enforcement of this Civil Code was promulgated in May 31,2011.However,the enforcement took six months later.Therefore, the 2007 civil code was applicable on December 21, 2011. Under the Civil Code,the provisions of any specific laws that conflict with those provisions in the 2007 Civil Code shall be repealed.

b. Code of Civil Procedures

The current Code of Civil Procedures was promulgated on July 6,2006 with the support and assistance from the Government of Japan. This Code entered into effect one year later on July 27,2007.

This Code of Civil Procedures is comprised of of nine books and has a total of 588 Articles.Book one of the Code is concerned with the general provisions.Book two specifies the procedure of the court of the first instance. Book three stipulates the appeal procedure. Book four describes the retrial procedure. Book five deals with demand procedure. Book six describes the compulsory execution.Book seven stipulates preservative dispositions.Book eight lays out the transitional provisions.Finally,Book nine specifies the final provisions.

c. Criminal Code

Cambodia's Criminal Code was promulgated on November 30,2009 with the technical support and assistance from the Government of France.

The 2009 Criminal Code consisted of six books and 672 articles. Book one stipulate the general provisions.Book two prescribes crimes against persons.Book three deals with offenses against property.Book four lays out the offenses against the nation. Book five refers the provisional provisions, and Book six is concerned with final provisions. This Criminal Code was adopted in response to the growing needs of the Cambodian society which requires a

---

① Hap Phalty, Legal System of Asian, A Short Guide, Introduction to Cambodia Law,Korea Legislation Research Institute,2016,p.34.

very comprehensive criminal law in order to combat new crimes in the modern Cambodia.

Although this Code came into effect one December 21,2009,only Book one relating to the general provisions was put into implementation,while the remaining parts were put into actual effect one year later,on December 21,2010.

d. Code of Criminal Procedure

Cambodia's Code of Criminal Procedures promulgated on August 10, 2007,also with the technical support and assistance of the Government of France.Unlike the Code of Civil Procedures,the Code of Criminal Procedures was put into implementation throughout the country after it entered into effect on August 31,2007.

This Code is comprised of eleven books with 612 Articles.Book one of this Code refers to criminal and civil actions.Book two stipulates the authorities entrusted with prosecution,investigation and interrogation powers.Book three describes the policy inquiry.Book four prescribes judicial investigation, while Book five describes judicial judgments.Book six is concerned with the Supreme Court.Book seven stipulates citations, summon and notifications. Book eight is concerned the enforcement procedure,and Book nine provides for special proceedings.Book ten sets out the transitional procedures,and the last Book is concerned with final provisions.

Ⅴ. Laws Making Procedures

a. Overview

This part will examine the law making procedures in narrow and broad means.In a narrow mean,the draft laws or proposed law required to be adopted by the National Assembly and to be approved by the Senate,and finally to be promulgated by the head of the state.In a broad mean,laws and other regulations promulgated by the head of the state,and issued by prime minister,ministers and other governmental organs.The constitution of the kingdom of Cambodia entitles the National Assembly,the Senate,and Prime

Minister to initiate the law.[①]

b. Legislative Procedure

i . Legislative Body (Draft Laws)

The members of the National Assembly have authority to initiate Draft Laws. The permanent standing committee of the National Assembly plays an important role to put forward a Draft Law. After the Draft Law has been prepared, they shall be submitted to the National Assembly Commission for review. Following the review, the Draft Law will be set for the discussion and adoption during the plenary sessions of the National Assembly. Then, the Draft Law has to be further forwarded to the Senate for review and adoption. After it is adopted by the Senate, the Draft Law will be forwarded to the head of the state for the promulgation. The table below provides an illustration of the law making process from the National Assembly through the promulgation by the head of state:

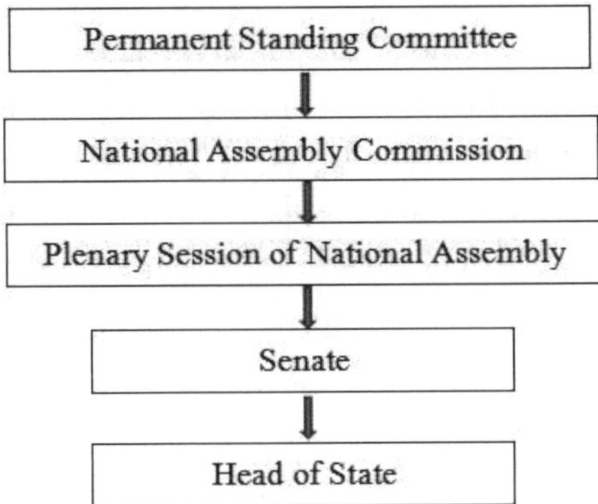

The 1993 constitution of Cambodia further provides that the senate to has an authority to initiate Draft Law. In this process, the permanent standing committee of the Senate prepares and puts forward Draft Law to the National Assembly Commission. The process will follow the same flow as the process flow when the Draft Law is initiated by the National Assembly.

---

① The Constitution of the Kingdom of Cambodia, 1993, Art.91.

The table below offers an illustration about the process for making laws that are initiated by the Senate:

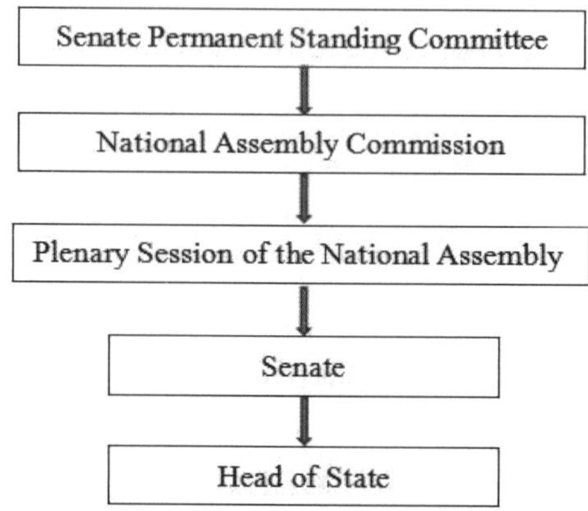

ⅱ. Executive Body (Proposed Laws)

It is the norm that the relevant ministries initiate Proposed Laws through their general and technical departments. After a Proposed Law is discussed and approved internally by a particular governmental Ministry, it will then be submitted to the specialized Council of Jurists of the Council of Ministers for technical and legal review. Following the review by the Council of Jurists, the Proposed Law shall be submitted for review and discussion by the Council of Ministers. It shall then be signed by the Prime Minister before it is forwarded to the National Assembly.

Upon receipt of the Proposed Law initiated by the government as the executive body, the National Assembly Commission will review the Proposed Law and will submit it to the plenary session of the National Assembly for deliberation and then adoption. The absolute majority vote of two thirds of the National Assembly is required for adoption of Proposed Law. Thereafter, the adopted Proposed will be further submitted to the Senate for deliberation and adoption. In terms of the final step, the adopted law will then be submitted for signature by the head of state for the purpose of promulgation.

ⅲ. Regulations (Executive Body)

The executive body, which is entrusted government organs, has full authority to enact and issue legal instruments. With regard to executive body

regulations or the legal instruments issued by the prime minister, the relevant Ministries prepare drafts of the regulations.

In the case that the legal regulations are concerned with the authorities of various ministries, those legal regulations are required to be discussed by the inter-ministries. When those legal regulations are finally discussed and are approved by the inter-ministries, then they will submitted to the Council of Jurists of the Council of Ministers for review.

Following the review by the Council of Jurists, the draft regulations are then discussed and approved by the Council of Ministers. The approval of the legal regulations approved by the Prime minister comes into effect on the date of signature.

Ⅵ. Court System

The Cambodia judicial system is consisted of the Provincial or Municipal Court, Military Court, Court of Appeals, and the Supreme Court.

a. Provincial Court (Court of First Instance)

The provincial or municipal court is the lowest court in Cambodia. The provincial or municipal court has the jurisdiction over the case in which occurs within its jurisdictional territory. Each province in Cambodia has one court of the instance.

Similar to the court of first instance is the military court. The military court has jurisdiction over the case only military offenses. The military offenses are involved military personnel, whether initialed or conscripted and which are concerned with disciplines of the armed force or harm to military property.①

b. Appeal Court

The appeal court reviews both matters of law and matters of law. Cur-

① Hor Peng, Kong Phallack, Jorg Menzel, Introduction to Cambodian Law, Konrad Adenauer Stiftung, 2012, p.11.

rently, Cambodia has one appeal court for the whole country. However, at present, the Ministry of Justice is planning to set up five regions of appeal courts in the country.

c. Supreme Court

The Supreme Court reviews only the matter of law, except in the case of a joint trial of the second grievance complaint. The Supreme Court may render final decisions on the questions of law and fact.①

Beside the court system above, there is also the Supreme Council of Magistracy. This organ has the power to ensure the independence of thejudiciary of the state.② The Supreme Council of Magistracy also has authority to decide and make proposals to the head of state for the appointment, delineation of duty, promote and dismissal, transfer, leave of absence of the Judges and Prosecutors of the country.③ In particular, this organ has the power to issue disciplinary action against delinquent Judges.④

The tables below show the hierarchy of the courts in Cambodia:

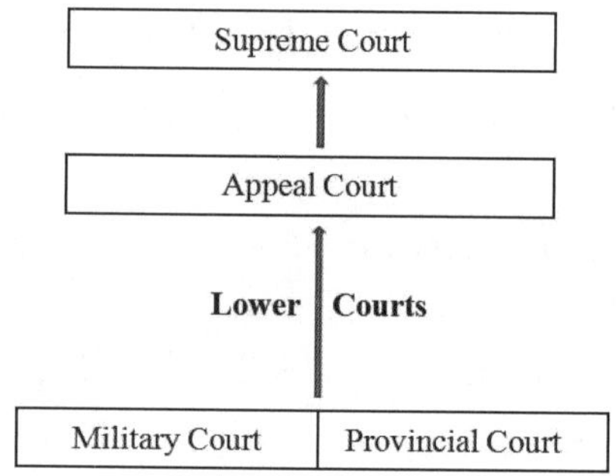

The table below shows the member of the Supreme Council of Magistracy:

---

① Hor Peng, Kong Phallack, Jorg Menzel, Introduction to Cambodian Law, Konrad Adenauer Stiftung, 2012, p.11.

② The Constitution of the Kingdom of Cambodia 1993, Art.132.

③ The Constitution of the Kingdom of Cambodia 1993, Art.134.

④ The Constitution of the Kingdom of Cambodia 1993, Art.133.

Member of Supreme Council of Magistracy	
—the King,	President
—the Minister of Justice,	Member
—the President of the Supreme Court,	Member
—the General Prosecutor of the Supreme Court,	Member
—a member appointed by the senate,	Member
—a member appointed by the National Assembly,	Member
—a member appointed by the Constitutional Council,	Member
—one prosecutor appointed by the Ministry of Justice	Member
—one judge appointed by higher courts	Member
—one prosecutor from higher prosecution	Member
—one judge appointed by lower courts	Member
—one prosecutor appointed by lower prosecutions	Member

References:

• The Constitution of the Kingdom of Cambodia, 1993.

• Hap Phalty, Legal System of Asian, A Short Guide, Introduction to Cambodian Laws, Korea Legislation Research Institute, 2016.

• Hor Peng, Kong Phallack, Jorg Menzel, Introduction to Cambodian Law, Konrad Adenauer Stiftung, 2012.

• Royal University of Law and Economics in Cooperation with Cultural Activities of French Embassy, Introduction Au Droit Cambodgien.

柬埔寨法律制度简介

Khim Kiri* 李冬梅**
郭梦盈*** 编译

内容摘要:本文以柬埔寨的法律制度为切入点,通过详细阐释和分析柬埔寨的法律制度,阐述了自1993年柬埔寨颁行现代国家宪法以来,柬埔寨的法律制度逐步完善,形成以宪法为中心,法律、皇家法令、政府法规、部门规章为体系的民主化法律构建的过程。

关键词:柬埔寨法律制度;民主化;司法制度;《柬埔寨王国宪法》

一、导言

本文旨在简要介绍柬埔寨现行法律制度及其立法程序。柬埔寨法律制度在很大程度上受到外国法律的影响,形成包括成文法和习惯法在内的各种形式。1863年到1953年,柬埔寨在法国政府的统治下,柬埔寨的法律体系和司法体系均受到法国的影响,甚至以法国的法律体系为基础建立本国的法律制度。从1970年至1993年,柬埔寨经历了几次由内部政治冲突导致的政权更迭,随着1993年现代国家宪法颁行,柬埔寨的法律和司法制度开始重新焕发活力,这为柬埔寨法律和司法制度发展奠定了民主和自由的基石。此外,在1998年,红色高棉政权结束了统治,国家实现了统一,政治稳定和团结协作促进了柬埔寨法律和司法制度加速改善。

---

* Khim Kiri,柬埔寨皇家法律经济大学国际关系处处长,西南政法大学国际法学院博士生。

** 李冬梅,西南政法大学国际法学院教师,中国法学会中国—东盟法律研究中心项目官员。

*** 郭梦盈,西南政法大学国际法学院2018级法律硕士研究生。

二、立法体系概述

柬埔寨的所有法律都由立法机关制定并由国家元首依照皇家法典颁布。自 1993 年以来，柬埔寨一直实行君主立宪制，国王是国家元首，实行终身制，"统而不治"。柬埔寨所有法律都必须符合宪法，由宪法授权的宪法委员会（由九名成员组成的宪法权力机构，每届任期九年）审查法律的合宪性。一般而言，所有基本法律必须提交给宪法委员会审查。柬埔寨政府加入的国际条约和公约，必须由政府提交给议会接受和批准。

根据宪法，议会由国会和参议院组成，国会所讨论和通过的所有法律，应送交参议院进一步审查和通过，参议院则根据宪法和法律的规定行使立法权，审查和评价国会提交的立法草案或拟议法律。

下列图表详细说明了国会向参议院提交法律的审查程序：

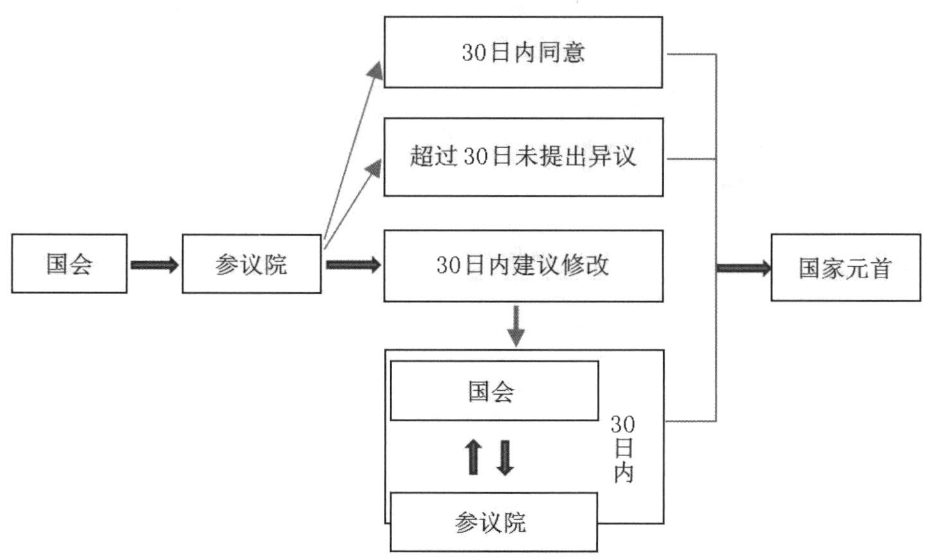

三、法律位阶

1.宪法

1993 年宪法是柬埔寨的最高法，法律、法规和国家机关作出的决定不得

抵触宪法。1993 年宪法规定了独立国家运作的基本制度,写明柬埔寨是君主立宪制国家,共包括柬埔寨国王、柬埔寨公民基本(根本)权利、政治制度、经济制度、立法机关(规定了国会、参议院、司法机关和国家行政机关的作用和职能)五个部分。

从 1947 年到现在,柬埔寨拥有过五部宪法。下表展示了这五种不同政体下的宪法:

<table>
<tr><th>序号</th><th>年份</th><th>政权名称</th><th>宪法颁行日期</th></tr>
<tr><td>1</td><td>1947—1970</td><td>柬埔寨王国</td><td>1947.5.6</td></tr>
<tr><td>2</td><td>1970—1975</td><td>高棉共和国</td><td>1972.6.10</td></tr>
<tr><td>3</td><td>1975—1979</td><td>民主柬埔寨</td><td>1976.1.5</td></tr>
<tr><td rowspan="2">4</td><td>1979—1989</td><td>柬埔寨人民共和国</td><td>1981.6.27</td></tr>
<tr><td>1989—1993</td><td>柬埔寨国</td><td>1989.4.30</td></tr>
<tr><td>5</td><td>1993—Present</td><td>柬埔寨王国</td><td>1993.9.24</td></tr>
</table>

1993 年现代宪法遇到了许多挑战,在 20 年的时间里已经被修改了 8 次,宪法修正案的日期如下表所示:

序号	国会通过宪法修正案日期	国家元首公布宪法修正案日期
1	1994.7.14	1994.7.14
2	1999.3.4	1999.8.8
3	2001.7.2	2001.7.28
4	2004.7.8	2004.7.8
5	2005.5.18	2005.6.19
6	2006.3.6	2006.3.9
7	2008.1.15	2008.2.15
8	2014.10.1	2014.10

作为国家的最高法,1993 年宪法取代了不符合宪法规定的法律和法规。下表反映了柬埔寨法律层次结构:

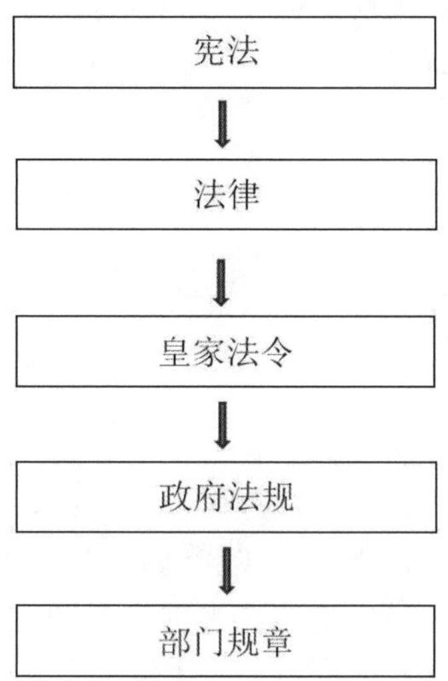

2.法律

法律是被立法机关通过后由国家元首颁布的法律规范，法律位阶在宪法之下。1993年宪法明确规定了每一项法律的生效时间。一般来说，法律在国家首都金边颁布10日后生效，颁布后20日在全国范围内生效。在紧急公布的情况下，法律在颁布日之后立即生效。

3.皇家法令

皇家法令被称为法律规则，在立法层级上低于法律。由部长会议提交国家元首签署，皇家法令生效。皇家法令分为两类，第一类是皇家法令可以任命、调任和解雇公务员、军队、外交大使、司法机关中的高级官员和部长会议成员。第二类是执行法令。

4.政府法规

政府法规（被称为"次级法令"）为法律和皇家法令之下的法律文书。政府法规是由有关部门制定的、部长会议或部长通过、由总理签署的行政法规。政府法规分为两类，即政府任命法规和政府执行法规。政府任命法规允许总理任命合适的人员在政府行政机构内担任任何职务，而政府执行法规则是与法律的执行有关的法规。

5.部门规章

部门规章是在部委层面制定的行政法，由有关部门编制，并由相应部长签署。部长们有权发布部门规章（所谓的"公告"），其法律位阶低于政府法规（次

级法令)。部门规章不能超出规定的部长职权范围,各部委和国家秘书处的结构组织和职能应由部门规章规定。

四、主要法律

柬埔寨主要法律渊源是《宪法》、《民法典》和《民事诉讼法》、《刑法》和《刑事诉讼法》,这些法律现行有效。

1.民法典

柬埔寨王国现行的《民法典》是在日本政府的技术支持和协助下于2007年12月8日公布的。2007年《民法典》由9编组成,共1305个条文。第一编涉及一般条款,主要规定在私法的一般原则;第二编描述了主体的概念(自然人和法人);第三以物权为核心;第四编规定了各种义务;第五编涉及各种类型的合同和侵权行为;第六编与证券有关;七本编是亲属关系;第八本编关于继承;第九编是最终条款。

2.民事诉讼法

现行的《民事诉讼法》是在日本政府的支持和协助下于2006年7月6日公布的,该法典于一年后的2007年7月27日生效,由九编组成,共588条。其中第一编是一般条款;第二编规定初审法院的程序;第三编规定上诉程序;第四编规定再审程序;第五编规定请求程序;第六编规定强制执行;第七编规定保全制度;第八编列出过渡条款;第九编是最终条款。

3.刑法典

2009年11月30日,在法国政府的技术支持和协助下,柬埔寨颁布了《刑法典》,该法由6编共672条组成。第一编规定一般条款;第二编规定人身性犯罪;第三编涉财产性犯罪;第四编列出了危害国家的罪行;第五编是暂行规定;第六编是最终条款。尽管《刑法典》在2009年12月21日生效,但只限于第一编与一般条款有关的条文,而其余部分则在一年后的2010年12月21日正式生效。

4.刑事诉讼法

柬埔寨得到法国政府的技术支持和协助,于2007年8月10日颁布《刑事诉讼法》,8月31日在全国范围内实施。《刑事诉讼法》由11编共612条组成,第一编是刑事和民事诉讼;第二编规定起诉、调查和审讯的权力机构;第三编描述了政策质询;第四编规定了司法调查,而第五编则描述了司法判决;第六编关于最高法院;第七编规定引用、传唤和通知;第八编是关于执行程序;第

九编规定特殊程序;第十编列出了过渡程序;第十一编是最终条款。

五、立法程序

1.概述

本部分将从狭义和广义的角度来审视立法程序。狭义上,法律草案或提议的法律须经国会通过并经参议院批准,最后由国家元首颁布。广义上的立法,指国家元首颁布的法律和其他法规,以及总理、部长和其他政府机关发布的规章。柬埔寨王国宪法赋予国会、参议院和总理权力来启动立法。

2.立法程序

(1)立法机构(起草法律)

国会议员有权提起法律草案,国会常设委员会在提出法律草案方面起着重要作用。法律草案草拟好后,将提交国会委员会审议。审查之后,将在国会全体会议期间讨论和通过法律草案。然后,法律草案必须进一步送交参议院审议和通过。经参议院通过后,该法律草案将送交国家元首公布。下面的表格说明了从国民议会到国家元首颁布的法律制定程序:

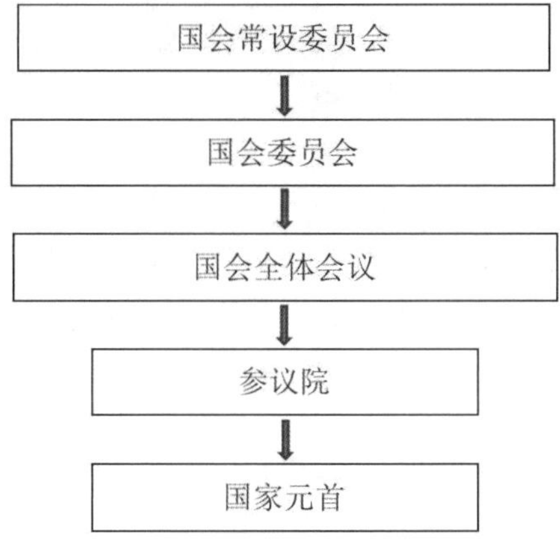

1993年宪法进一步规定,参议院有权起草法律草案。在这一过程中,参议院常设委员会草拟并向国会委员会提出法律草案。此过程与法律草案由国会发起的程序相同。下面的表格说明由参议院发起的法律制定程序:

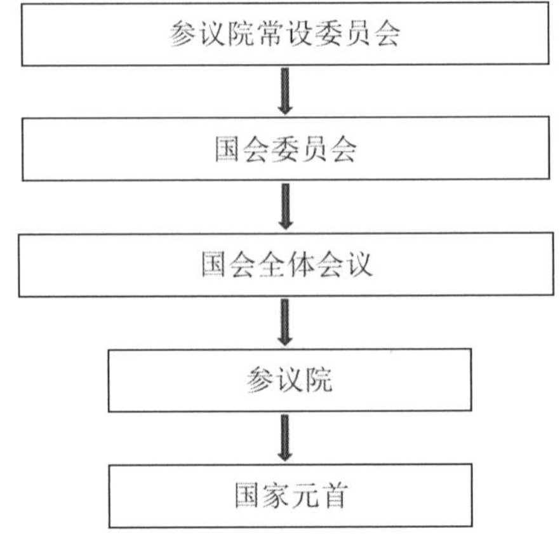

(2)行政机构(法案)

依照规定,有关部委可通过其综合或专业组成部门提出拟议法案。一项拟议法案经特别政府部门讨论和通过后,将提交给部长理事会的法学家专门理事会进行技术和法律审查。根据法学家理事会的审查,拟议法案应提交部长理事会审查和讨论,然后由部长签署后提交国会。在收到政府作为行政机构提出的法案后,国会委员会将审查该拟议法案,并将其提交国会全体会议审议后通过,通过拟议法案必须获得国民大会三分之二的绝对多数票。此后,通过的拟议法案将进一步提交参议院审议和通过。最后,通过的法案将由国家元首签署公布。

(3)规章(行政机构)

受政府机关委托的行政机构有充分的权力制定和发行法律文书。行政部门规章或者部长发布的法律文书,由有关部委编制法律草案。在拟制定的法律法规涉及多个部委的情况下,必须由各部委共同讨论。当这类法律法规最终被讨论并经各部委批准后,将向部长理事会的法学家理事会提交审查。经法学家理事会审查后,法律草案由部长理事会讨论和批准。经部长批准的法律规章,自签字之日起生效。

六、司法制度

柬埔寨司法系统由省、市法院、军事法庭、上诉法院和最高法院组成。

1.省级法院(一审法院)

省或市法院是柬埔寨最低层级法院,省、市法院对在其管辖范围内发生的

案件有管辖权，柬埔寨的每个省都有一个法院。军事法院类似一审法院，军事法院对军事违法案件有管辖权，即自愿或者征召入伍的军事人员，违反军队纪律或对损害军事财产的案件。

2.上诉法院

上诉法院审查法律和法律问题。目前，柬埔寨全国有一个上诉法院，但司法部正计划在全国设立 5 个地区上诉法院。

3.最高法院

最高法院一般只审查法律问题，除非是对第二次申诉的联合审判。最高法院可就法律和事实问题作出最终决定。除了上面的法院系统，还有最高裁判法院，该法院有保证国家司法独立的权力。最高裁判法院也有权决定和向国家元首提出法官和检察官任命、划分职责、升职、解雇、调任、辞退的建议。特别的是，该法院有权对失职法官进行纪律处分。下表为柬埔寨的法院等级示意图：

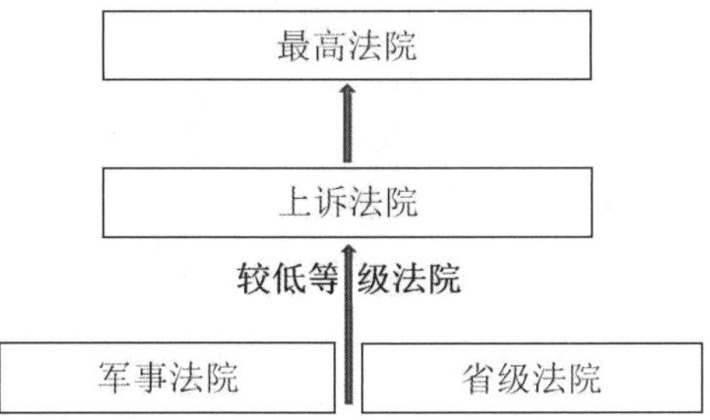

下表为最高裁判法院的成员名单：

最高裁判法院的成员名单	
一国王	主席
一司法部部长	成员
一最高法院院长	成员
一最高法院检察长	成员
一一名参议院任命的成员	成员
一一名国会任命的成员	成员
一一名宪法委员会任命的成员	成员
一一名司法部任命的检察官	成员
一一名上级法院任命的法官	成员
一一名上级检察院任命的检察官	成员
一一名下级法院任命的法官	成员
一一名下级检察院任命的检察官	成员

Introduction to Contract and Tort Law Under Cambodia Civil Code

Ung Radsorin*

Ⅰ. Introduction

The Civil Code of Cambodia (the "Civil Code") was adopted by RoyalKram No.NS/RKM/1207/030 dated 8 December 2007 as part of the first phase of the Plan of Action for Implementing the Legal and Judicial Reform Strategy which was implemented by the Royal Government of Cambodia on 29 April 2005.Defined as both a fundamental law(together with the Criminal and Civil Procedure Codes and the Criminal Code)as well as a strategic objective of the Council for the Legal and Judicial reform, the Civil Code did not take effect until the law on its implementation had also been promulgated. This-the Law on the Implementation of the New Civil Code(the "Implementation Law")was promulgated by the King on 31 May 2011 which set the effective date for the implementation of the Civil Code at 21 December 2011.

The stated purposes of the Implementation Law are to ensure continuity in legislation governing civil matters and to guarantee the proper enforcement of the provisions of the Civil Code and of any matter related to the implementation of the Civil Code.The Implementation Law reflects three salient principles for the enforcement of the Civil Code: the principle of non-retroactivity, the continuity of the rule of law and legal consistency. According to these principles, although the Civil Code will not apply to any

---

* Ung Radsorin is Assistant to H.E Minister of Justice of the Ministry of Cambodia and a Ph.D candidate of the International Law School, SWUPL.

transaction(or contractual or similar arrangement) that completed prior to the effective date of the Civil Code, to the extent a transaction(or contractual or similar arrangement) was ongoing (and not completed) as at that date, it would be subject to the provisions of the Civil Code on and from that date(even though these obligations may have been entered into prior to that date).

Further to the implementation of the Civil Code, a number of provisions in existing Cambodian laws will be abrogated or amended. This special edition of our monthly pointer is intended to reflect a high-level summary on the areas that the provisions of the Civil Code will have a major impact.①

Currently, contracts and other liabilities are governed by Decree Law No.38(the "Contract Law"), dated 28 October 1988②. The Contract Law provides general rules on the formation and execution of contracts, special contracts and other civil and non-contractual obligations. On 21 December 2011, the Contract Law will be replaced by the comprehensive provisions of the Civil Code, except for the provisions applicable to Carriage Contracts.

In this regards, I will highlight the main key changes which will be implemented by the Civil Code in relation to contracts and obligations.

Ⅱ. Validity of Contract

The Civil Code introduces the concept of the formation of a contract based on an offer and acceptance. Generally, the formation of a contract is based on the principle of consent. Unlike the Contract Law, no writing is generally required, except for some specific contracts. Writing and/or authentication is one of the requirements for the validity of a contract if it is specifically required by this Civil Code or other specific laws, such as is the case with a loan with interest rate exceeding the legal interest rate or the sale of immovable property.

According to the Civil Code, a contract may be voided, among other reasons, if it is concluded, (ⅰ) as a result of mistakes relating to substantial

① See Civil Code of Cambodia (2007).

② See Decree Law No.38 Contract Law (1988).

terms of the contract; (ii) fraud; (iii) misrepresentation; (iv) abuse of circumstances; (iv) duress; (v) act of making excessive benefits; (vi) mental reservation; (vii) fictitious declaration of intention; (viii) initial impossibility; or if it is (ix) illicit or contrary to the public order and good morals or (x) not in conformity with the general interest or moral principles of society①.

Ⅲ. Breach of Contract

Once a contract is effective, the parties are obliged to adhere to its provisions. A breach of contract occurs when there is no performance, late performance or an inability to perform the obligations expressed in the contract. Where an obligor fails to perform an obligation, the oblige may demand specific performance, damages, or termination of the contract. In cases of a breach of contract, the aggrieved party is entitled to compensation covering not only the value of the contract, but also any expenses or charges suffered as a result of non-performance. The court may also decide upon any moral damages claimed by the aggrieved party. Additionally, the obligor and oblige may separately, and in advance, establish conditions for the payment of damages and an amount to be paid; however, a special agreement exempting the obligor from liability for non-performance that is either intentional or the result of gross negligence is void②.

Ⅳ. Statute of Limitations

Unlike the Contract Law, the Civil Code provides more kinds of statute of limitations on extinctive prescription, such as claims for compensation for damages, right for termination of a contract and right to the claim. This statute of limitations is fixed to five years. Additionally, the extinctive prescription period for a claim pertaining to the price of a product or service sold or provided by a manufacturer or merchant to a non-merchant is two

① See Civil Code of Cambodia (2007), art.345.

② See Civil Code of Cambodia (2007), art.365.

years but the right of a non-merchant to make a claim against a merchant or manufacturer is five years. Apart from the above, the extinctive prescription for property rights, other than claims and ownership, is fixed for 10 years.

Ⅴ. Assignment of Claims, Obligation and Contract

There is no specific provision under the Contract Law on the assignment, and therefore, under the current Contract Law. The assignment must be agreed by the assignor, assignee and the other contracting party. However, under the Civil Code, claims, obligations, or contracts may be assigned unless the nature of a claim or a contract is inconsistent with such an assignment, or otherwise restricted by an agreement.

The assignment of a contract or claims shall take effect only through agreement between the oblige seeking to assign the claims or contract and the assignee. However, in order to assert the assignment of a claim or a contract against the obligor, the assignor must give notice thereof to the obligor or the obligor has consented thereto to the assignor or the assignee and it shall have effect against third parties only when the notice or the obligor's consent is notarized by a notary public.

However, the assignment of obligations alone is valid between the obligor and the assignee only and not binding against oblige and third parties. In this case, the obligor and the assignee are jointly and severally liable for performance of obligations for the obliged.

Ⅵ. Special Contracts

The Contract Law provides provisions on sales and purchase contracts, interest bearing loans, secured personal property, contractor contracts, carrier contracts, bailment contracts, and loans for use, leases and personal guarantee contracts. Except for the carrier contract, the Civil Code provides further provisions on Gifts, Profit-Sharing Leases, Mandates, Partnerships, Life Annuities and Compromises. In addition to this, the Civil Code provides more complete and comprehensive provisions on a secured transaction[①].

Ⅶ. Loans for Consumption with Interest

A loan for consumption exists when a person borrows money, food-related products, paddy or other fungible objects from another and returns objects of the same type, quality and quantity as those originally received from the lender at the expiry of the term. Interest may be charged on a loan for consumption only if it is made in writing. The interest rate may be determined by the parties to the contract or, if not specified in the agreement, by law. Where parties to a contract fail to specify a rate of interest to be charged, the Civil Code provides for an interest of 5% per annum. However, if the rate of interest agreed on by the parties exceeds 5%, it must still comply with a maximum rate which will be fixed by the Ministry of Justice ("MOJ") between 10% and 30% per annum (the "Ceiling Rate"). In the event the interest rate charged exceeds the Ceiling Rate, the portion of interest paid in excess of the Ceiling Rate shall either be abrogated or applied to repayment of the loan principal.

Additionally, under the Civil Code, the interest on interest is expressly allowed. Where the payment of interest is in arrears for one year or more, if the obligor fails to pay such interest after receiving a demand of payment from the oblige, the oblige may include the amount of such interest in the principal.

Furthermore, a pre-agreed amount of compensation for damages or clause on damages penalty interest on late payment (the "Penalty Rate") is expressly allowed by the Civil Code; however, the Penalty Rate must not exceed the ceiling Penalty Rate which will be fixed by the MOJ at a limit of 1.2 to 2 times of the Ceiling Rate.

---

① See Civil Code of Cambodia (2007), art.365.

Ⅷ. Other Liabilities

Like the Contract Law, the civil liabilities on damages caused by a person's acts, including involuntary acts such as carelessness or negligence is expressly stated. However, other civil liabilities stated in the Contract Law are limited to the act of property, act of animal, fault of private employees or government officials and fault of minors. In addition to the Contract Law, the Civil Code provides further provisions on the management of affairs without mandate, unjust enrichment, dangerous defect products, dangerous things and structure affixed to land①.

Under the Contract Law, any person who has caused damage to others is not liable to bear the responsibility resulting from such damages if (ⅰ) the damage was caused by a force majeure; or (ⅱ) the damage was caused entirely by the fault of the victim. However, under the Civil Code, the following may be grounds for excuse of liabilities:

(ⅰ) A tortfeasor shall be excused from responsibility for harm caused by the tortfeasor where the injured party consented to or assumed the risk of such harm;

(ⅱ) A person who causes harm while engaged in justifiable self-defense or emergency escape shall not be held responsible for harm that results therefrom;

(ⅲ) A person who commits an act that is deemed reasonable and acceptable under prevalent social standards shall not be held responsible for the harm caused thereby;

(ⅳ) A tortfeasor shall be excused from responsibility for harm caused by the tortfeasor where the injured party consented to or assumed the risk of such harm; or

(ⅴ) A person who causes harm while engaged in justifiable self-defense or emergency escape shall not be held responsible for harm that results therefrom.

---

① See Civil Code of Cambodia (2007), art.742.

Like the Contract Law, under the Civil Code, where a thing is destroyed or damaged by atortious act, the injured party may seek compensation for the price of the damaged or destroyed thing, the cost of repair, etc. However, in the event where the injured party dies as the result of a tortious act, such injured party's successors shall acquire the right to demand damages for economic harm and emotional distress suffered prior to death. Additionally, where an injured party suffers bodily harm as the result of a tortious act, the injured party may demand damages for economic harm and emotional distress suffered thereby. Furthermore, where one's honor or reputation is damaged by a tortious act, the injured party may seek damages for mental or emotional distress accompanying the drop in one's social standing. The damages for emotional distress or mental damages, damage of honor or reputation are not expressly treated in the current Contract Law.

柬埔寨民法典中的合同与侵权法

Ung Radsorin*
王颖**编译

内容摘要：本文以柬埔寨新民法典的颁行与生效，有关旧民法典中关于合同的规定将被取代为切入点，通过详细阐释和分析柬埔寨新旧民法典中合同规定的变化窥见了柬埔寨司法改革的重心，论证了柬埔寨新民法典更加注重保护公民私权利、新民法典对合同的规定更加的细致的观点。

关键词：柬埔寨民法典；合同法；债权；利率

一、引言

《柬埔寨民法典》(以下简称《民法典》)于 2007 年 12 月 8 日由第 NS/RKM/1207/030 号王令颁布通过。该《民法典》作为柬埔寨王国政府执行 2005 年 4 月 29 日的"执行法律和司法改革战略行动计划"第一阶段的一部分。《民法典》具有基本法(与民事和刑事诉讼法典和刑法典一道)和"法律与司法改革委员会"战略目标的双重意义。这部新民法典的实施法(以下简称"实施法")由国王于 2011 年 5 月 31 日颁布，生效日期为 2011 年 12 月 21 日。

"实施法"的颁布是为了保证民事活动立法管理的连续性和确保民法典的规定与实施中的相关事项得到适当的处理。"实施法"反映了《民法典》实施中的三项突出原则：1.法不溯及既往；2.法律的联系性；3.法律的一致性。根据这些原则，虽然《民法典》不适用于在《民法典》生效之前完成的交易(合同或类似协定)，但某种程度上，自《民法典》生效之日起，生效之日前继续履行的(未完

---

* Ung Radsorin，柬埔寨司法部司法部长助理，西南政法大学国际法学院博士生。

** 王颖，西南政法大学国际法学院 2018 级法律硕士研究生。

成)的交易(合同或者类似协定)将受到《民法典》条款的约束(尽管义务可能已经在生效之日前履行完毕)。

为了进一步贯彻实施民法典,柬埔寨现行法律中的一些条款将会被废除或修改。因此,政府颁布特别的“每月指南”,以期对《民法典》条款适用产生重要影响的领域进行高度总结。现行合同和其他债权、债务问题由1988年10月28日颁布的第38号法令(以下简称《合同法》)所规制。

现行《合同法》规定了合同的订立和执行、特殊合同和其他民事和非合同义务的一般规则。自2011年12月21日起,除适用于运输合同的规定外,《合同法》的相关规定将由《民法典》全面取代。在这方面,本文将重点介绍《民法典》在合同和义务实施方面的关键变化。

二、合同的效力

《民法典》引入了以要约和承诺为基础的合同订立概念,一般来说合同的订立是以协商一致原则为基础的。与《合同法》规定不同的是,除了一些特定的合同之外,一般情况下合同不要求以书面形式订立。当《民法典》和特定法律有要求的情况下,书面形式和(或)认证才是合同有效的条件之一,例如在贷款利率超过法定利率或出售不动产的情况中。

根据《民法典》规定,合同的无效可由以下原因导致:1.合同实质条款产生错误;2.欺诈;3.虚假陈述;4.滥用合同;5.胁迫;6.过度牟利;7.意思保留;8.虚伪意思表示;9.合同自始不能实现;10.违法或者违背公序良俗;11.违背社会公共利益和道德原则。

三、合同的违反

一旦合同生效,各方有义务遵守合同约定。当合同未实际履行、迟延履行或者一方当事人无力履行合同义务时,就产生了违反合同情形。当履行义务的一方不履行其义务时,另一方可要求继续履行、损害赔偿或者终止合同。在违反合同的情况下,受害方有权要求损害赔偿,且赔偿额度不仅包括合同标的金额还可扩大至因合同未能履行所导致的其他损失金额和费用。法庭还可决定是否给予受害方要求的精神损害赔偿。另外,履行义务的一方和另一方可另行约定,并预先确定损害赔偿金的支付条件和数额。但免除履行义务方因故意或重大过失而不履行合同的责任的特定协议无效。

四、时效

与《合同法》不同,《民法典》在时效方面规定了更多的时效消灭情形,如损害赔偿索赔权,合同的解除权和请求权,此类权利的时效为 5 年。此外,与制造商或商户出售或提供给非商家的产品或服务的价格有关的索赔的时效为两年,但是非商家向商家或制造商提出索赔的时效为 5 年。除上述规定外,财产权、其他索赔和所有权的时效为 10 年。

五、债权、债和合同的转让

现行《合同法》中没有关于转让的具体规定。转让必须经转让人、受让方和缔约另一方协商一致。但根据《民法典》,债权、债和合同可以转让,除非债权或合同的性质不适用于转让,或受到协议的限制。

合同或债权的转让只能通过寻求转让债权或合同的一方与受让方达成的协议才能生效。但是,为向债务人主张债权或合同已转让,转让方必须向债务人发出转让的通知或者转让方或受让方取得债务人同意,并只有在对通知或债务人的同意公证后方可对抗第三人。

但债务人和受让方间单独就债务进行转让是有效的,仅对债权人和第三方没有约束力。在这种情况下,债务人和受让人对债务的履行皆负义务。

六、特殊合同

《合同法》就买卖合同、生息贷款、有担保的个人财产、承揽合同、运输合同、保管合同、使用借贷、租赁和保证合同做出了相关规定。除运输合同外,《民法典》还对赠予、租赁、委托授权、合伙、人寿保险做出了进一步规定。此外,《民法典》就担保交易做出了更为完善的规定。

七、有利息的消费借贷

消费借贷指自然人向他人借用金钱、食物、稻谷或其他可替代之物,并在借贷期限届满前返回与借贷物相同种类、质量和数量的种类物。消费借贷中的利息只能以书面形式做出。利率可由合同当事方决定,若合同未作规定,则

依照法律确定。若合同当事方未就利息做出明确规定,《民法典》规定的年利息为5%。但若双方约定的年利率超过5%,仍可按照最高年利率计算,最终由司法部("MOJ")在10%至30%("最高利率")的年利率中确定的一个固定值。若收取的年利率超过最高利率,则超出部分应不予支持或用于偿还贷款本金。

此外,《民法典》准许计算复利。凡应支付利息的款项拖欠一年或以上,若债务人收到还款通知后仍未支付利息,则债权人可将利息包含在本金中。

再者,《民法典》也明确允许双方提前约定损害赔偿金或逾期付款的损害惩罚金比例("罚金率"),但罚金率不能超过由司法部确定的1.2至2倍的上限。

八、其他责任

就《合同法》而言,就个人对他人造成的损害,包括因疏忽等非故意行为造成的民事责任也明确做出了规定。但是,《合同法》中规定的其他民事责任仅限于因财产、动物、私人劳务关系或政府官员的过错以及未成年人的过错导致的。除《合同法》外,《民法典》还就无因管理、不当得利、缺陷产品、危险物和土地附着物做出了进一步的规定。

根据《合同法》的规定,在下列情形中加害人免责:

(ⅰ)损害是由不可抗力造成的;或

(ⅱ)因受害人过错。

而《民法典》规定的免责事由为以下几种:

(ⅰ)若受害方同意或愿意承担此种损害导致的危险,则侵权人可免责;

(ⅱ)因正当防卫或者紧急避险造成的损害,免责;

(ⅲ)按照普遍认同的社会标准认为是合理和可接受的行为,行为人无需对损害承担责任;

(ⅳ)侵权人可因受害方同意或愿意承担损害的危险而免责;或

(ⅴ)因正当防卫或者紧急避险造成的损害不承担责任;

与《合同法》相同的是,根据《民法典》,凡某物因侵权行为而遭受损坏,受害方可要求侵权人赔偿被损坏物的价值、修理等费用。但若受害方因侵权行为而致死,受害方的继承人有权要求赔偿因损害行为造成的经济损失和精神损害。此外,若因侵权行为而遭受人身损害,受害方也可要求赔偿经济损失和精神损害。再者,若某人的名誉因侵权行为受到损害,受害方可因其社会地位的下降而造成的精神损害寻求赔偿。但现行《合同法》中没有明确规定对精神以及名誉损害的损害赔偿。

Introduction to the Civil Tort in Cambodia

Lay Nisay* and Li Dongmei**

Introduction

In the daily living, we all cannot avoid the civil tort in everyday life, even though it is a petty or heavy tort. According to the glossary of Cambodia Civil Code, it has given the definition of Tort as the act of an unlawful abuse of rights or interests of others people. In additional, in the Civil Code of Cambodia has clearly stipulated on the elements of general tort and burden of proof that is a person who intentionally or negligently infringes on the right and benefits of the another people in violation of law is reliable for the payment of damages for any harm occurring as a result. In the light of this law, even a mistake or infringement permit by a person is petty but as a result, if damages or harm occurring to another person is huge, the person who had committed will be reliable to all the huge damages to the victim. The victim or injured party caused by tortious act must proof that the damage prove by intent or negligence of the tortious actor by any means according to the laws.

* Lay Nisay is a legal official of the Minister's cabinet of the Ministry of Justice of Cambodia and a Master Student of the International Law School, SWUPL.

** Li Dongmei is Program Director of the China-ASEAN Law Research Center, SWUPL.

1. The Sort of Reliable to the Civil Tort

In the civil matter, the responsibility to the damage may happen in so many forms by the mistake of human, product, animal or other materials. In the wide scope of action to the tort, we cannot fully determine the exact action caused by civil tort to define the reliable of the tort. Anyway, according to the civil code of Cambodia, the responsibility of the civil tort has divided in to several kinds as following;

- The reliable to the its own acts
- The reliable to other people acts
- The reliable to the acts of animals and objects
- Other reliable.

1.1 The Reliable to Its Own Acts

The person who intentionally or negligently committed the acts of infringement to the right and obligation of other person shall be responsible to the damages which occurring from its infringement. However, the Code also provide the exception to limited capacity to responsible for its acts to the person who is under 14 years old and a person who due to mental defect or other causes lack of capacity to understand legal ramification of their action when committing a tortious.①

1.2 The Reliable to Other People's acts

The reliable to other people's acts is the reliability of persons who are having a duty to supervise to minor or other people for their acts such as to reliable to the damages for any harm caused to another people by the action s of the minor or person lacking of capacity to understand legal ramifications because they have got mental diseases or other caused stipulated by existing law. The responsibility between the people who having a duty to supervise and people who are under his/her supervise is depend on the legal relationship

① See Cambodian Civil Code 2006, article 745, para.1, 2.

and condition of the parties as following;

1.2.1 Supervision's Liability

Pursuant to the Civil Code, a person who has legal duty to supervise a minor[①] has to responsible for the damages of any harmful caused to other person by the minor actions as following;

- A supervision of a minor who age under 14 has to responsible for all the damages cause to another person made by a minor. In this regard, the minor under 14 have no legal capacity to responsible to their action at all.
- A person who has a legal duty to supervise a minor 14 years old or older is jointly responsible with the minor for damages for any harm caused to other by the actions of the minor.

1.2.2 Employer's Liability

A person who hires an employee to perform work is reliable for damages caused in violation of law to another in the performance of that work by employee through the employee intention or negligence. Moreover, a person who is in charge of performing supervision of the employee place on behalf of the employer bears the same liability as the employer. However, a person who performs employer supervision shall not bear with the damage if the supervision was properly performed.

1.2.3 Tortious Act of the Legal Person

Legal Person is also reliable to the damage caused harmful to another through the act of the representative person such as director or other representative in their duty for the organization. In this case, the legal person that reliable for any remedies according to the acts of their representative of the organization may demand compensation from their representative who committed the tortious act.

1.2.4 Tortious Act of the Public Official

The official who exercises public possessed by the national government or a governmental entity harms to another unlawful in term of his duties, the national government or governmental entity is responsible for the payment of damages but they can ask for compensation in return from that official. In

---

① According to the Cambodian civil law, a minor is a person under the age of eighteen.

the light of Cambodia Criminal law of Cambodia has provided the definition of public official as following[①];

ⅰ.A person who works for executive or legislative or judiciary branch which was permanently or not permanently appointed by legal instrument whether receive salary or not.

ⅱ.Other people who work for Civil Servant factor including government agency,government entity or other state organ provided by Law.

ⅲ.People who was elected to be a member of senate, parliamentary, council of municipality,council of province,council of city,council of district and council of commune and other people who was elected and work in other civil servant matter.

1.3 The Reliable to the Act of Animals and Objects

1.3.1 Liability of Animal Possessor

The possessor of the animal is liable for the damages for any harm caused to another person by their animal.On the other hand,the civil code is not clearly demonstrated what if the animal which has no owner or wild animal,who shall be reliable for the tortious act commit by such an animal.

1.3.2 Liability of Producer to Its Product

The producer of the product shall be reliable for its own production as following;

- Unreasonable dangerous,caused harmful or damages to people
- The manufacture movable product from mixing raw material where it is dangerous and caused harmful to other people.
- Importer of the dangerous product is considered as producer.
- A person who affixes his name on a movable as a manufacturer or distributor shall be deemed the manufacturer.

1.4 Other Reliable Action

1.4.1 The Responsibility of Dangerous Item

A person who owns or manages an automobile or other transportable or

① Cambodia Criminal Law 2009,article 30.

apparatus, an explosive item, radioactive substance or a toxic chemical or other highly dangerous item is reliable to any harm caused by another excepted the caused or harmful due to unavoidable force, force measure or by the act of the injured party or a third party.

1.4.2 The Responsibility of Structure Affixed to Land

The manager of the installed structure and the owner of the land shall jointly respond for a failure in the installation or control of affixed to or appurtenant to land which caused damage to others. However, the manager of in the installed structure shall be exemption from the responsibility if he proof that he had exercised proper control to the structure. In case of jointly reliable of manger of the installed structure and the owner of the land must be determined in according to the proportion contribution to the failure in the installation or control of the structure.

1.4.3 Tortious Act on Fetus

A Tortious act commit on a fetus at the time of existence can be entitled to seek damages for a harm arising from such act after it born. Cambodia civil law fully recognize the right natural person. Natural person shall require legal capacity by birth and loss their right and obligation by death. However, the right and obligation of the natural person's comprehensive when they become adult[①].

1.4.4 Joint Tort

Where the joint is caused by the acts of several persons, each person has to:

- Jointly reliable for resulting harm
- Reliable according to the percentage contribute to the harm.

In case a joint tort voluntarily pays the entire amount of damage, then he can demand indemnification from other people in joint tort in according to their proportion contribute to the harm.

---

① In the light of article 17 of the Cambodian civil law: Minors are persons under the age of eighteen. According to this article, we can presume that an adult is a person the age of eighteen or beyond this.

2. Element of Tort

In order to define tort in term of civil matter, there are several elements to be considered by the relevant parties, which will clearly demonstrate in this following part. Mainly, the act presumes as the Tortious act shall have 3 main factors such as Mistake, Relationship between the fact and result and Damage.

2.1 Mistake

Mistake is the act of the person intentionally or negligently such as not obey their obligations caused harmful or damages to another person. Generally, Mistake can be divided in to two kinds, such as intentional mistake and negligent mistake.

2.1.1 Intentional Mistake

In the light of the civil code, the action that caused harm or damage to another where the people who had committed has foreseen the particular result that would generally come out after the action and accepted the occurrence of such result.

2.1.2 Negligent Mistake

The act deemed to be negligent mistake is the act of a person having the same profession or experience that could have foreseen the particular result that would normally occur from the act, but fail to foreseen the result due to their negligent or can be avoid but not avoid the occurrence of such a result.

2.2 Damage

In the Principle of Civil Tort, the damage must be real and caused by the tortious act. The damage may occur immediately after the tortious act or in the period of time in the future. Generally, in the civil tort causes damage to the people in so many different forms. In this regard, regularly there are 3 significant damages occurring from civil tort.

2.2.1 The Damage of Item

Whenever a thing is destroyed by a tortious act, victim who is suffer by

loss or destruction of a thing can seek for compensation for the price of the loss or damaged thing or the cost of repair, etc.

The evaluation of the compensation cannot be measured by law, but it can be measured by the result of the tortious act. If the tortious act provides a huge loss or damage, the compensation will be calculates accordingly.

2.2.2 Physical Damage

The victim who has suffered from the tortious act can seek for compensation to the damage occurring from injuring or injured to death. These injures are including to economic harm during injure and emotional distress suffered prior to death. In term of Economic harm is also includes medical expenses which have been paid and injured person should have been paid from the date of tortious act until the date of death as well as other expenditure which the injured person unable to obtain while suffering by tortious.

2.2.3 Mental Damage

Mental Damage is the damage affect to the understanding in mental way to the victim caused by tortious act. In this concern, the victim and victim's relatives can claim for compensation occurring from tortious act after victim suffered to death.

2.3 Relationship Between the Fact and Result

In according to the civil principle of tortious act, mistake and damage have to be absolute elements and the fact must be reflected to the absolute result. The fact and result must be true and direct. The relationship between the fact and result means that mistake must lead to damage or harmful and the damaged must be result from directly tortious act of the committer.

3. Grounds for Avoiding Responsibility of the Tortious Act

3.1 Capacity

Pursuant to Civil code, article 14 provided that lack of capacity, the act commit by natural person who was unable to understand and recognize the legal consequences that occurring from his act is voidable. Furthermore, the code provides that there are several kinds of limited capacity person, minors, adults in guardianship and a person under curatorship. These sort of natural persons are incompetent to do his act fully and independently.

3.2 Justifiable Self-Defense and Emergency Measure

3.2.1 Justifiable Self-Defense

A person who commits Tort in term of justifiable self-defense is not reliable to such an act of tort. Justifiable self-defense is a harmful act that is made against an unlawful harmful conduct but necessary in order to defense the physical well-being or the property of one's self or another from such a conduct. In term of justifiable self-defense, there two legitimate elements, firstly, the act of committing tort against such an unlawful harmful conduct are closely related in time. Secondly, there shall be no disparity in the mean of self-defense employed and the severity of harmful conduct.

3.2.2 Emergency Escape

A person who commit tortious act in term of emergency escape is not reliable to any damages caused by such act. Emergency escape is an act that cause harm to another in necessary way in order to defend the physical well-being or the property of one's self or another from current or impending danger. In term of emergency escape shall involve a situation in which there is no disparity in the means of emergency escape and severity of the danger[①].

3.3 Victim's Mistake

A person who commits tortious act shall be excused from responsibility for harm caused by his act where the injured party consented to or assumed the risk of such harm. However if the consent or assumption of risk contravenes prevalent social standards, a person who committed the tortious act cannot be excused from reliable for such act.

① Cambodian Civil Code 2006, article 755 (definitions of justifiable self-defense and emergency escape), para.2.

3.4 Force Majeure

Force Majeureis unforeseeable or unpredictable situation that prevent someone from achieving a contract or obligations or irresistible compulsion.

A person who had committed tortious act in term of Force Majeure resulted damage or harmful caused by force measure to other person shall not be reliable to such damages or harmful[①].Commonly, natural disaster is the main ground to avoiding responsibility in the contact.

3.5 Minor under the age of 14 years old

In the Criminal law, the Minor who committed crime is subject to be observation, education, protection and assistance to rehabilitate and integrate them into society. In this connection the court may declare criminal punishment on the minor who his age from 14 years old depending on the circumstance of the crime and personality of the minor[②].

In the civil matter, the lack of competence to assume responsibility is defined under the age of 14 years old. A minor under the age of 14 years old who committed in tortious act cannot be held reliable in tort. However, in the light of the civil law, minors who are age 14 years old or older shall be reliable for his act through intention or negligence.

4. The Calculation of Damages and the Extinctive Prescription

In the principle of paying for damages including tangible asset, physical or mental damages, shall be in money. In some case in which money cannot be as appropriate remedy, victim or injured party may demand restitution or injunction relief. However, in the civil code does not stipulate clearly whether the award of restitution remedy for the torts is whether they are accessible for the tort once he committed or whether they are only available in the sort

① Law on Contract and Responsibility out of the Contract 1988, article 133, para.1.

② Cambodia Criminal Code 2009.

of certain torts.

4.1 The Calculation of Damages due to the Tortious Act

4.1.1 Item Damages

The calculation of damage shall be determined by the economic loss of the victim or injured party due to the tortious act.The cost of paying damage shall be evaluated by the presumption of the existence of the tortious act on the victim and how much if he would have earned if the tortious act not occurred.The evaluation also focuses on other documents,calculation by using statistic and materials to the possible extent.

4.1.2 Damage for Mental or Emotional Distress

The Damage for mental or emotional distress caused by the tortious act can be calculated by the amount of damages and other factors related.In this regard, there are three main factors to determine the amount of compensation such as;

- The degree of mistake commit by Tortfeasor,according to this degree the judge may consider on the mistake whether it is an intentional or negligence action
- The sort of tortious act
- The degree of harm whether it is serious harm or not.

In short,these three elements are significant measure to evaluate the amount of money or other compensation for remedy caused by tortious act affected on mental understanding of a victim or an injured party.

4.1.3 Harm for Honor or Reputation

In case of honor or reputation of a person under threatening or caused damage in term of tortious act,victim or injured party may demand a person who committed such act to reliable for compensation.Additional to this damage of the reputation,the Tortfeasor shall take any measure to fix or restore the injured party's honor or reputation,in particular,provided by the article 757(2)of the Cambodia Civil code,the measure to restore reputation of injured party can be done such as public apologize.

5. Extinctive Prescription

The victim or injured party in term of tortious act has the right to claim his compensation. However, the right to claim shall be just and in the reasonable period prescribed by law.

The demand for compensation can be seen into two possible ways as following;

• the right of the complainant will be exhausted by Prescription upon the expiration of 3 years from the time that the victim or injured party or his representative awards that he has right to seek for compensation from tortfeasor caused damages by tortious act.

• And 10 years after the time of the tortious act happened.

These above ways provide the victim or injured party to claim compensation legally and also reasonably for the defendant to compensate in the appropriate time.

Conclusion

The responsibility to the tortious act is significantly to all the people in society to live carefully in their daily life to avoid such a mistake occurring from their negligently or wrong doing. Tortious act was shown the way and how to reliable to such a mistake whether occurring intentionally or negligently infringes on the rights and interests of other people.

Generally, the principle of the Civil Code provided that, even though the mistake was small but result in a huge damage, a person who had committed shall reliable to those results. Contrary, if the mistake was huge but result in a small damage, the person who had committed shall responsible for such a result.

References:

• Criminal Code 2009

• Cambodia Civil Code 2007

• Law on Contract and Responsibility out of the Contract 1988

柬埔寨民事侵权导论

Lay Nisay* 李冬梅**
马逸璇*** 编译

内容摘要:本文以《柬埔寨民法典》为依据,通过分析《柬埔寨民法典》中有关民事侵权的一系列内容,包括民事侵权类型、一般侵权行为的责任构成要件以及行为人对其故意或过失下不法侵害他人权利或权益而导致的任何损害结果承担责任的证明责任分配等,来描绘出柬埔寨民事侵权行为的法律架构,为社会中每个人避免故意或过失行为造成他人损害提供预防建议。

关键词:柬埔寨民法典;民事侵权;侵权责任

引 言

日常生活中,轻微或严重的民事侵权行为随处可见。根据《柬埔寨民法典》术语解释,侵权系不法侵害他人权利或权益的行为。此外,《柬埔寨民法典》明确规定了一般侵权行为的责任构成要件,以及行为人基于故意或过失不法侵害他人权利或权益而导致的任何损害结果承担责任的证明责任分配。根据该法,即使行为人的侵权行为轻微,只要导致严重损害结果,则行为人仍须对全部损害负责。同时,根据该法,被侵权方还须通过各种方式证明侵权行为人的故意或过失。

* Lay Nisay,柬埔寨司法部部长办公厅法律官员,西南政法大学国际法学院硕士生。

** 李冬梅,西南政法大学国际法学院教师,中国法学会中国—东盟法律研究中心项目官员。

*** 马逸璇,西南政法大学2014级学术人才实验班学生。

一、民事侵权类型

在民事领域，侵权责任可能会由于人的过错行为、产品的缺陷、动物致害等原因而产生。总的来说，具体侵权行为难以完全界定，责任承担亦是如此。但《柬埔寨民法典》将民事侵权责任区分为以下几类：自己责任、替代责任、动物及物件致害责任及其他责任。

(一)自己责任

行为人因故意或过失侵害他人权利及义务(译者注：应为权益)的，应对由此产生的损害承担侵权责任。然而，《民法典》同样具有例外规定，未满14周岁与由于存在心理疾病等致缺乏法律后果理解力之人侵权责任能力有限。

(二)替代责任

替代责任是指具有监护或管理职责之人对未成年人、缺乏法律后果理解能力之人实施侵权行为而造成的损害承担责任。这主要是因为行为人具有心理疾病或现行法律另有规定。监管人与被监管人之间的替代责任产生于如下当事人的法律关系及法定条件：

1.监护人责任

根据《柬埔寨民法典》，法定监护人对以下未成年人侵权行为造成的损害承担责任：

(1)未满14周岁的未成年人造成他人损害的，由监护人承担侵权责任。易言之，未满14周岁之人为无侵权责任能力人。

(2)已满14周岁的未成年人造成他人损害的，监护人与该未成年人承担连带责任。

2.雇主责任

雇员基于故意或过失，不法执行工作任务造成他人损害的，由雇主承担责任。监督雇员的雇主代表人对此承担同样的责任，已尽到合理监督职责的除外。

3.法人责任

董事或其他法人代表造成他人损害的，由法人承担责任，法人可就其补救行为向做出侵权行为的法人代表追偿。

4.公职人员责任

国家政府或政府实体的公职人员因不法行为造成他人损害,由国家政府或政府实体承担责任,并可向做出侵权行为的公职人员追偿。《柬埔寨刑法》对公职人员界定如下:

(1)在行政、立法或司法部门永久或非永久性、有偿或无偿工作,为司法文书所任命的工作人员;

(2)在包括政府机构、政府实体或其他国家机关含有公务性质的机构工作的其他人员;

(3)当选为参议院、国会、直辖市议会、省议会、区议会议员或公社委员会委员的人员,以及选举产生的其他履行公务事务的人员。

(三)动物及物件致害责任

1.动物所有人责任

饲养的动物致人损害的,动物所有人承担责任。但是,《柬埔寨民法典》尚未规定无主动物或野生动物致人损害的责任承担者。

2.产品生产者责任

产品生产者在以下情况下承担侵权责任:

(1)不合理的危险致害;

(2)利用危险原料制造可移动产品,对他人造成伤害;

(3)危险产品进口商视为生产者;

(4)在可移动产品上以制造商或经销商名义之身份署名者应被视为生产商。

(四)其他责任

1.高度危险责任

汽车或其他运输工具或器械、爆炸物、放射性物质、有毒化学物质或其他危险性高的物品致人损害,由所有人或管理人承担责任,但由于不可抗力、强制措施、被侵权人自身行为或第三方行为之人损害的除外。

2.建筑物损害责任

建筑过程致人损害或土地附属设施管理不当致人损害,建筑物管理人与土地所有者承担连带责任,但建筑物管理人能证明自己尽到管理责任的除外。建筑物管理人与土地所有者内部责任比例按过错程度分担。

3.对胎儿的侵权(译者注:应为“对胎儿侵权的责任”)

胎儿因侵权行为受到损害,娩出后为活体的,具有损害赔偿请求权。《柬

埔寨民法》对自然人的认识充分且正确。自然人的民事权利能力始于出生，终于死亡，但只有成年人才享有完全民事行为能力。

4.共同侵权（译者注：应为“共同侵权责任”）

二人及二人以上共同侵权，每一侵权人：

（1）承担连带责任；

（2）按各自过错比例承担内部责任。

连带责任人自愿支付全部赔偿数额的，有权向其他连带责任人追偿。

二、侵权责任构成要件

在民事案件中界定侵权责任，当事人要考虑诸多构成要件，以下将重点阐述。侵权责任有三个主要构成要件，过错行为、损害结果，以及过错行为与损害结果之间的因果关系。

（一）过错行为

过错行为是指行为人因故意或过失违反义务致人损害的行为。过错行为通常可分为故意的过错行为和过失的过错行为两种。

1.故意的过错行为

根据《柬埔寨民法典》规定，故意的过错行为系侵权行为人已经预见其侵权行为通常会产生的后果并接受该结果的侵害他人的行为。

2.过失的过错行为

过失的过错行为系具有相同专业或经验的人可以预见该行为通常会导致的后果，但由于疏忽而未能预见，或已经预见但轻信可以避免而实施的行为。

（二）损害结果

侵权原则要求损害结果必须是真实存在且是由侵权行为导致的。损害结果可能在侵权之后随即产生或在未来特定时间内产生。通常而言，侵权行为产生的损害结果有诸多不同形式，以下三种最为常见。

1.财产损害

侵权行为造成被侵权人财物灭失或毁坏，被侵权人有权请求侵权人赔偿财物损失或修复费用。

赔偿数额通过侵权行为的损害结果计算，而非法律。如果侵权行为导致巨大损失，赔偿额也会据此计算。

2.人身损害

侵权行为造成被侵权人人身伤害或伤害致死,受害者有权请求侵权人赔偿损失。这些损失包含死亡前由于人身伤害损失和精神痛苦导致的经济损失。经济损失包括被侵权日起至死亡期间所支付的医疗费用以及由于被侵权而在该期间不能获取的利益。

3.精神损害

精神损害,是指侵权行为所导致的受害者心理或情感遭受创伤和痛苦的损害。因此,受害人可以请求精神损害赔偿;受害人死亡的,受害人近亲属可以请求精神损害赔偿。

(三)过错行为与损害结果之间的因果关系

根据侵权责任法原则,过错行为与损害结果是侵权责任的必备要素,不法行为的结果也必须体现在明确的损害结果上。过错行为与损害结果必须真实且直接。过错行为与损害结果之间的因果关系表明,过错行为必须是有害的或者能导致损害结果,并且损害结果必须是由侵权行为人的侵权行为直接导致的。

三、侵权责任法上的责任阻却事由

(一)行为能力

根据《民法典》第 14 条,不能辨认自己行为的人为无民事行为能力人,无民事行为能力人实施的法律行为无效。此外,民法典规定了几种限制民事行为能力人,如未成年人(译者注:已满 14 周岁的未成年人)、被监护或被管理的成年人。限制民事行为能力人不能完全独立进行民事法律行为。

(二)正当防卫与紧急避险

1.正当防卫

因正当防卫造成损害的,侵权人不承担责任。正当防卫是为对抗非法有害行为而做出的有害行为,但为防止本人或他人的人身、财产免受不法侵害而所必须。正当防卫具有两项法律构成要件:首先,防卫行为必须与过错行为具有时间上的紧密相关性;其次,防卫的手段不能超过必要限度。

2.紧急避险

因紧急避险造成损害的，侵权人不承担责任。紧急避险是指为使本人或他人的人身、财产免受正在发生的或迫切的危险而不得已采取的行为。紧急避险要求其手段不超过必要限度。

(三)受害人过错

受害人同意或自愿承担损害风险的，侵权人对其所造成的损害免除责任。然而，如果受害人同意或承担风险的程度违反普遍的社会标准，侵权人的责任并不当然免除。

(四)不可抗力

不可抗力是指无法预见的情况，其能阻碍合同成立及履行。

因不可抗力致人损害的，侵权人不承担责任。通常情况下，自然灾害是合同履行中免责的主要原因。

(五)未满 14 周岁的未成年人

在刑法中，犯罪的未成年人应受到关注、教育、保护和协助，使其康复并融入社会。在这方面，法院可以依据未满 14 周岁未成年人的犯罪情况及性格特征，考虑是否判处刑罚。

在民事案件中，未满 14 周岁的未成年人没有责任能力，即未满 14 周岁的未成年人不必对其侵权行为承担责任。然而，《民法典》规定，已满 14 周岁的未成年人需对故意或过失的侵权行为负责。

四、损害计算与诉讼时效

(一)侵权行为导致的损害计算

1.物质损害

损害是通过计算侵权行为造成受害人或受害方的经济损失来确定的。赔偿的数额应当基于侵权行为的损害以及在没有侵权行为情况下受害人原本所能获得的利益来评估。当然，赔偿数额的评估也注重其他证明材料，例如采用统计资料和其他材料来计算可能的损失程度。

2.精神损害

侵权行为造成的精神或情绪困扰的损害可以通过损害金额及相关因素来

量化确定。在这方面,确定损害赔偿金额有三个主要因素:

(1)侵权人的过错程度,即法官根据侵权人的过错行为属于故意还是过失进行过错程度判断;

(2)侵权行为类型;

(3)伤害的严重程度。

简而言之,上诉三项是评估赔偿给受害者或受害方的精神损害赔偿金的重要要素。

3.荣誉或名誉损害

如果由于侵权行为威胁或损害到权利人的荣誉或名誉,受害者或受害人有权向侵权方索赔。除了名誉损失赔偿额外,侵权人还应采取措施恢复受害者的荣誉或名誉,特别是根据《柬埔寨民法典》第757条第2款,通过诸如公开道歉等方式恢复受害者名誉。

(二)诉讼时效

受害者或受害方有权向侵权人索赔,但权利应当在法律规定的合理期间内行使。

权利人应在以下两个时期内进行索赔:

(1)自受害者、受害方或其代理人有权向侵权人索赔之日起3年内,超过3年诉讼时效,权利人权利消失;

(2)以及自侵权行为发生之日起10年内。

受害者或受害方可在上述期间向被告合法合理索赔,并给予被告一定时间履行。

结　论

侵权责任承担对社会上每个人而言都至关重要,每个人在生活中都要小心谨慎,避免故意或过失的行为。无论过错行为是故意的抑或是过失的,侵权行为总会侵害他人的权利或利益。

根据《柬埔寨民法典》的原则,即使过错行为轻微,倘若造成严重损害,行为人也应为此负责。与此相反,严重的过错行为仅造成轻微损害,行为人同样要对该结果负责。

Domestic Adoption in Cambodia

Chan Sotheavy*

Adoption is the establishment of family relations and family relations, the same as the relationship of parents and children as well, therefore, in the state's obligations related to the protection and ensuring the higher interests of the child. States must set a good system to care for children so that children grow and develop in a family with warm and no abuse rights.

In contrast, the care of children in a family is not appropriated, it will affects the rights and interests of the child as a factor leading affect society in the future, because children are the national successor.

Relevant to the systems and regulations related to this adoption according to research have shown that the system and regulations often change and evolve with period, situation and progress in society and to state party of international legal instruments(such as treaties, conventions, pacts, etc.)

Ⅰ. The Objective to Create the Adoption System

In creating or organizing any system, the first is to reflect the key necessary to create a system that responds all main requirements and be able to solve the real problems or issues that may occurs in society.

Obviously to create a system of adoption beside the purpose to create relationships between the children with relatives of a foster family, the main

* Chan Sotheavy is Secretary of Sate of the Ministry of Justice of Cambod, and a Ph.D candidate of the School of International Law, SWUPL.

objectives and priorities to find a solution by providing a family of children who do not have proper maintenance status of biological parents. Children who need the special protection or children are at risk, so that those children have developed a complete family atmosphere of happiness, love and understanding by taking the higher interests and the protection of fundamental rights of the children.

Ⅱ. Types of Domestic Adoption in Accordance with the Civil Law

In accordance with the Civil Code in 2007, that provision that related to the adoption stimulated on Book 7 Chapter 4 Section 2 that divided into 2 parts:

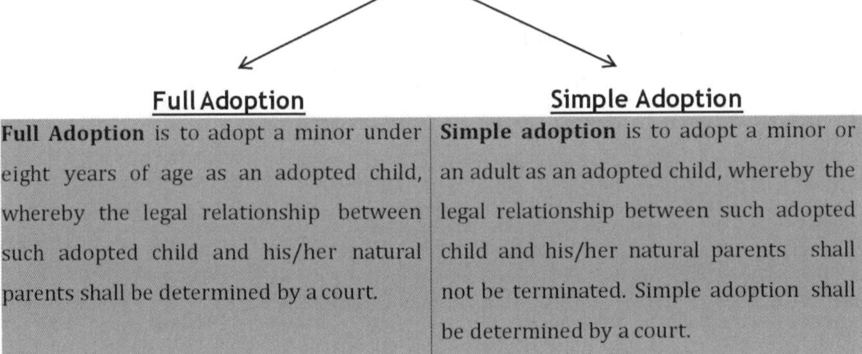

Full Adoption	Simple Adoption
Full Adoption is to adopt a minor under eight years of age as an adopted child, whereby the legal relationship between such adopted child and his/her natural parents shall be determined by a court.	**Simple adoption** is to adopt a minor or an adult as an adopted child, whereby the legal relationship between such adopted child and his/her natural parents shall not be terminated. Simple adoption shall be determined by a court.

1. Common Points

Domestic adoption, no matter whether full adoption or simple adoption, has common points as follows:

• The formation of domestic adoption needs to have a court's decision in accordance with legal process.

• Domestic adoption createsa permanent parent-child relation between an adopted child and adoptive parents, and places the adopted child in this relation.

2. Differences

There are some differences between full adoption and simple adoption as follows:

• In case of full adoption, an adopted child must be a minor below eight years of age. In case of simple adoption, no matter whether a minor or an adult, any person is eligible to become an adopted child if he/she is younger than adoptive parents.

• Full adoption shall terminate the legal relationship between an adopted child and his/her natural parents. Simple adoption shall not terminate the legal relationship between an adopted child and his/her natural parents.

In summary, full adoption is a scheme to provide a family composed of a father and a mother with sufficient stability for a child who is not under the care of his/her natural parents.

Full adoption will terminate the legal relationship between an adopted child and his/her natural parents. Then, the adopted child will obtain a status as a natural child of adoptive parents, and have a legal relationship with all family members of the adoptive parents.

1) Full Adoption

A. Formalities for Creation of Full Adoption

Article 1007 of the Civil Code provides that, in order to create full adoption, it is necessary to fulfill the requirements as follows:

a. There must be a motion by the person(s) who will become the adoptive parent(s).

b. All conditions provided in Article 1008 through Article 1012 of the civil Code mustbe fulfilled.

c. A court must issue a ruling which admits the full adoption.

Among the provisions from Article 1008 through Article 1012, each Article stipulates about the following points:

a. Article 1008 and Article 1009 stipulate about conditions for the adoptive parents.

b. Article 1010 stipulates about conditions for the adoptive child.

c. Article 1011 stipulates about consent to the adoption.

d. Article 1012 stipulates about criteria for determination of creation of the full adoption.

Therefore, in accordance with all of the above-mentioned Articles, the flow chart for creation of full adoption is shown as below:

a. A montion shall be filed to a court.

b. The motion shall fulfill all of the following conditions:

-Conditions for the adoptive parents(s)

-Conditions for the adoptive child.

-Consent to the adoption.

-Criteria for determination for creation of creation of full adoption.

c. The court issues a ruling which admints the full adoption.

d. The full adoption is created.

B. Conditions for Adoptive Parents

(1)Joint Adoption by Married Couple

Article 1008 of the Civil Code provides that, in principal, a person who will become an adoptive parent must have a spouse. The purpose of full adoption is to provide a family composed of a father and a mother with sufficient stability for an unfortunate child. Thus, the Civil Code has adopted the principle of joint adoption by married couple. For this reason, one spouse alone may not become an adoptive parent when the other spouse does not become an adoptive parent.

• Principle of Joint Adoption by Married Couple

A person who will become an adoptive parent must have a spouse. Thus, if a person does not have a spouse, this person may not become an adoptive parent.

One spouse alone may not become an adoptive parent when the other spouse does not become an adoptive parent.

• Exception for Principle of Joint Adoption by Married Couple

In cases where one spouse becomes an adoptive parent of a natural child of the other spouse, it is not necessary for a married couple to jointly adopt the child. This means that, in the above-mentioned cases, one spouse alone can become an adoptive parent of a natural child of the other spouse.

(2) Age of Adoptive Parents

• Minimum Age of Adoptive Parents

Article 1009 of the Civil Code provides that an adoptive parent must be no less than 25 years of age. Thus, the minimum age of adoptive parents is 25 years. This requires that adoptive parents have mental and physical maturity enough to provide actual and adequate care to a baby or young infant.

Each of adoptive parents must fulfill this minimum-age requirement.

This minimum-age requirement is a requirement for creation of full adoption. Thus, at the moment the court issues a ruling which admits full adoption, the adoptive parents need to be no less than 25 years of age. This means that at the moment the adoptive parents file a motion to a court, they do not have to be no less than 25 years of age.

• Minimum Difference of Age Between Adoptive Parents and Adopted Child

Article 1009 of the Civil Code provides that an adoptive parent must be at least 20 years older than the adopted child. Thus, the minimum difference of age between an adoptive parent and the adopted child is 20 years.

Each of adoptive parents must fulfill this requirement of minimum difference of age between an adoptive parent and the adopted child.

• Maximum Age of Adoptive Parents

The Civil Code does not have any conditions about maximum age of adoptive parents. Thus, an elderly person could become an adoptive parent by means of full adoption.

However, if a married couple wants to adopt a child, but they are so old that they lack sufficient capacity to take care of the child until he/she reaches the age of majority, then the court cannot admit full adoption by this couple. That is because full adoption by such an elderly couple is not contributory to the child's interests (Article 1012 of the Civil Code).

• Adoptive Parents' Capacity to Act

The Civil Code does not have any conditions about adoptive parents' capacity to act. Thus, a person who has a limited capacity to act, such as a person under general guardianship and a person under curatorship provided in Article 16 of the Civil Code, could become an adoptive parent by means of full adoption.

However, a person under general guardianship or a person under curatorship usually lacks sufficient capacity to take care of a child. Therefore, full adoption by a person under general guardianship or a person under curatorship is not contributory to the child's interests (Article 1012 of the Civil Code). In this case, the court cannot admit full adoption.

C. Conditions for the Adopted Child

(1) Age of the Adopted Child

Article 1010 of the Civil Code provides that the adopted child must be less than 8 years of age. Full adoption is a system to provide parents to a young infant who needs care and support. Thus, in principle, the Civil Code limits to a child who is less than 8 years of age.

However, if an adopted child is less than 8 years of age at the moment when a motion for full adoption is filed to a court, then the court can issue a ruling which admits the full adoption even though the adopted child has already attained 8 or more years of age at the moment when the ruling is issued. That is because, in order to create full adoption, there must be at least 6 months as the trial period of care (Article 1013 of the Civil Code). Thus, the Civil Code anticipates that there will be some cases where the court proceedings for full adoption need to take a very long time such as one year, two years, or longer. For this reason, we have to interpret that, if an adopted child is less than 8 years of age at the moment when a motion for full adoption is filed to a court, and then this is sufficient to fulfill the requirement of age of the adopted child.

(2) Number of the Adopted Children

The Civil Code does not have any restriction to the number of the adopted children. Thus, adoptive parents can adopt one child or more, and take care of the child/children by means of full adoption. Moreover, a married couple who has one or more natural child/children of them can adopt another child/children and take care of the child/children by means of full adoption.

However, if a married couple has one child or more, no matter whether a natural or adopted child, who is/are subject to parental responsibility, the court should take the number of the couple's children into consideration when the court determines whether the couple has sufficient capacity to take

care of another child or not. In case where the court understands that the couple does not have sufficient capacity to take care of another child, the court cannot admit full adoption. That is because the full adoption by the married couple is not contributory to the child's interests (Article 1012 of the Civil Code).

D. Consent to Adoption

Article 1011 of the Civil Code provides that in order to create full adoption, in principle, the consent of the natural parents of the child to be adopted must be given. Full adoption terminates the relation with the natural parents, and aims to have the adopted child completely enter the family of the adoptive parents. Thus, in principle, it is necessary to obtain the consent from the natural parents who have deep relation and strong interests with the child to be adopted.

(1) Consent from Natural Parents

In cases where the natural father and mother of the child to be adopted are alive, in principle, the consent should be given by both the natural father and the natural mother.

In cases where either the natural father or mother of the child to be adopted is dead, in principle, it is sufficient to obtain consent from only the remaining natural mother or father who is still alive.

• Consent in Exceptional Cases to Principle of Joint Adoption by Married Couple

In cases where one spouse becomes an adoptive parent of a natural child of the other spouse, it is not necessary for a married couple to jointly adopt the child (Sentence 2, Paragraph 2, Article 1008 of the Civil Code). This means that, in the above-mentioned cases, one spouse alone can become an adoptive parent of a natural child of the other spouse by means of full adoption, and in principle, it is necessary and sufficient to obtain consent from the other spouse alone.

(2) Cases Where Consent of Natural Parents Is Unnecessary

As explained above, in order to create full adoption, in principle, the consent of the natural parents of the child to be adopted must be given. However, there are some cases where it is difficult to obtain the consent from natu-

ral parents. In addition, there are other cases where the natural parents have refused to give consent, and this refusal is detrimental to the interests of the child to be adopted, or harmful to the health, safety or morality of the child.

In these above-mentioned cases, it is not necessary to obtain the consent of the natural parents in accordance with the second sentence of Article 1011 for the purpose of protecting the interests of the child to be adopted.

a. Cases where parents are incapable of declaring their intention

The second sentence of Article 1011 provides that in cases where the natural parents are incapable of declaring their intention, it is not necessary to obtain the consent from the natural parents. The words "cases where the parents are incapable of declaring their intention" can include the cases where the locations of the natural parents are not certain.

b. Cases where the parents have abused the child, abandoned the child in bad faith, or there is any other cause that is extremely detrimental to the interests of the child who will be adopted.

The second sentence of Article 1011 also provides that it is not necessary to obtain the consent from the natural parents in the following cases:

• The natural parents have abused the child;

• The natural parents have abandoned the child in bad faith; or,

• There is other cause that is extremely detrimental to the interests of the child who will be adopted.

(3) Consent from Guardian of the Minor

As explained above, in order to create full adoption, in principle, the consent of the natural parents of the child to be adopted must be given. However, there are some cases where both of the natural parents passed away because of disease or accident. In addition, there are other cases where the natural parents who have parental authority have been suspended or divested of their parental authority (Article 1048 of the Civil Code) In these cases, there is no one who exercises the parental authority. Therefore, a guardian of a minor must be designated in order to protect the minor (Article 1067 of the Civil Code).

In cases where a guardian of a minor has been designated for the minor

who will be adopted, it is necessary to obtain consent from the guardian of the minor in order to create full adoption (Article 1011 of the Civil Code).

• Cases Where Guardian of Minor Refuses to Give Consent

If a guardian of a minor has been designated, it is necessary to obtain consent from the guardian of the minor in order to create full adoption. However, there are some cases where it is difficult to obtain the consent from the guardian of the minor. In addition, there are other cases where the guardian of the minor has refused to give consent, and this refusal is detrimental to the interests of the minor to be adopted, or harmful to the health, safety or morality of the minor.

Even though there are such cases as mentioned above, the second sentence of Article 1011 cannot apply to those cases. That is because the second sentence of Article 1011 shall apply to only "parents."

Therefore, if the guardian of the minor is incapable of declaring his/her intention, or if the guardian of the minor has refused to give consent without good reason, then the court can dismiss the guardian of the minor (Article 1073 of the Civil Code). Then, the court must designate a new guardian of the minor (Paragraph 2 of Article 1068 of the Civil Code). In this way, the consent can be obtained from the guardian of the minor.

• Cases Where Natural Parents Have Withdrawn Their Consent

In cases where the natural parents have withdrawn their consent, in principle, the court cannot admit full adoption.

However, if the withdrawal of consent is detrimental to the interests of the child to be adopted, or harmful to the health, safety or morality of the child, then the second sentence of Article 1011 can apply to the withdrawal. Thus, the court can admit full adoption even if there is no consent from the natural parents.

• Cases Where the Guardian of the Minor Has Withdrawn His/Her Consent

In cases where the guardian of the minor has withdrawn his/her consent, in principle, the court cannot admit full adoption.

Moreover, even though the withdrawal of consent is detrimental to the interests of the minor to be adopted, or harmful to the health, safety or morality of the minor, the second sentence of Article 1011 cannot apply to the

withdrawal. That is because the second sentence of Article 1011 shall apply to only "parents."

However, if the guardian of the minor has withdrawn his/her consent without good reason, the court can dismiss the guardian of the minor (Article 1073 of the Civil Code). Then, the court must designate a new guardian of the minor (Paragraph 2 of Article 1068 of the Civil Code). In this way, the consent can be obtained from the guardian of the minor, and then the court can admit full adoption.

E. Criteria for Determination of Creation of Full Adoption

Article 1012 of the Civil Code provides the substantive criteria for the court to decide creation of full adoption. In order to create full adoption, it must satisfy all of the following two requirements provided in Article 1012:

(1) The court must find that:

a. It is extremely difficult for the natural parents to are for the child to be adopted, or

b. It is inappropriate for the natural parents to care for the child.

c. There are any other special circumatances, and

(2) The court must find that full adoption is specifically necessary for the interests of the child.

Only if all of the two requirements as mentioned above are satisfied, the court can decide the creation of the full adoption.

F. Trial Period of Care

In principle, the period of trial care must be at least 6 months after the adoptive parents filed a motion for full adoption to a court. The court can, if necessary and appropriate, set a definite period of trial care longer than 6 months in order to evaluate whether or not the full adoption would meet the interests of the child.

However, if there has already been a record showing the circumstances of the adoptive parents' care and custody of the adopted child in advance, and the court can obtain this record as resources for determination, then the court can use this record. In this case, the court can calculate the trial period of care by starting from the date when the adoptive parents had begun to provide the care and custody of the adopted child.

2) Simple Adoption

A. Formalities for Creation of Simple Adoption

Article 1020 of the Civil Code aims to establish the system of simple adoption in Cambodia which eases the strict conditions of full adoption putting an adopted child into the exclusive custody of the adoptive parents and terminating the whole legal relationship between the adopted child and his/her natural parents.

Therefore, in cases where an adopted child does not wish to be detached totally from his/her natural parents and put him/herself into the whole custody of the adoptive parents, the system of simple adoption can be used under the supervision of a court in order to establish some effect of legal family relationship such as succession and family supports.

In order to create simple adoption, it is necessary to fulfill the requirements as follows:

a. There must be a motion by the person(s) who will become the adoptive parent(s), together with a person to become an adopted child.

b. All conditions provided in Article 1020 through Article 1025 of the Civil Code must be fulfilled.

c. A court must issue a ruling which admits the simple adoption.

When a person who will become the adoptive parent files a motion for simple adoption together with a person to become an adopted child, there must be a mutual agreement on the creation of simple adoption between the person who will become the adoptive parent and the person to become an adopted child. Thus, we can say that simple adoption is an adoption based on the agreement. This means that simple adoption must be established upon the mutual agreement on the adoption between the both parties.

Therefore, the flow chart for creation of simple adoption is shown as below:

a. There must be a mutual agreement on the creation of simple adoption betweenthe both parties.

b. The both parties file a motion to a court.

c. The motion must fulfill all conditions provided in Article 1020 through Article 1025 of the Civil Code.

d. The court issues a ruling which admits the simple adoption.

e. The simple adoption is created.

• Cases Where the Person to Become an Adopted Child is a Minor

In cases where the person to become an adopted child is a minor, the parental authority holder or huardian of such minor must file a motion for simple adoption in the capacity of the minior's statutory agent(Paragraph 2 of Article 1020).

B. Conditions for Adoptive Parents

(1)Conditions for Adoptive parents

Paragraph 1 of Article 1020(Motion for simple adoption) provides that person ages 25 years or more, together with a person to become a adopted child, may file a motion to the court for creation of simple adoption.

Thus, simple adoption has the age limitation of the adoptive parent as 25 years old or more. A person aged 25 years old or more can become an adoptive parents no matter whether such person a spouse or not.

(2)Cases Where the Person to Become an Adoptive Parent Has a Spouse

Article 1021 of the Civil Code requires the joint adoption by a married couple in cases where a person with a spouse wishes to adopt a minor. Adopting a minor is surely a significant matter for both of the spouses. Moreover, when they adopt a minor, they have to maintain the stability of their family and guarantee a good environment for taking care of the minor. For these reasons, this article requires the joint adoption by a married couple.

However, in cases where a person with a spouse adopts a child of his/her spouse or where his/her spouse is insane, or where his/her spouse is incapable of declaring her/his own intention because the spouse's location is unknown, such person alone can adopt a minor without the joint filing of the motion.

C. Conditions for the Adopted Child

The Civil Code does not have any conditions regarding the age of an adopted child. Therefore, in principle, any person can become an adopted child no matter whether such person is a minor or an adult. This means that adopting an adult is permissible.

However, the second sentence of Paragraph 1 of Article 1020(Motion

for simple adoption)provides that the person to become an adopted child may not be an ascendant or senior of the person to become an adoptive parent. Thus, the Civil Code prohibits any person from adopting his/her ascendant or senior.

D. Consent to Adoption

(1)Consent to Simple Adoption

Simple adoption is an adoption based on the agreement. This means that simple adoption must be established upon the mutual agreement on the adoption between the person to become an adoptive parent and the person to become an adopted child.

For this reason, in principle, it is not necessary to obtain consent to the simple adoption from any third party.

(2)Cases Where the Person to Become an Adoptive Parent Has a Spouse

Article 1022 of the Civil Code provides that if a person with a spouse files a motion for simple adoption, the consent of such spouse must be obtained. This is because in cases where a person with a spouse adopts another person by means of simple adoption, such adoption can significantly affect the succession, family support, family name, family's daily life, and so on.

The case under Article 1022 of the Civil Code is different from the case where a person with a spouse adopts a minor in accordance with Article 1021 (The case where the person to become an adoptive parent has a spouse). If a person with a spouse adopts an adult, the joint adoption by a married couple is not required. That is because one spouse alone can adopt the adult by means of simple adoption with the consent of his/her spouse.

- Cases Where the Consent of Spouse Is Not Necessary

In cases where a married couple files a motion jointly or where the spouse is incapable of declaring his/her intention, the consent of the spouse is not necessary(The second sentence of Article 1022).

(3)Cases Where the Person to Become an Adopted Child is a Minor

In cases where a person to become an adopted child is a minor, the parental authority holder or guardian of such minor must file a motion for simple adoption in the capacity of the minor's statutory agent(Paragraph 2 of Article 1020).

However,if such minor has attained the age of 15 years,it is necessary to obtain consent from the minor in order to create simple adoption(Paragraph 3 of Article 1024).

E. Criteria for Determination of Creation of Simple Adoption

(1)Criteria for Determination of Creation of Simple Adoption

Article 1023 of the Civil Code provides the criteria for determination of creation of simple adoption.

Simple adoption will establish a legal parent-child relationship.Thus,in order to create simple adoption,Article 1023 requires that the parties truly have the intention to establish a parent-child relationship(Paragraph 1 of Article 1023).

In addition,Article 1023 prohibits the parties from abusing the system of simple adoption for any immoral purposes,such as a camouflage of a parent-child relationship or a homosexual marriage(Paragraph 2 of Article 1023).

(2)Cases Where the Person to Become an Adopted Child is a Minor

Article 1024 of the Civil Code provides that in adopting a minor,the court may admit the creation of simple adoption only if the court finds that such simple adoption is especially necessary for the benefit of the minor(Paragraph 1 of Article 1024).Thus,the court must make a determination on whether or not the simple adoption will be beneficial to the minor to be adopted.

• Cases Where the Natural Parents of the Adopted Child Have Divorced

Paragraph 2 of Article 1024 provides that in cases where the person to become an adopted child is a minor whose natural parents have divorced,the court shall hear the opinion of the parent without parental authority in making its decision on whether or not the adoption will be beneficial to the minor to be adopted.

When a divorce between the father and mother occurs,the father and mother must determine through mutual consultation which of them is to become the parental authority holder of the minor child(Article 1037).And if such minor child is to become an adopted child,his/her parental authority holder must file a motion for simple adoption in the capacity of the minor's

statutory agent(Paragraph 2 of Article 1020).

However, simple adoption sometimes can be used for the purpose of disturbing the parent without parental authority from meeting and socializing with his/her minor child. Thus, even though it is not necessary to obtain consent from the parent without parental authority, the court needs to hear the opinion of the parent without parental authority (Paragraph 2 of Article 1024).

• The Court Must Respect the Child'S Intention Regarding Adoption.

Paragraph 3 of Article 1024 provides that if the minor has attained the age of 15 years, it is necessary to obtain consent from the minor in order to create the adoption(The first sentence). In addition, Paragraph 3 of Article 1024 provides that even if the minor is less than 15 years old but can express his/her intention, the court must hear the minor's opinion in making its decision on whether or not the adoption will be beneficial to the minor to be adopted(The second sentence).

Paragraph 3 of Article 1024 is a provision requiring the court to respect the child's intention regarding adoption in order to guarantee the child's right to express his/her opinion.

(3) Adoption Between Guardian and the Person Under Guardianship

Article 1025 of the Civil Code provides an adoption between a guardian and the person under guardianship.

In cases where a guardian files a motion to adopt the person under his/her own guardianship, no matter whether guardianship for a minor or general guardianship, there can be a case in which the guardian abuses his/her superior status which has authority to administer property and take care of the person under guardianship.

For this reason, Article 1025 provides that the court must consider the fiduciary relationship between a guardian and the person under guardianship, and can admit the creation of adoption only if the court confirms that there is no unlawfulness or other problem in such fiduciary relationship.

柬埔寨的国内收养制度

Chan Sotheavy*
贾亚辉**编译

内容摘要:本文以《柬埔寨民法典》为依据,通过阐述《柬埔寨民法典》中有关国内收养制度的规定,包括国内收养制度的两种类型中完全收养和简单收养构成关系的条件、手续和标准等,为社会中的弱势群体儿童给予保护并保证其获取更好的权益,同时为缺乏亲生父母照顾的儿童营造充满幸福、爱和理解的家庭气氛。

关键词:柬埔寨民法典;国内收养制度

收养是指将他人子女收为自己子女,从而形成一种类似于父母子女间的关系。国家有义务保护收养儿童并保证其获得更高的权益,各国应当建立良好的收养制度从而保证儿童在温暖的环境中成长。

一、收养制度的目标

建立任何制度的目标是在于解决社会中现实发生或可能发生的问题,显而易见,建立收养制度的目标在于为需要被收养的儿童寻找到一个合适的家庭,并且通过法律制度建立起被收养人和收养人之间的权利义务关系,从而实现对被收养人的保护。

---

* Chan Sotheavy,柬埔寨司法部国务秘书,西南政法大学国际法学院博士生。

** 贾亚辉,西南政法大学国际法学院 2018 级硕士研究生。

二、收养的种类

根据2007年《民法典》第7部分第4章第2节将收养分为两种类型，即完全收养和简单收养。完全收养是指收养八岁以下的未成年人，从而导致被领养的儿童与其亲生父母的法律关系依法庭的裁决而终止。简单收养是指收养未成年人或成年人，而此种收养将不会因法庭的裁决导致被收养子女与其亲生父母之间的法律关系的终止。

完全收养和简单收养的共同点在于：第一，收养关系的成立需要经过法律程序裁决；第二，均会导致养子女和养父母的父母子女关系的成立。

完全收养和简单收养的不同点在于：第一，完全收养要求被收养的儿童必须是八岁以下的未成年人，而简单收养则无此要求，无论是未成年人还是成年人，只要被收养人比养父母年轻，就有资格被收养；第二，完全收养将终止被收养子女与其亲生父母之间的法律关系，而简单收养则不会。

1.完全收养

(1)建立完全收养关系的手续

根据《民法典》第1007条的规定，成立完全收养关系应当满足：第一，养父母有收养意愿；第二，符合《民法典》第1008条至第1012条的规定条件；第三，必须经过法院裁决。

据此，建立完全收养关系的手续如下：首先，养父母应当提交收养申请书，收养申请书中应当表明作为养父母的条件，作为被收养人的条件，收养的同意以及确定完全收养的标准；其次，由法院做出建立完全收养关系的裁决，完全收养关系遂成立。

(2)成为养父母的条件

第一，根据《民法典》第1008条的规定，要求成为养父母的人必须有配偶，即无配偶之人不得成为养父母。

第二，根据《民法典》第1009条的规定，养父母年龄不得小于25岁。此处25岁是指在法庭做出完全收养裁决之时满25岁，即不要求收养人在递交申请书时就已满25岁。同时，该条还规定了养父母双方和被收养子女年龄均相差20岁。该条文并未规定养父母年龄的上限。

(3)成为被收养儿童的条件

根据《民法典》第1010条的规定，被收养儿童必须8岁以下。此处的8岁是指法庭做出完全收养裁决之时满8岁。同时，《民法典》未做出对收养儿童数量的限制,法官应当根据收养人的收养能力做出裁决。

(4)收养的同意

根据《民法典》第 1011 条的规定,为建立完全收养,原则上应当经过被收养儿童的亲生父母同意。若亲生父母一方死亡,则应当经未死亡一方同意。

同时,建立完全收养在以下情形中,无须获得被收养儿童的亲生父母同意:第一,被收养儿童的亲生父母缺乏表意能力;第二,被收养儿童的亲生父母存在虐待,遗弃或者其他有害于被收养儿童的情形。

根据上述规定,收养的成立原则上应当经过被收养儿童的亲生父母的同意。那么,当存在被收养儿童双亲皆已不在或者亲生父母的监护权被剥夺的情形时,为保护被收养儿童,根据《民法典》第 1067 条,此时应当为被收养儿童指定监护人。在存在指定监护人的前提条件下,根据《民法典》第 1011 条,该收养关系的成立应当经过被收养儿童监护人的同意。

若被收养儿童的监护人不同意收养或者要求撤回收养,而这种不同意或者撤回会损害未成年人的利益,但此时并不能适用《民法典》第 1011 条第二项的规定,因为此处的监护人不同于“父母”,在这种情况下,法庭可因监护人无正当理由不同意或撤回,剥夺该监护人的监护权,从而实现收养。

如果亲生父母要求撤回收养,法庭原则上不再准许完全收养,但若存在不同意收养将导致损害未成年人的利益,法院可以根据《民法典》第 1011 条第二项的规定,不经过父母的同意即裁决该收养的成立。

(5)完全收养的实质条件

根据《民法典》第 1012 条的规定,完全收养应当满足两个实质性要件:第一,必须经过法庭的裁决;第二,该裁决必须是为了保护未成年人的利益所必要的。

同时,《民法典》也规定了 6 个月的考察期,该考察期自收养人提出收养申请时起算。

2.简单收养

根据《民法典》第 1020 条的规定,在法庭的监督下,可以简化收养的要求,在某些情形下,被收养子女不完全独立于亲生父母,被收养子女仍然可以与亲生父母保持如继承、家庭援助等关系。

(1)建立简单收养关系的手续

简单收养关系应当满足以下三个条件:第一,必须由养父母和被收养子女共同申请,这意味着简单收养必须建立在双方协议之上;第二,符合《民法典》第 1020 条至第 1025 条的规定条件;第三,必须经过法院裁决。因此,简单收

养实际上是以协议为基础的收养。

(2)成为养父母的条件

根据《民法典》第1020条,简单收养只需要收养人满足25周岁的要求,并未对是否有配偶做出要求,只要收养人同被收养人达成协议收养人即可满足成为养父母的条件。若收养人已婚,则法律要求夫妻双方共同收养。

(3)成为被收养人条件

法律并未对简单收养中的被收养人的年龄做出限制,故未成年人和成年人都可以成为被收养的对象。但是,《民法典》第1020条第二款规定,不得收养长辈。

(4)简单收养的准许

简单收养由于是基于收养协议而成立的,所以一般不存在第三方同意的情形,只需要收养人和被收养人之间达成协议。当收养人存在配偶的情况下,应当经过配偶的同意。若配偶无表意能力时,则无须征得配偶同意。

当被收养人是未成年人的时候,此时未成年人的亲生父母应当以法定代理人的形式来进行简单收养程序。当未成年人已满15周岁,则须经未成年人同意才可成立简单收养。

(5)简单收养的实质条件

为避免双方滥用简单收养达成不法目的,法庭应当考察双方的真实目的,同时,当被收养人是未成年人时,根据《民法典》第1024条,法庭应当考察简单收养对未成年人的利益是否必要。

当未成年人亲生父母存在离异的情形,法官在判断是否有必要利益时,应当同时听取不具有抚养权一方的意见。同时,当未成年人未满15周岁,但具有表达自己意思的能力的前提条件下,法庭也应当听取未成年人的意见。

当监护人在监护人申请收养他人,并建立监护关系时,无论是与未成年人建立监护关系还是一般的监护关系,均可能会出现监护人利用监护关系在管理被监护人财产和看管被监护人时滥用自己的监管权的情况。根据《民法典》第1025条的规定,在监护关系中法庭必须考虑监护人和被监护人之间的信托关系,并且只有在确认不存在违法且在其他信托关系中不存在问题时,法庭才可以准许建立收养关系。

Important Judicial Officers in Criminal Procedure of the Court of First Instance in Cambodia

Nup Sothunvisoth*

Introduction

The purpose of Code of Criminal Procedure of the Kingdom of Cambodia aims at defining the rules to be strictly followed and applied in order to clearly determine the existence of a criminal offense. The power and the responsibility of the state officers are provided by this law in order to process a smooth procedure on any criminal case, as well as to find justice for both victims and the accused. Although those officers are provided the power to investigate or to prosecute or to put somebody in jail, their power is restricted very strictly according to the law. There are some important judicial officers who involving in criminal procedure, however this paper focus only the most important person such as Judicial Police, Prosecutors, Investigating Judge, and the Trial Judge of the Court of First Instance.

A-Judicial Police

According to article 56 of Criminal procedure of Cambodia "The judicial police perform their duties in support of the judicial body. The judicial police have the duty to examine felonies, misdemeanors and petty offenses, to iden-

* Nup Sothunvisoth is Director of the Department of Research, Publishing and Training on Penal Law of the Ministry of Justice of Cambodia and a Ph.D candidate of the International Law School, SWUPL.

tify and arrest offenders and to collect evidence".

Who Can Be a Judicial Police?

A Judicial Police is a National Police Officer or Military Officer who hold the grade of at least major lieutenant and who have at least two year of work experience in the service and after obtaining a Higher Diploma of the Judicial Police or other particular Officer who is authorized to examine offenses in the scope of their territorial jurisdiction. Moreover, some other important positions are automatically classified as judicial police such as Governor and deputy governor of provinces and municipalities, governor and deputy governor of District and Khan, Chief of commune and chief of Sangkat; Director and deputy director of the Central Department of Judicial Police; and other high positions.

Supervision of Judicial Police and Misconduct

The Judicial Police shall be monitored and controlled by the General Prosecutor attached to the Court of Appeal. The General Prosecutor attached to the Court of Appeal shall be empowered to take disciplinary actions against judicial police (Article 59 of CCP).

Disciplinary Procedure

All cases in which a judicial police officer has committed misconduct during the performance of his duty shall be reported by the Royal Prosecutor or the investigating judge to the General Prosecutor attached to the Court of Appeal. Depending on the circumstances, the General Prosecutor attached to the Court of Appeal notifies the Minister of Interior or the Minister of National Defense in order to take disciplinary action. The General Prosecutor attached to the Court of Appeal shall be informed about the results of the disciplinary action (Article 64, CCP). The disciplinary actions could be Disciplinary Sanctions or Prohibition of Judicial Police Officers, but these disciplinary actions shall not be an obstacle to criminal action provided that a criminal offense has been committed by the respective officer.

Missions of Judicial Police Officers

The fundamental mission of judicial police officers includes:

• Recording the offenses by receiving complaints or denunciations in order to examine offenses.

• Undertaking flagrant enquiry or preliminary enquiry under the conditions that the case is a Flagrant Felony or Misdemeanor, or the case is just a common case which require preliminary inquiry.

• When a judicial investigation has been initiated, judicial police officers enforce interrogating letter issued by the investigation judge.

Actions Taken After Receipt of Complaints (Article 74, CCP)

A judicial police officer who receives a complaint shall either immediately initiate a police inquiry or send the record of the complaint to the Prosecutor who makes a decision on how to proceed. Before initiating a police inquiry, the judicial police officer may ask for advice from the Prosecutor. When receiving a denunciation which is not manifestly unfounded, the judicial police officer shall inform the Prosecutor and request for his advice.

Authority of Judicial Police Officers

In the case of a flagrant felony or misdemeanor, the power of judicial police is becoming more forceful than the case classified as a common one. The definition of Flagrant felony or misdemeanor is stipulated in Article 86 of CCP, stated that a crime which committed during the commission of a crime; immediately after the commission of a crime; a suspect is being in a hot pursuit by the public; a person is found to have an object, or a scar, mark or any other evidence from which it can be concluded that he committed or participated in the commission of an offense. In contrast, other crimes beside these conditions are considered as common crimes.

Conduct a Search

In any kind of case, judicial police can conduct a search. However, if the offense of a Flagrante Delicto Case, they may conduct a search when they re-

ceived the authorization from the Royal Prosecutor even if the authorization is verbal. The search must be in the presence of the occupant of the place to be searched. In the absence of such person, the search shall be done in the presence of two witnesses. The witnesses shall be appointed by the judicial police officers and they shall not be police or military police who are participating in the search operation. On the other hand, if the offense is a common crime and when the preliminary inquiry involved, the search of the judicial police shall be changed to softer operation. Judicial police officers shall seek an express and real approval from the occupant of the premises. The approval may be hand-written by the occupant of the premises. If the occupant of the premises is absent or denies the search, the President of the Court of First Instance which has territorial jurisdiction on the case may authorize the search upon a Prosecutor's request. The Prosecutor shall personally lead this search. Judicial police officer shall conduct the search at the presence of the occupant of the premises, or if he is absent, at the presence of two witnesses. The witnesses shall be assigned by the Prosecutor; they cannot be judicial police or military police who are participating in the search. The search cannot be conducted before six o'clock in the morning and after six o'clock in the evening.

Police Custody

In order to respond to the needs of an inquiry, judicial police officers may remand in custody a person suspected of participating in the commission of an offense, judicial police officers may also remand in custody individuals who may provide them with relevant facts that this individual may provide information but refuses to do so. This kind of custody must be provided in writing by a Prosecutor. Judicial police officers shall immediately report any measure of police custody to the Royal Prosecutor and shall deliver to him all relevant evidence that led the police to take the custodial action. The maximum duration of any police custody is 48 hours. The duration shall commence from the time when the detained person arrives at the police or military police office. More interestingly, the custody duration may be extended to 24 hours more if the measure is necessary to conduct the inquiry properly. However, an extension is not permitted if the detained person is a minor. The duration shall be reduced according to the age of the detained person who is a minor, from 18 to 14 years old. In addition, assistance of lawyer is provided during police custody after 24 hours and the assistance of medical doctor is also available to examine the detained person at any time.

B-Prosecutors

Authorities Entrusted with Prosecution, Investigation, and Interrogation Powers

The prosecution brings charges of criminal offense against charged person and asks for the application of laws by the court; prosecutors are responsible for the implementation of orders of the criminal court on criminal offenses, including the dissemination of arrest warrants. In performing his duties, a prosecutor has the right to directly mobilize public forces. A prosecutor shall attend all hearings of the trial court in criminal cases.

The Prosecutors include:

1. The General Prosecutor, Deputy General Prosecutors and Prosecutors attached to the Supreme Court;

2. The General Prosecutor, Deputy General Prosecutors and Prosecutors attached to the Court of Appeal;

3. Royal Prosecutor and Deputy Prosecutor attached to a Court of First Instance.

Hierarchy of Prosecution

Technically, the Minister of Justice can denounce to the General Prosecutor attached to the Court of Appeal or to any Royal Prosecutor any offense that the minister has knowledge of, make a written injunction on the case file to initiate proceedings, or render other orders which he thinks are appropriate.

The General Prosecutor attached to the Court of Appeal has power over all Prosecutors who are under his territorial jurisdiction. He can issue an in-

junction to such Prosecutors to initiate proceedings against someone or to make conclusions that he thinks are appropriate.

The Royal Prosecutor has power over Prosecutors who are under his territorial jurisdiction. He can issue an injunction to such Prosecutors to initiate proceedings or to make conclusions that he thinks are appropriate.

However, the General Prosecutor, Deputy General Prosecutors and Prosecutors attached to the Supreme Court represent the prosecution body at this court and they participate in requests for application of the law in the appeal to the Supreme Court, motions for review of a decided case or other claims made to the Supreme Court. In practice, the General Prosecutor of Supreme Court has no power over all Prosecutors in Appeal Court and the Court of the First Instance on technical prosecution and investigation, but he holds a top position as a member of the Council of Magistrate automatically. This position leads the General Prosecutor to make decision to appoint or remove judges and prosecutors.

Powers of Prosecutor

The Royal Prosecutor leads and coordinates the operations of all judicial police agents and judicial police officers within his territorial jurisdiction. He exercises all authority designated to the judicial police officers. In special circumstances, a Prosecutor can revoke delegated investigative powers from the judicial police agents and officers and arrange for their replacement. At any time he can inspect a judiciary police unit and can participate in interviews. He can examine the implementation of any police custody, especially to ensure compliance with the legal procedures and the rules for custodial management.

Processing of Criminal Proceedings

The Royal Prosecutor shall consider written complaints and protests that have been received by him or that have been directly submitted by judicial police officers. He can decide to either hold a file without processing or to conduct proceedings against the offenders. Filing the case without processing shall be based on grounds of law and fact. Filing without processing does not have the effect of *res judicata*; it means that the Prosecutor may always change his decision as long as the criminal action has not been extinguished. If the Prosecutor decides to conduct proceedings against the offenders, there are three types of proceeding he can operate. 1-Conducting through the opening of judicial investigation, 2-through a citation, 3-through the procedure of immediate appearance.

1. Opening of Judicial Investigation

In the case of a felony, the Prosecutor shall open a judicial investigation. The judicial investigation shall be based upon the initial submission provided to the investigating judges. The judicial investigation may be opened against identified or unidentified individuals. Also in the case of a misdemeanor, the Prosecutor may open a judicial investigation. But he has other options such as directly summons the accused to appear before the Court of First Instance with the exact date or he can order the accused to immediately appear before the Court of First Instance.

2. Prosecution through citations

A citation is an order made to the accused to appear before the Court of First Instance. A citation shall include the relevant court, its location, and the date and time of trial. The citation shall specify that the accused may be defended by a lawyer. Moreover, in case of petty offense, the Prosecutor shall issue a citation for the accused to appear before the court. This process aims to speed up the case by handing the case to trial judges to render final judgment.

3. Prosecution through immediate appearance

Prosecutors may order the accused to appear before the Court of First Instance immediately if all of the following requirements are satisfied:

- The offense is flagrant crime, flagrant felony or misdemeanor
- The offense carries a sentence of imprisonment for less than one year and not greater than five years;
- The accused reaches a legal age; and
- There are substantial facts to be tried.

C-Investigating Judge

Investigating judge is a judge who responds to conduct an investigation a case which is a felony but it is optional for a misdemeanor. The investigating judge is seized with the facts specified in the introductory submission by the Prosecutor. An investigating judge, in accordance with the law, performs all investigations that he deems useful to ascertaining the truth. He has the obligation to collect both*inculpatory* evidence and *exculpatory* evidence. It means that investigating judge as an impartial body to investigate and collect the evidence which presented by the Prosecutor aiming to put pressure on the accused, and at the same time investigating judge is obligated to investigate and collect evidence which discovered by the accused.

Assistance of Court Clerks

An investigation judge shall be assisted by a clerk. In any case, the clerk cannot perform the duties of the investigation judge himself. The clerk shall be kept by the clerk. If possible, the clerk shall make copies of each record. The clerk shall certify that the copied records are true copy of the original. The copies shall be kept in a reserve file. The clerk shall assign code number for all records in a chronological order. The original records and the reserve copies of the records shall be stored in the clerk's office, in the investigating judge's office, or in any room of the court with sufficient security conditions. The lawyer or his secretary may be authorized by the investigating judge to copy the record at his own cost under the supervision of the clerk. In some circumstances, an investigating judge may visit any site, after inform the Royal Prosecutor, always accompanies by his clerk in the territorial jurisdiction of the Court of First Instance.

Security Measures of Investigating Judge

In order to ensure the effectiveness of the investigation, an investigating judge has power to issue subpoena, orders to bring someone before the judge, issues arrest warrants and detention orders.

Subpoena

Perhaps at the begging of the investigation, an investigating judge shall be entitled to issue a subpoena. A subpoena is an order to a person to appear before the investigating judge and this order may be issued against a charged person or any person against whom there is evidence of guilt. However, this measure is not always applied. For instance, in case that there is a strong evidence which indicate that the accused has committed the crime and sometime the accused run away, an investigating judge shall issue an arrest warrant directly. This is because of the urgency of the case which requires quick respond.

Order to Bring Issued by Investigating Judge

An investigating judge shall be entitled to issue an order to bring which order public forces to arrest and bring a person before the investigating judge. An order to bring may be issued against a charged person or any person against whom there is evidence of guilt. This order shall be executed by the judicial police. In case of urgency, it shall be published by all means to police units or military police units. Sometimes, the cited person cannot be brought before the investigating judge immediately after the arrest, that person shall be brought to the police unit or military police office in the detention center or prison. In the next day, he shall be brought before the judge. But if the appearance does not occur, the cited person shall be released in liberty.

Arrest Warrants

An arrest warrant may be issued against a charged person or any person against whom there is evidence of guilt. An investigating judge can issue an arrest warrant only if the offense in question is a felony or misdemeanor punishable by imprisonment and the suspect has fled or his whereabouts are unknown or is staying outside of the territory of the Kingdom of Cambodia. The arrest warrant is an order to the public security forces to search for, arrest and bring the charged person to a prison or detention center. The chief guard

of a prison or detention center is obligated to receive and detain that person.

Detention Orders

The investigating judge shall be entitled to issue a detention order. This order is happened only if the charged person is the subject of a provisional detention order. It means that provisional detention may be ordered only in case of a felony or of misdemeanors involving a punishment of imprisonment of one year or more. There are several reasons for judge to detent someone such as to stop the offense or prevent the offense from happening again, prevent any harassment of witnesses or victims or prevent any collusion between the charged person and accomplices, preserve evidence or exhibits, guarantee the presence of the charged person during the proceedings against him, protect the security of the charged person, and to preserve public order from any trouble caused by the offense. In contrast, investigating judge can also decide not to detent the charged person even if he received an application from the Royal Prosecutor requesting provisional detention. This decision shall be opened to appeal from the Royal Prosecutor.

In principle, the charged person shall remain at liberty. However, if the charged person is detained, he also can be released by the investigating judge or by the request of the royal prosecutor or by the request of the charged person. The release decision is made by the investigating judge with the approval from the royal prosecutor.

Termination of Investigations

When an investigating judge considers that the judicial investigation is terminated, he shall notify the Royal Prosecutor, the charged person, the civil parties and the lawyers. The investigating judge issues Closing Order. It means that if the judge considers that the facts constitute a felony, a misdemeanor or a petty offense, he shall decide to indict the charged person before the trial court. The order shall state the facts being charged and their legal qualification. But the investigating judge can also issue a non-suit order if he considers that the facts do not constitute a felony, misdemeanor or petty offense or the perpetrators of the committed acts remain unidentified or there is insufficient evidence for a conviction of the charged person.

D-Trial Judge

The Court of First Instance shall judge upon felonies, misdemeanors and offense. Three judges of the Court of First Instance sit in a felony and single judge sits at misdemeanors and petty offenses. Any sitting judge who has been acting as a Prosecutor or investigating judge upon a certain case may not participate in the adjudication of that case, otherwise the judgment shall be deemed null and void. A criminal case can be brought to trial in three ways: firstly the investigating judge's order or the Investigation Chamber's decision to forward the case for trial (indictment); secondly, the citation of the Royal Prosecutor; thirdly, the written record of immediate appearance submitted by the Royal Prosecutor.

To conclude

The Code of Criminal Procedure of Cambodia has given a clear power and responsibility to the state officers who working in this field. It is not only for the smooth process, but it is also for the purpose of finding justice to all involving people. Although those officers are provided the power to investigate or to prosecute or to put somebody in jail, their power is restricted very strictly according to the law. This is because of the purpose of this law is to balance between the power of the authority and the fair trial rights of citizens.

柬埔寨初审法院刑事程序中的重要司法官员简介

Nup Sothunvisoth*
黄鹏伟**编译

内容摘要:本文以《柬埔寨王国刑事诉讼法》为依据,阐释了柬埔寨刑事诉讼程序中涉及到的许多司法工作人员如司法警察、检察官、调查法官和审判法官在该各自领域内被明确赋予的权力和责任,同时这些权力也被严格限制在了法定范围之内。这样规定的目的一方面有助于刑事程序的顺利推进,确保刑事程序的公正性,另一方面,也能平衡权力机关的权力和公民接受公平审判的权利。

关键词:柬埔寨王国刑事诉讼法;司法官员;权力

简　介

《柬埔寨王国刑事诉讼法》的主旨意在明确规则的遵守和适用,以确定是否存在刑事犯罪。该法赋予了执法者权力和责任,意在推进刑事程序的顺利进行,也意在为受害者和被告人双方之间寻求正义。尽管执法者们被赋予了检察控诉,甚至是判刑入狱的权力,但是这些权力都被严格地限制在了法定范围之内。刑事诉讼程序中涉及许多重要的司法工作人员,本文将着重讨论其中最为重要的人,如刑事一审程序中的司法警察、检察官、调查法官及审判法官。

* Nup Sothunvisoth,柬埔寨司法部刑法研究出版和培训局局长,西南政法大学国际法学院博士生。

** 黄鹏伟,西南政法大学国际法学院硕士研究生。

一、司法警察

根据《柬埔寨王国刑事诉讼法》第56条规定:“司法警察的主要职责系负责支持司法机关,司法警察应当负责调查重罪、轻罪、轻微罪行以及逮捕罪犯和收集证据。”

(一)什么人可以成为司法警察

司法警察应当为至少拥有少校军衔的国家警察或者军官,并且要求服役满两年且获得国家司法警察高级文凭,又或者其他被授权审查其辖区内罪行的特别官员。此外,一些重要的职务如直辖市市长、副市长或者省长、副省长,又如司法警察局局长、副局长以及其他领导职务,会被自动赋予司法警察的权力和职责。

(二)司法警察及其渎职行为的监督

司法警察应由对应的上诉法院的总检察官进行监督和管理。上诉法院的总检察长有权对司法警察采取纪律措施(《刑事诉讼法》第56条)。

(三)纪律处分程序

司法警务人员在履行职责期间犯有不当行为的所有案件,应由皇家检察官或者调查法官向上诉法院的总检察长报告。根据情况,上诉法院的总检察长将告知内政部长或国防部长,以便采取纪律措施。纪律措施的结果应向上诉法院的总检察长通报(《刑事诉讼法》第64条)。纪律措施可以是纪律处分或停职。相应的官员行为触犯刑事犯罪的,纪律措施的采取不阻碍刑事责任的追究。

(四)司法警察的使命

司法警察的基本任务包括:

1.记录收到的投诉或者告发,以便后续的犯罪调查。

2.根据案件是恶劣的重罪或轻罪亦又或是一个仅需初步调查的普通案件的不同,对案件进行公开调查或初步调查。

3.在司法调查开始后,调查法官签发审问令,并由司法警察将其执行。

（五）收到投诉后采取的行动（《刑事诉讼法》第74条）

受理投诉的司法警官应立即发起警察调查，或者将申诉记录发送给检察官，由检察官决定如何开展后续工作。在开始调查之前，司法警官可以向检察官征求意见。当收到的告发并非显然没有根据时，司法警察应当通知检察官并征求其意见。

（六）司法警察的权力

在案件为恶劣重罪或轻罪案件的情况下，司法警察的权力要比处理普通案件时大。《刑事诉讼法》第86条规定了恶劣重罪和轻罪的定义，它们是指：在犯罪过程中犯下的罪行；犯罪后立即实施的罪行；犯罪人正在被通缉的；嫌疑人被发现持有某样物体、一个伤疤、标记或任何其他证据，从中可以断定他犯了罪或参与了犯罪行为的。除此之外的其他罪行都被认为是普通罪行。

（七）实施搜查

在任何案件中，司法警察都可以进行搜查。在现行犯的情况下，一旦他们收到皇家检察官的授权，即使是口头的，也可以进行搜查。搜查必须在被搜查场所的居住人在场的情况下进行。如果居住人或者占有人不在场，则须在两名见证人在场情况下进行搜查。见证人由司法警察指定，不得是参与搜查行动的警察或宪兵。另一方面，如果犯罪是一种普通犯罪，在采取初步调查时，司法警察的搜查应当温和进行。司法警察应寻求居住人或者占有人的明示和批准。批准可由该处所的居住人手写。如果该处所的居住人不在场或拒绝搜查，对该案具有地域管辖权的初审法院院长，可根据检察官的请求授权搜查。检察官应亲自领导搜查，搜查应由司法警察在居住人或占有人在场的情况下进行，不在场的，应当要有两名见证人在场。见证人应由检察官指派；他们不能是参与搜查的司法警察或宪兵。早上六点之前和晚上六点之后不得进行搜查。

（八）羁押

为了应对调查的需要，司法警察可以对涉嫌参与犯罪的人进行羁押，司法警察还可以羁押他们有理由相信可以提供信息却拒绝提供的人。这种羁押必须由检察官书面提出。司法警察应立即向皇家检察官报告任何警察的羁押措施，并向其提供所有致使警方采取羁押行动的相关证据。警方羁押的最长期

限为48小时。羁押期限自拘留人员到达警察局或宪兵局之日起开始。值得注意的是,为满足调查的需要,羁押期限可以延长24小时。但是,如果被羁押的人是未成年人,则不允许延期。羁押的期限应根据被羁押的未成年人的年龄从18岁到14岁依顺序递减。此外,对于羁押超过24小时的人应当提供律师,同时,医疗协助也应当随时待命以提供给被拘留人。

二、检察官

(一)起诉、调查和审讯的权力

检察机关对被控人提起刑事犯罪指控,要求法院依法适用法律;检察官负责执行刑事法院关于刑事犯罪的命令,包括逮捕令的发布。检察官在履行职责时,有权直接调动公共力量。检察官应当参加审判庭审理刑事案件的全部听证会。

检察官包括:

1.最高法院总检察长、副检察长和检察官;

2.上诉法院的总检察长、副检察长和检察官;

3.初审法院的皇家检察官和副检察官。

(二)检察系统的等级制度

理论上讲,司法部长可以通过签发书面命令对上诉法院的总检察长或者任何皇家检察官或者任何部长知晓的案件启动诉讼,或提出他认为适当的其他命令。

上诉法院的总检察长领导其辖区内的所有检察官。他可以向这些检察官发出命令以启动诉讼,或作出他认为适当的结论。

皇家检察官领导其其辖区内的所有检察官。他可以向这些检察官发出命令以启动诉讼,或作出他认为适当的结论。

然而,最高法院的总检察长、副检察长和检察官只代表最高院的检察机关。他们只参与向最高法院上诉的法律申请、案件的复审决议或向最高法院提出的其他要求。实际上,最高法院总检察长无权干涉对上诉法院和初审法院的所有检察官进行起诉和调查,但他作为最高法院法官的一员自动被赋予了最高地位。这导致总检察长有权决定任命或撤销法官和检察官。

(三)检察官的权力

皇家检察官领导和协调辖区内所有司法警察和司法警官的行动。他行使司法警官的一切权力。在特殊情况下,检察官可以撤销司法警察和警务人员被授予的侦查权,并安排其更换。在任何时候,他都可以视察司法警察部门,并参与审讯。他可以审查任何警察拘留的执行情况,主要是为了确保其遵守法律程序和拘留管理规则。

(四)刑事诉讼程序

皇家检察官应认真对待他收到的或由司法警察直接提交的书面申诉和抗议。他可以决定要么不予审查,要么对违法者提起诉讼。不予审查结案的案件应当以法律和事实为根据,但并不代表对案件具有既判力的效果。它意味着只要刑事诉讼尚未终结,检察官可能随时可以改变他的决定。如果检察官决定对违法者提起诉讼,他可以采取三种诉讼程序。1.通过启动司法调查;2.通过传票;3.通过立即出庭的程序。

1.通过启动司法调查

在重罪案件中,检察官应进行司法调查。司法调查应以向调查法官提交的初步意见为基础。司法调查可以针对已身份确认或者身份不明的人适用。此外,在轻罪案件中,检察官可以进行司法调查。但他还有其他选择,例如直接传唤被告在初审法院在确定的日期出庭,或命令被告立即在初审法院出庭。

2.通过传票

传票是向被告提出的在初审法院出庭的命令。传票应包括有关法院、其所在地和审判日期及时间。传票应载明被告可由律师辩护。此外,在轻微罪行的情况下,检察官应发出传票,要求被告出庭。这个程序旨在通过将案件移交审判法官作出最终判决来加速案件的审理。

3.通过立即出庭的程序

如果满足下列要求,检察官可以责令被告立即出庭;

(1)犯罪是恶劣罪行、恶劣重罪或轻罪。

(2)该罪判处监禁不少于1年,不超过5年;

(3)被告达到法定年龄;以及

(4)有大量事实需要审理。

三、调查法官

调查法官是指对重罪案件进行调查的法官,但对于轻罪调查法官也可以选择进行调查。调查法官从检察官的介绍性陈述中提炼事实。根据法律,调查法官可以采取他认为对查明真相有用的所有调查。他有义务收集定罪证据和无罪证据。这意味着作为一个公正审判的主体,在调查和收集检察官提出的不利于被告的证据的同时,调查法官也有义务调查和收集被告自己提出的证据。

(一)法院书记员的协助

书记员应当协助调查法官。在任何情况下,书记员不能履行调查法官本人应承担的职责。而书记员的工作也应当由书记员自己完成。有条件的,书记员应将记录复印留存。书记员应证明复印的记录是原件的真实副本。书记员应按时间顺序为所有记录指定代码编号。原始记录和保留副本应保存在书记员办公室、调查法官办公室或法院的任何有具备充分安全条件的房间。律师或其秘书可由调查法官授权,在书记员的监督下自费复印记录。在某些情况下,调查法官可在通知皇家检察官后,在其书记员的陪同下访问其初审法院辖区内内任何地点。

(二)调查法官的强制措施

为了确保调查的有效性,调查法官有权发出传票,命令将某人带到法官面前,发出逮捕令和拘留令。

(三)传票

有时出于调查需要,调查法官有权发出传票。传票是指一个人被要求前来面见调查法官的命令,该命令可能针对被控人或任何已有证据表明其犯罪的人发出。然而,这一措施并非总是适用。例如,如果有确凿的证据表明被告犯有犯罪或者有时被告逃走情况下,则调查法官应直接签发逮捕证。这是因为案件的紧迫性要求其迅速作出反应。

(四)调查法官的传唤命令

调查法官应当有权发出命令,命令公共力量逮捕并将某人带到调查法官

面前。命令可以针对被控人或任何已有证据表明其犯罪的人发出，并由司法警察执行。遇有紧急情况时，应尽所有方式向警察单位或宪兵局公布。有时被逮捕的人不能在逮捕后立即被带到调查法官，则该人应被带到拘留中心或监狱的警察局或宪兵局。次日，应当将其带至法官面前。但是如果传唤事由消失，被传唤的人应当被释放。

(五)逮捕令

对被指控的人或有任何证据表明其犯罪的人，可以发出逮捕令。只有当所涉罪行为重罪或轻罪，或该罪可被判处监禁的，且疑犯已潜逃或下落不明或逗留在柬埔寨王国领土外时，调查法官才可发出逮捕令。逮捕令是要求公安机关搜查、逮捕被控告被羁押人并带至监狱或者拘留中心的命令。监狱或拘留中心的警卫队长有义务接收和拘留该人。

(六)拘留

调查法官有权发出拘留令，且该命令仅当被控人系临时拘留令的拘留对象时才生效。这意味着临时拘留仅适用重罪案件或涉及处罚一年以上有期徒刑的轻罪。法官在以下情况下可以拘留某人，如阻止犯罪或防止犯罪再次发生，防止证人或受害者受到任何骚扰或防止被控人和同伙勾结，保存证据或现场，保证被控人在起诉过程中在场，保护被控人的安全，防止因犯罪造成的引发麻烦而扰乱公共秩序。相反，调查法官也可以决定不拘留被控人，即使皇家检察官请求临时拘留。皇家检察官有权提出上诉。

原则上，被控的人应给予行动自由。但是，如果被控的人被拘留，他也可以根据调查法官或皇家检察官的请求或被指控者自身提出的请求而被释放。调查法官在皇家检察官批准的情况下作出是否释放的决定。

(七)终止调查

调查法官认为司法调查终结时，应当通知皇家检察官、被告人、民事诉讼人和律师。调查法官应发布结案。这意味着，如果法官认为事实构成重罪、轻罪或轻微的罪行，他应决定向审判法庭起诉被控人，该命令应当说明其所指控的事实及其法定资格。但是，如果调查法官认为事实不构成重罪、轻罪或轻微罪，或犯下罪行的肇事者仍然不明身份，或没有足够证据证明被控人有罪，则也可以决定不予起诉

四、审判法官

初审法院应当评定重罪、轻罪和一般违法行为。重罪案件的应当由初审法院的三名法官担任审判工作,轻罪及轻微违法案件则只需要一名法官。担任某一案件的检察官、调查法官的审判人员不得参与该案件的审理,否则判决无效。刑事案件可通过三种方式接受审判。首先是调查法官的命令或调查庭将案件提交审判的决定。其次是皇家检察官的传票。最后是皇家检察官提交的要求立即出庭的书面记录。

结　论

《柬埔寨王国刑事诉讼法》赋予了在该领域工作的国家官员明确的权力和责任。这不仅是为了刑事程序的顺利推进,也是为了公正地为所有涉案人员伸张正义。虽然这些官员有权调查或起诉或将某人关进监狱,但他们的权力受到法律的严格限制。这是因为本法旨在平衡权力机关的权力和公民接收公平审判的权力。

Effective Measurement for International Cooperation in Cambodia in the Context of Corruption Case

Ku Khemlin*

1. Introduction

In general there are several characteristic of corruption which occurred in the world as corruption against development of prosperity which is affecting developed and developing countries alike, corruption unduly influences a wide range of both public and private sector activities, hampers sustainable social, economic and political development and represents serious obstacle to improving the lives of the poorest segments of the population and corruption against democracy and justice and rules of law which is one of the main obstacles to peace, security, stability, democracy and human rights globally. It may weaken democratic institutions both in new and in long-established democracies. Corruption in the environmental sector can have a devastating impact during the initial stages of the resource exploitation process as well as during operations. Such practices include grand corruption in the issuance of permits and licenses for natural resources exploitation, petty bribery of law enforcement and embezzlement during the implementation of environmental programmes. The health and education sectors are one of the largest budget items in many countries, presents many opportunities for corrupt practices due to huge among of budget expenditure.

The Cambodia government set up in its own strategy plan to fight a-

* Ku Khemlin is Deputy Director General of Justice Development of the Ministry of Justice of Cambodia and a Ph.D candidate of the International Law School, SWUPL.

gainst these corruptions as priority in the 5 th mandate of the Royal government including the legal and judicial reform.The judicial system in Cambodia is composed of court of first instances, appeal court and a Supreme Court, The supreme court is highest level the of the court system and located in the Phnom Penh that can received and reviewed complaints of a party that is not satisfied with the judgment of the appeal court and has authority as final judgment in the cases.The appeal court has the mandate to decide on the appeal against the case is not satisfies with the judgment of the court first instance of its jurisdiction both civil and criminal cases including extradition whether decide to extradite or not of the chamber of investigation chamber's decision.The first instance court is a low level court with full capacity to make decision all provisions and laws with respect to each court's own jurisdiction and this court has the authority to handle all cases.The new Administration secretariat attached to all courts which play role as administrative affairs and coordinate between people to court and bring information to public so that it may easy to people access to the court.

2. Extradition and Transfer of Sentenced Person

a. Extradition

Extradition is the formal process by which one jurisdiction asks another for the enforced return of a person who is in the requested jurisdiction and who is accused or convicted of one or more criminal offences against the law of the requesting jurisdiction. The return is sought so that the person will face trial in the requesting jurisdiction or punishment for such an offence or offences and is also a tool of international cooperation; its roots can be traced to antiquity.Originally designed to seek the return of persons alleged to have committed political offences, the concept has grown and evolved so that it now covers a plethora of criminal offences, and obligations related thereto have been solidified by way of bilateral, regional and multilateral treaties.Extradition shall be subject to the conditions provided for by the domestic law of the requested State Party or by applicable extradition treaties, including,

inter alia, condition in relation to the minimum penalty requirement for extradition and the ground upon requested State Party may refuse extradition.

Depending upon the domestic legislation of the State, a number of factors may be considered by a requested State when dealing with an extradition matter. The decision to surrender a person to another State is usually the result of a bifurcated system involving the judiciary at the outset of the process and the executive branch during the latter part of the process. Depending on the jurisdiction, the courts may consider a number of different factors in deciding to extradite, among them dual criminality, identity, sufficiency of the supporting evidence and the existence of an extradition treaty. Once the case is turned over to the executive, the Government representative responsible for extradition matters may, before ordering surrender, consider other issues, such as human rights concerns, that are separate from those considered by the court. In some jurisdictions, the decisions of either the court or the executive can be appealed or reviewed, with further litigation arising as a result. The process is subject to strict timelines for filing documents, perfecting appeals, bringing the suspect before court and surrendering the suspect if ordered to do so. The process can seem quite complex to those unfamiliar with a particular legal system, and there is a high degree of risk that attempting to navigate a foreign process without constant consultation with the central authority will lead to failure.

So far there is no specific law on Extradition in Cambodia but the extradition and the procedures are including in the Criminal Procedures Code[①] and based *on principal of reciprocity, nationality and dual criminality, and in the spirit good cooperation*. As practice, the implementation may agree to extradite to a foreign State a foreign citizen who is currently present in the Kingdom of Cambodia and who is subject to criminal proceedings in that State and convicted to imprisonment by a court of that State. The extradition may provide legal framework of cooperation among regional and international assistance to each countries in combating the trans-boundary crime including the corruption and assets recovery to their own country. The

① Criminal Procedures Code, Article 566-594, 2007.

best way to implement such kind of assistance is governed by the provisions of international conventions and treaties ratified by the Kingdom of Cambodia and if no treaties and conventions the criminal procedure code may applied(*If Cambodia is the requested State*:*The diplomatic procedure precedes judicial procedure. The competent authorities of requesting State must approach Cambodia by diplomatic channels* (*Embassy and Ministry of Foreign Affairs* (*MFA*))by written request accompanied by supporting documents.Once received the request,the MFA will forward this request to the Ministry of Justice(MOJ)which will verify regularity of the request. Upon verification,the MOJ may request the Prosecutor General of Court of Appeal to issue an arrest or detention order of interested person staying in the territory of Kingdom of Cambodia.If Cambodia is the requesting State: The judicial procedure precedes the diplomatic procedure. The concerned court of Cambodia must sent request with supporting documents to the MOJ which will refer the dossier to the MFA for launching diplomatic actions. Once received the request of Cambodia,the competent authorities of the requested State will verify regularity of the request for further action).

There are several extradition treaties between Cambodia namely,China, South Korea,Viet Nam,Thailand,Lao,French and Russia.

b. Transfer of Sentenced Person

The nature of transnational organized crime means that it is increasingly common for criminals involved to be convicted and sentenced in foreign countries.International transfer of sentenced prisoners not only facilitates the fair treatment and social rehabilitation of prisoners,but is also a tool of international cooperation.Generally it is preferable that prisoners are imprisoned or otherwise deprived of liberty in their own countries, where they have access to visits from their families and where their rehabilitation,re-socialization and reintegration is aided by familiarity with the local community and culture.However,where prisoners are inappropriately deported or otherwise removed to serve their sentences in their home countries,the result may be that they avoid punishment completely and simply resume their criminal activities.Alternatively,where prison conditions in the prisoner's home country

are substandard, his or her imprisonment or deprivation of liberty may amount to violation of his or her fundamental human rights. States are forbidden from transferring persons in such situations.

The Agreement between the Kingdom of Cambodia and the Kingdom of Thailand on the transfer of sentenced persons and on co-operation in the enforcement of penal sentences in 2009 gives foreigners who are deprived of their liberty as a result of their commission of a criminal offence the opportunity to serve their sentences within their own society.

In addition, there are several conditions[①], a sentenced person may be transferred based on the act or omission on account of which the sentence has been imposed constitute a criminal offence according to the law of the reserving party, or would constitute such a criminal offence if committed on the territory of the receiving party. This condition shall not be interpreted to require that the offence described in the laws of both Parties be identical, the sentenced person in a national of the receiving Party, the sentenced person has at least one(1) year remaining to be served at the time of receipt of the request for transfer and the requirement may be waived by agreement of the Parties, in exception cases. The judgment is final and no other legal proceedings pending in respect of this person in the territory of the transferring Party and the transferring and receiving Parties and the sentenced person all consent to the transfer. Where the sentenced person is incapable of giving consent under the law of the transferring Party, consent may be given by a person entitled to act on their behalf.

3. Mutual Legal Assistance and Free Asset and Asset Recovery

a. Mutual Legal Assistance in Criminal Matter

There is a strong basis under bilateral and multilateral treaties for Cambodia and the other countries to provide international legal cooperation to in-

① The transfer of sentenced persons between the Kingdom of Cambodia and the Socialist Republic of Vietnam, Article 4, 2016.

vestigate and prosecute offences relating to corruption. Under international legal standard, each country is required to facilitate cross border cooperation for extradition and mutual legal assistance in criminal matters in case relating to trans-national crime. A regional ASEAN treaty on mutual legal assistance in criminal matters is also in place, however all ASEAN members have not implemented yet①. Informal cooperation between law enforcement agencies is also an essential tool in fighting crime. Informal cooperation-also "police to police" or "agency to agency" (along border) assistance-typically does not require a legislative basis, and facilitate a wide measure of information sharing between primary law enforcement agencies of different countries. Informal cooperation allows police to share the law enforcement intelligence (for example, criminal histories and movement records) during investigation stage, while evidence is still being gathered. The importance of informal law enforcement cooperation is more appropriate, because of its closer link comparing with the formal mechanism of extradition and mutual legal assistance.

b. Asset Seizure and Asset Recovery

Requests involving the seizure or freezing of property are, by their very nature, complex undertakings requiring accurate descriptions of the property to be seized or frozen and coordination of effort by agencies tasked with seizing, freezing and potentially disposing of or returning the property in the requesting and requested State.

When a person is found guilty of corruption, the court shall confiscate all his/her corruption proceeds including property, material, instrument that is derived from corruption act and the proceeds shall be transformed into state property. If the above seized asset is transferred/ changed into different property from the original asset nature, this transformed asset will become the subject of seizure② at the place where it locates. If the corruption proceeds make more benefits or other advantages, all of these benefits and advantages

① ASEAN Treaty on Mutual Legal Assistance in Criminal Matters, 2004.

② Anti-Corruption Law, Article 28.

will be seized as well. If the corruption proceeds disappear or lose value, the court may order the settlement of the proceeds. The procedures of seizure shall be follow criminal procedure code①.

If assets and corruption proceed are found kept in foreign countries, the competence authority of Cambodia shall take measure to claim those assets and to repatriate them back to Cambodia by using the international cooperation. In addition, handing over of Property which is the result of crime, the

4. Law Enforcement Cooperation

a. Law Enforcement Cooperation

In term of cooperation within the judiciary activities the Central Authority has been established since 2011 in the Ministry of Justice, which play role as coordinating agency for relevant activities as well as mutual legal assistance, extradition, transfer of sentenced person, civil and criminal matter with foreign countries.

To meet requirement of current situation of Cambodia the Ministry of Justice has updated Prakas on organization and functioning of the Central Authority in 2017② which lead by the Minister of Justice to review and facilitate request in mutual legal assistance in criminal, civil commercial extradition and transfer of sentenced person.

The Anti-corruption Law was promulgated by the Royal Kram on 17 April 2010, it is substantive law that is applicable to all forms of corruption in all sections and all levels throughout the country. The law provide mandate to Anti-corruption Unit for investigating corruption offences and play roles as judicial police to investigate corruption offences. The criminal code is a framework of investigation in corruption offence. The court authority of the Kingdom of Cambodia may delegate power to competent court authority of

---

① Criminal Procedure Code, 2007.

② Ministry of Justice, Prakas on Organization and Functioning of the Central Authority, 2017.

any foreign state and may also obtain power from court authority of any foreign state, in order to collect evidence/proof or answer/response through court means①. It highlighted the need to gather information on different types of money-laundering, to analyse legal and regulatory frameworks and to recognize the responsibility of the financial sector. It stressed the importance of close cooperation, trust and exchange of knowledge, information between competent authorities in requesting and requested States.

b. Investigation Technique

The official of the Anti-corruption Unit are accredited as judicial police take charge of investigation corruption offences. If difference offences are found during the course of a corruption offence investigation, and if the facts are related to the offence being investigated by the anti-corruption agency, officials of the anti-corruption agency may continue the investigation of the offences until the final stage. The Anti-corruption cannot investigate other offences that are unrelated to corruption unless the agency is order by the court to do so②.

The investigating judges are assigned by the Court President, and they open judicial investigations against one or more person until there is a introductory submission from the Royal Prosecutor. He/ she has obligation to collect "charge"(incriminatory) and "uncharged"(exculpatory) evident. The investigation judge may make site visit or observation and may search and seize exhibits with the court clerk and informing the prosecutor thereof. In implantation an investigating judge may issues letters rogatory asking another judge or judicial police to undertake the investigation instead of him③.

5. Conclusion

The corruption offence is a main problem that threat to economic devel-

---

① Anti-Corruption Law, Article 51.

② Anti-Corruption Law, Article 25.

③ Criminal Procedure Code, Article 131, 2007.

opment, prosperity, democratic by effect to electoral process in selecting right leading in the country, and justice and rules of law by creating bureaucratic quagmires whose only reason for existence is the soliciting of bribes. The effective measures to combating the corruption is set up clear policy and sufficient measure to craft down roof of corruption by using the exiting national legal framework and also close cooperation among regional and international scheme for quickly response to the offences. The strengthening network among execution agencies is also a crucial tool help facilitate mutual legal assistance without the need for a formal request.

References:

- Law on Anti-Corruption, Cambodia
- Criminal Procedures Code, Cambodia, 2007
- Law on Suppression of Human Trafficking and Sexual Exploitation, 2008
- United Nations Convention Against Corruption, 2014
- ASEAN Agreement on Mutual Legal Assistant in Criminal Matter
- Prakas on Organization and Functioning of the Central Authority of Ministry of Justice, 2017
- Manual on Mutual Legal Assistance and Extradition, UNODC, 2012

柬埔寨在反腐败国际合作中的有效措施

Ku Khemlin*
郭雅菲**编译

内容摘要:本文通过详细介绍柬埔寨现有的法律体系中存在着的有关反腐败的明确的政策和有效的措施,包括引渡和移交被判刑者、司法互助、财产没收与追缴以及反腐败调查等执法合作方式,力图在地区性和国际性体制间建立反腐败国际合作机制,目的在于迅速应对腐败犯罪,推翻腐败根基,并恢复国家在经济、政治和法治公正性上的正常运转。因此,在柬埔寨第五项皇家政府命令中,有关反腐的立法司法改革列为国家战略计划首要内容。

关键词:反腐败;引渡;措施;执法合作

通常来说,发生在世界各国的贪污腐败都有一些相同的特点。比如无论对发展中国家还是发达国家来说,贪污腐败都会影响国家的繁荣昌盛,同时还会影响公共部门和私营领域,阻碍社会、经济和政策的可持续发展,也是改善最贫困人口生活的巨大障碍。同时,贪腐挑战着国家的民主、正义和法治,也是影响全球和平、安全、稳定、民主和人权发展最主要的障碍之一。不仅如此,它还可能削弱新兴民主国家和传统民主国家的民主制度。在自然资源开发初期和运营期间,环境部门里的贪腐将会给其带来毁灭性的影响。目前在现实社会中既有涉及签发自然资源开采许可证的大宗腐败案件,也有环境项目执法过程中的小额贿赂与侵占。在许多国家,卫生与教育部门也滋生出大量的贪污腐败行为,因为他们拥有大量的财政预算项目。

在柬埔寨第5项皇家政府命令中,立法司法改革名列其中,反腐成为战略

---

* Ku Khemlin,柬埔寨司法部司法发展总局副局长,西南政法大学国际法学院博士生。

** 郭雅菲,西南政法大学2014级涉外法律人才实验班学生。

计划首要内容。柬埔寨的司法系统由一审法院、上诉法院和最高法院组成。最高法院在首都金边，是法院系统中最高的一级，它接受和复审上诉法院中一方当事人对判决不满意的案子，并有权做出最终判决。上诉法院有权决定重审初级法院管辖的民事和刑事方面的案件，包括有权决定是否引渡和做出法庭调查以及判决。一审法院是最低一级的法院，其有权在其管辖范围内办理所有案子并适用所有法律作出判决。新的政府秘书处隶属于所有法院，它扮演着处理法院行政事务、向公众发布信息、协调法院与人民间的事务的角色，旨在令人民在法院办事更加方便快捷。

一、引渡和移交被判刑者

（一）引渡

引渡是指一国把在该国境内被他国指控为犯罪或已被他国判刑的人，根据有关国家的请求移交给请求国审判或处罚的程序，被引渡人所犯的罪行将会在请求国面临审讯和处罚。这是在加强惩罚犯罪方面国际合作的一种手段，可以追溯到很久之前。引渡制度最开始是用于两国之间归还政治犯，后来这个概念逐渐发展演变，现在开始涵盖大量的刑事犯罪，与此相关的责任和义务已通过双边、区域和多边条约得到巩固。引渡应当遵守被请求国的国内法或适用条约规定的条件，尤其包括引渡的最低限度处罚要求以及被请求国拒绝引渡的理由。

根据国家的国内立法，在处理引渡问题时，被请求国需要考虑若干因素。将一个人引渡到另一个国家的决定通常是一个过程分为两部分的结果。这个过程开始涉及司法部门，之后又涉及行政部门。根据管辖权，法院或许要考虑众多不同的因素来决定是否引渡，比如：是否是双重犯罪、身份的验证问题、支持证据充分与否以及是否有引渡条约的存在。一旦案件进入行政部门执行阶段，负责引渡的政府部门在下令移交人员前，会有与法院完全不同的考虑，例如人权问题等。在一些辖区，法院和行政部门的决定也可以经由上诉或复审引起进一步的诉讼。在这个过程中，归档文件、完善上诉、将嫌犯带到法庭庭审以及命令下达后按照程序移交嫌犯都有严格的时间要求。对于那些不熟悉特定法律体系的人来说，这一过程似乎相当复杂，而且在没有与中央政府持续协商的情况下，试图操纵一个涉外流程风险很高，可能一着不慎就会导致引渡失败。

迄今为止，柬埔寨还没有针对引渡的专门法条，但是基于互惠原则、属人原则及双重犯罪原则，本着与他国良好合作的精神，引渡以及引渡程序均包括在2007年《刑事诉讼法》第566～594条当中。实践中，柬埔寨可能同意将在该国境内被他国指控为犯罪或已被他国判刑的人引渡回请求国。引渡可以为各国在区域性与国际性援助合作中提供法律框架，尤其是在打击跨国犯罪方面，包括贪腐案件和海外财产追缴。实施这种援助最好的方法是适用柬埔寨加入并同意使用的条约以及公约，如果没有条约和公约，还可以适用柬埔寨国内刑事诉讼法让请求国提交书面请求并提供证明文件(如果柬埔寨是被请求国：外交程序先于司法程序。请求国的主管机关必须通过外交途径与柬埔寨大使馆和外交部接触)。一旦收到请求，外交部将会把它移交给司法部进行审查，经核查后，司法部可要求上诉法院总检察长签发对留在柬埔寨境内的利害关系人的逮捕或拘留令。如果柬埔寨是请求国：司法程序先于外交程序。柬埔寨的有关法院将会把附有证明文件的请求递交给司法部，司法部会把详细卷宗转交给外交部进行外交行动。一旦被请求国收到柬埔寨的请求，其主管部门也会先行审查，以此来进一步采取行动。

柬埔寨与中国、韩国、越南、泰国、老挝和俄罗斯之间均签有引渡条约。

(二)移交被判刑者

跨国有组织犯罪的性质意味着牵涉的罪犯越来越多地在国外被定罪和判刑。对被判刑的国际囚犯进行引渡移交，不仅有利于囚犯得到公正待遇并在国内完成社会改造，也是国际合作的一种手段。通常，囚犯更加愿意在本国被监禁或者被剥夺自由，因为在那里，他不仅可以和他的家属会见，而且他们也熟悉当地的社区和文化，这有助于他们改造并重新回归社会。但是，如果囚犯被不当地驱逐出境或以其他方式在其本国免于服刑，那最终可能会导致囚犯彻底逃避惩罚并且重新走上犯罪道路。另一方面，如果请求国的监狱条件不合格，那么将他引渡回国坐牢或者剥夺其自由就可能会侵犯基本人权。因此，这种情况下被请求国也有权拒绝引渡。

柬埔寨与泰国于2009年签订了一份关于移交被判刑者及合作执行刑事判决的协议。该协议给了因犯罪而被剥夺自由的外国人一次在自己的国家服刑的机会。

但是，根据2016年《缅甸与越南社会主义共和国引渡条约》第4条的规定，引渡需要符合下列条件：基于扣留国的法律，被引渡人的作为或不作为足以构成刑事犯罪；或者，在扣留国的领土内进行的作为或不作为将构成刑事犯

罪。本条件不应被理解为双方法律所述罪行相同；被判刑者须为接收方国家公民；接受移交请求之时，被判刑者应还有至少一年的服刑期。当然在特殊情况下，双方可通过协议放弃这些要求。判决为终审判决，且在被请求国不应还有关于该被引渡者的未决诉讼。此外，请求国、被请求国和被引渡者均须同意引渡。如果依据被请求国的法律，该人无法表示同意，那么可以由有权代表他们行事的人作出同意决定。

二、司法互助、自由财产与财产追缴

（一）刑事案件中的司法互助

依据双边和多边条约，柬埔寨和其他国家之间在调查、起诉与腐败相关的犯罪案件方面有着强有力的国际法律合作基础。依据国际法律标准，在跨国犯罪案件中，每个国家都需要促进引渡和司法互助的跨境合作。目前有关刑事案件的地区性东盟司法互助条约也已到位。然而，并不是所有的东盟成员国都加入了2004年《东盟关于刑事案件的司法互助条约》。执法机关之间的非正式合作也是打击犯罪的重要工具。非正式合作也称为“警警合作”或者“机构合作”。这种合作通常无徐以条约为基础，这就促进了不同国家主要执法机构之间大量的信息共享。非正式合作可以让警方在调查阶段搜集证据的时候共享执法情报（例如嫌疑人犯罪历史记录与案底）。与正式的引渡和司法协助机制相比，非正式执法合作可能更加重要，因为是机构间的联系更为紧密。

（二）财产没收与追缴

由于性质原因，请求没收或者冻结财产本身就是一项复杂的工作。这项工作需要对所没收或冻结的财产进行准确的评估，并且在请求国与被请求国间进行没收、冻结、潜在处理或者归还财产需要双方机构通力合作，协调行事。

根据《反腐败法》第28条规定，如果发现某人犯了贪腐罪，法院应当没收其所有腐败所得，包括通过腐败行为取得的财产、物资和作案工具。最终这些腐败所得将收归国库。如果上述所没收的财产已经转变为其他不同类型的财产，则转换后的财产将成为其所在地的没收对象。腐败所得产生的更多或者其他的利益也会同样予以没收。如果腐败所得已经不存在或者贬值，法院可以下令对这些腐败所得进行结算。没收程序应当遵守《刑事诉讼法》的规定。

如果在国外发现了相关财产和腐败所得,柬埔寨的主管部门会通过国际合作对这些财产进行追缴并将其收回柬埔寨。

三、执法合作

(一)执法合作

在司法合作的基础上,中心局作为有关活动以及司法协助、引渡、被判刑人移交与外国民刑事案件交接事宜的协调机构,自 2011 年起便在司法部设立。

为了适应柬埔寨目前的情况,司法部在其部长的领导下于 2017 年修订了《关于中心局的组织和职能的部门规章》,以审查和便利涉及刑事、民商事的引渡与被判刑人移交的司法互助的请求。

2010 年 4 月 17 日,皇家克朗姆(国王议会)颁布了一部适用于全国各地各类腐败的实体法——《反腐败法》。这部法律赋予了反腐败组织调查腐败犯罪的职权,以及与司法警察同样的调查腐败案件的权力。而《刑法典》则是腐败犯罪调查的一个框架。根据《反腐败法》第 51 条规定,柬埔寨法院机关为了通过法庭手段收集证据/证明或答复/反应,可将权力授予外国的法院机关或者从外国的法院机关获取权力。这突出了收集不同类型洗钱的信息、分析法律和监管框架以及发现金融部门责任的必要并彰显了请求国和被请求国主管当局之间密切合作、信任和信息交流的重要性。

(二)调查技术

根据《反腐败法》第 25 条规定,反腐败部门的官员被授予司法警察的权力,有权负责调查腐败犯罪。如果在腐败犯罪调查过程中发现其他犯罪,除非有法院的命令,否则反腐败部门不能调查与腐败无关的其他罪行。但只要事实与反腐败机构正在调查的罪行有关,则反腐官员可以继续对这些罪行进行调查,一直到最后阶段。

根据《刑事诉讼法》第 131 条规定,负责调查的法官由同一级法院院长指定,他们可以一直对一名或多名人员进行司法调查,直到收到皇家检察官引导性意见为止。他们有义务同时收集有罪与无罪的证据。调查法官可以进行现场调查或勘测,以及与法庭书记搜查和扣押物证,并通知这个案件的检察官。如需中途更换调查人员,调查法官可以签发调查委托书,要求另一名法官或司

法警察代替他进行调查。

四、结论

腐败犯罪如今成为一个重要问题，它不仅威胁到国家经济的发展、繁荣，也充斥于国家大选的选举过程中，严重影响着国家的民主，更重要的是，它腐蚀着国家政治阶层，让一个国家没有了法治与公正。打击腐败的有效措施是通过利用国家现有的法律体系来制定明确的政策和充分的措施以推翻腐败的根基，并在地区性和国际性体制间建立密切合作以迅速应对这类犯罪。在没有必要提出正式请求的情况下，加强执行机构间的网络沟通也是促进司法互助的一种重要手段。

图书在版编目(CIP)数据

中国—东盟法律评论.第8辑/张晓君,昂翁·瓦塔纳〔柬埔寨〕主编.—厦门:厦门大学出版社,2018.12
ISBN 978-7-5615-7299-3

Ⅰ.①中… Ⅱ.①张…②昂… Ⅲ.①法律—中国、东南亚国家联盟—文集
Ⅳ.①D92-53②D933-53

中国版本图书馆CIP数据核字(2018)第302254号

出版人 郑文礼
责任编辑 甘世恒

出版发行 厦门大学出版社
社址 厦门市软件园二期望海路39号
邮政编码 361008
总编办 0592-2182177 0592-2181406(传真)
营销中心 0592-2184458 0592-2181365
网址 http://www.xmupress.com
邮箱 xmup@xmupress.com
印刷 厦门市金凯龙印刷有限公司

开本 720 mm×1 000 mm 1/16
印张 14.25
插页 3
字数 246千字
版次 2018年12月第1版
印次 2018年12月第1次印刷
定价 78.00元

厦门大学出版社
微信二维码

厦门大学出版社
微博二维码